StartUp

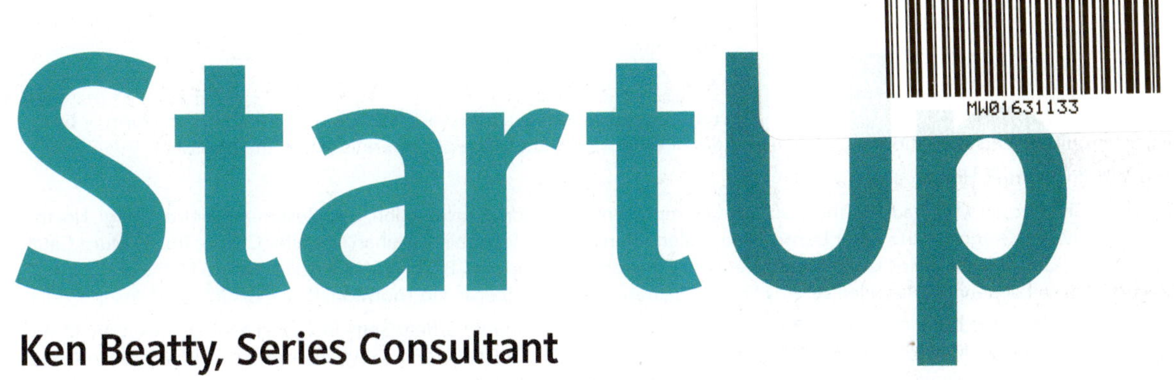

Ken Beatty, Series Consultant

4

Lynn Bonesteel
Sharon Goldstein
Nancy Blodgett Matsunaga
Kimberly Russell
Jessica Williams

StartUp 4

Pearson, 221 River Street, Hoboken, NJ 07030

Staff credits: The people who made up the StartUp team representing editorial, production, and design are Pietro Alongi, Héctor González Álvarez, Gregory Bartz, Peter Benson, Magdalena Berkowska, Stephanie Callahan, Jennifer Castro, Tracey Munz Cataldo, Dave Dickey, Gina DiLillo, Irene Frankel, Sarah Henrich, Christopher Leonowicz, Bridget McLaughlin, Kamila Michalak, Laurie Neaman, Alison Pei, Jennifer Raspiller, Jeremy Schaar, Katherine Sullivan, Stephanie Thornton, Paula Van Ells, and Joseph Vella.

Cover credit: Front cover: Javier Osores/EyeEm/Getty Images. Back cover: Klaus Vedfelt/Getty Images (Level 1); Alexandre Moreau/Getty Images (Level 2); Matteo Colombo/Getty Images (Level 3); Javier Osores/EyeEm/Getty Images (Level 4); Liyao Xie/Getty Images (Level 5); Ezra Bailey/Getty Images (Level 6); guvendemir/Getty Images (Level 7); Yusuke Shimazu/EyeEm/Getty Images (Level 8); tovovan/Shutterstock (icons)

Text composition: emc design ltd

Library of Congress cataloging-in-publication data on file.

Photo and illustration credits: See pages 167–168

Printed in the United States of America

ISBN-10: 0-13-736019-3

ISBN-13: 978-0-13-736019-2

3 2023

ISBN-10: 0-13-736051-7 (with Online Practice)

ISBN-13: 978-0-13-736051-2 (with Online Practice)

3 2023

ACKNOWLEDGMENTS

We would like to thank the following people for their insightful and helpful comments and suggestions.

Maria Alam, Extension Program-Escuela Americana, San Salvador, El Salvador; **Milton Ascencio**, Universidad Don Bosco, Soyapango, El Salvador; **Raul Avalos**, CALUSAC, Guatemala City, Guatemala; **Adrian Barnes**, Instituto Chileno Norteericano, Santiago, Chile; **Laura Bello**, Centro de Idiomas Xalapa, Universidad Veracruzana, Xalapa, México; **Jeisson Alonso Rodriguez Bonces**, Fort Dorchester High School, Bogotá, Colombia; **Juan Pablo Calderón Bravo**, Manpower English, Santiago, Chile; **Ellen J. Campbell**, RMIT, Ho Chi Minh City, Vietnam; **Vinicio Cancinos**, CALUSAC, Guatemala City, Guatemala; **Viviana Castilla**, Centro de Enseñanza de Lenguas Extranjeras UN, México; **Bernal Cespedes**, ULACIT, Tournón, Costa Rica; **Carlos Celis**, Cel. Lep Idiomas S.A., São Paulo, Brazil; **Carlos Eduardo Aguilar Cortes**, Universidad de los Andes, Bogotá, Colombia; **Solange Lopes Vinagre Costa**, Senac-SP, São Paulo, Brazil; **Isabel Cubilla**, Panama Bilingüe, Panama City, Panama; **Victoria Dieste**, Alianza Cultural Uruguay-Estados Unidos, Montevideo, Uruguay; **Francisco Domerque**, Georgal Idiomas, México City, México; **Vern Eaton**, St. Giles International, Vancouver, Canada; **Maria Fajardo**, Extension Program-Escuela Americana, San Salvador, El Salvador; **Diana Elizabeth Leal Ffrench**, Let's Speak English, Cancún, México; **Rosario Giraldez**, Alianza Cultural Uruguay-Estados Unidos, Montevideo, Uruguay; **Lourdes Patricia Rodríguez Gómez**, Instituto Tecnológico de Chihuahua, Chihuahua, México; **Elva Elizabeth Martínez de González**, Extension Program-Escuela Americana, San Salvador, El Salvador; **Gabriela Guel**, Centro de Idiomas de la Normal Superior, Monterrey, México; **Ana Raquel Fiorani Horta**, SENAC, Ribeirão Preto, Brazil; **Carol Hutchinson**, Heartland International English School, Winnipeg, Canada; **Deyanira Solís Juárez**, Centro de Idiomas de la Normal Superior, Monterrey, México; **Miriam de Käppel**, Colegio Bilingüe El Prado, Guatemala City, Guatemala; **Ikuko Kashiwabara**, Osaka Electro-Communication University, Neyagawa, Japan; **Steve Kirk**, Nippon Medical School, Tokyo, Japan; **Jill Landry**, GEOS Languages Plus, Ottawa, Canada; **Tiffany MacDonald**, East Coast School of Languages, Halifax, Canada; **Angélica Chávez Escobar Martínez**, Universidad de León, León, Guanajuato, México; **Renata Martinez**, CALUSAC, Guatemala City, Guatemala; **Maria Alejandra Mora**, Keiser International Language Institute, San Marcos, Carazo, Nicaragua; **Alexander Chapetón Morales**, Abraham Lincoln School, Bogotá, Colombia; **José Luis Castro Moreno**, Universidad de León, León, Guanajuato, México; **Yukari Naganuma**, Eikyojuku for English Teachers, Tokyo, Japan; **Erina Ogawa**, Daito Bunka University, Tokyo, Japan; **Carolina Zepeda Ortega**, Lets Speak English, Cancún, México; **Lynn Passmore**, Vancouver International College, Vancouver, Canada; **Noelle Peach**, EC English, Vancouver, Canada; **Ana-Marija Petrunic**, George Brown College, Toronto, Canada; **Romina Planas**, Centro Cultural Paraguayo Americano, Asunción, Paraguay; **Sara Elizabeth Portela**, Centro Cultural Paraguayo Americano, Asunción, Paraguay; **Luz Rey**, Centro Colombo Americano, Bogotá, Colombia; **Ana Carolina González Ramírez**, Universidad de Costa Rica, San José, Costa Rica; **Octavio Garduno Ruiz**, AIPT Service S.C., Coyoacán, México; **Amado Sacalxot**, Colegio Lehnsen Americas, Guatemala City, Guatemala; **Deyvis Sanchez**, Instituto Cultural Dominico-Americano, Santo Domingo, Dominican Republic; **Lucy Slon**, JFK Adult Centre, Montreal, Canada; **Scott Stulberg**, University of Regina, Regina, Canada; **Maria Teresa Suarez**, Colegios APCE, San Salvador, El Salvador; **Daniel Valderrama**, Centro Colombo Americano, Bogotá, Colombia; **Kris Vicca**, Feng Chia University, Taichung, Taiwan; **Sairy Matos Villanueva**, Centro de Actualización del Magisterio, Chetumal, Q.R., México; **Edith Espino Villarreal**, Universidad Tecnológica de Panama, El Dorado, Panama; **Isabela Villas Boas**, Casa Thomas Jefferson, Brasília, Brazil

LEARNING OBJECTIVES

WELCOME UNIT

page 2 In the classroom | Learn about your book | Learn about your app

Unit	Vocabulary	Grammar	Conversation/ Speaking	Listening
1 What are your favorite things? **page 5**	• Personal interests • Fashion accessories • Adjectives for describing objects	• No article • Restrictive relative clauses • Sequence of adjectives	• Talk about your interests • Talk about accessories • Describe personal objects **Skill** Talk about your interests	• Listen to a radio show about memories **Skill** Visualize what you hear
2 What is the weather like? **page 17**	• Weather conditions • Dangerous weather • Effect of dangerous weather	• *Must / may / might / could* for conclusions • Present perfect and present perfect continuous • Expressing cause and effect with *so / such…that*	• Talk about the weather • Report dangerous weather • Discuss the effects of weather **Skill** Express relief	• Listen to a news report about weather **Skill** Listen for organization
3 How well do you work together? **page 29**	• When things go wrong • Ways to avoid problems • Words related to understanding	• Object complements • Making suggestions • Imperatives in reported speech	• Discuss problems at work • Talk about avoiding problems • Talk about a misunderstanding **Skill** Show agreement	• Listen to stories about problems **Skill** Listen for cause and effect
4 How do you relax? **Page 41**	• Ways to connect • Entertainment • Movies	• *Used to* and *would* • *So, neither, too,* and *either* with simple present action verbs • Simple present and simple past passives	• Talk about how life has changed • Talk about what you like • Talk about a movie review **Skill** Ask for clarification	• Listen to a movie review **Skill** Draw inferences
5 What are we eating? **page 53**	• Restaurant experiences • Categories on a menu • Party food	• Tag questions • Expressing preference with *would rather* and *would prefer* • Quantifiers	• Discuss restaurant experiences • Talk about food preferences • Tell a story about a party **Skill** Talk about preferences	• Listen to a radio show about a party **Skill** Listen for time words

Pronunciation	Reading	Writing	Media Project	Learning Strategy
• Main stress • Intonation in compliments	• Read about making choices **Skill** Find the main idea	• Write about a friend **Skill** Use a main idea and supporting details	• Make a video about important items and memories	**Grammar** • Use good examples to make new sentences
• Pronouncing *th* • Stressed and unstressed words	• Read about extreme weather **Skill** Identify examples as supporting details	• Write about a weather event **Skill** Organize one idea per paragraph	• Describe photos of a time when weather changed your plans	**Vocabulary** • Make a vocabulary word web
• Stress and word endings • Numbers and moving stress	• Read about creative thinking **Skill** Understand extended definitions	• Write about communication skills **Skill** Develop an argument	• Describe photos of co-workers and friends	**Pronunciation** • Listen, read, and say
• Blended pronunciation of *used to* ("useta") • Sentence rhythm	• Read an interview with a location scout **Skill** Make predictions based on text features	• Write a movie review **Skill** Use contrast to express your opinion	• Describe photos about your favorite band, book, or movie	**Grammar** • Find grammar examples in real-life English
• The sounds /ʃ/, /ʒ/, /ʧ/, and /ʤ/ • The sounds /u/, /ʊ/, and /ʌ/	• Read a restaurant review **Skill** Identify author's opinion with key words	• Write a food blog **Skill** Use specific details	• Make a video of your favorite meal	**Vocabulary** • Use new vocabulary in daily life

Unit	Vocabulary	Grammar	Conversation/ Speaking	Listening
6 How do you stay healthy? **page 65**	• Fitness activities • Managing stress • Staying healthy	• Gerunds as subjects and objects • Past forms of *be* + *going to* for past intentions • Prepositions of time	• Talk about fitness activities • Talk about managing stress • Give advice on staying healthy **Skill** Reply questions	• Listen to a podcast about exercise **Skill** Listen for enumeration
7 How do you do this? **page 77**	• Technology verbs • Describe work and co-workers • Phrasal verbs	• Embedded *wh-* questions • Comparisons with *as…as* • Phrasal verbs with objects	• Ask about how to do something • Talk about expectations • Give instructions **Skill** Respond to "thank you"	• Listen to voicemail messages **Skill** Listen for instructions
8 How are you feeling? **page 89**	• Common health problems • The flu • When you are sick	• *May / might / could* with the continuous to show possibility • Subordinating conjunctions in time clauses • Future real conditional	• Talk about feeling sick • Talk about the flu • Discuss what happens when you get sick **Skill** Show concern	• Listen to a podcast about the flu **Skill** Listen for signal words
9 Can you tell me a story? **page 101**	• Adjectives to describe • Morning routines • Verbs for thinking and understanding	• Reflexive pronouns • Past continuous with *while* and *when* • Infinitives of purpose	• Tell a personal story • Retell a story • Explain how you learned to do something **Skill** Show interest	• Listen to a podcast about learning **Skill** Listen for details
10 What will the future bring? **page 113**	• Dreams and ambitions • Helping others • Making decisions	• Noun clauses with *that* • Present unreal conditional • Past perfect	• Discuss hopes and dreams • Talk about *what if* situations • Tell someone's success story **Skill** Respond with encouragement	• Listen to a podcast about someone's life **Skill** Listen for key words in questions and answers

Pronunciation	Reading	Writing	Media Project	Learning Strategy
• Linking identical consonants • Blended pronunciation with *to*	• Read about fitness apps **Skill** Identify comparison and contrast	• Write about health and fitness **Skill** Show cause and effect	• Describe photos of how to reduce stress	**Vocabulary** • Group words
• Stress and linking in comparisons with *as…as* • Stress in phrasal verbs	• Read about good work habits **Skill** Synthesize information	• Write about how people learn **Skill** Show comparison and contrast	• Make a video about showing how to do something	**Grammar** • Grammar challenge
• Silent letters • *Can* and *can't*	• Read about keeping cool **Skill** Identify cause and effect	• Write about being sick **Skill** Use formal and informal writing	• Make a video about staying healthy	**Vocabulary** • Connect vocabulary to personal experience
• Consonant groups • Intonation to end or continue a thought	• Read about the power of stories **Skill** Find supporting evidence	• Write about a funny experience **Skill** Show sequence	• Describe photos of working hard to learn something	**Pronunciation** • Watch TV or a movie in English
• Blended pronunciation of *would you* ("wouldja") and *did you* ("didja") • Thought groups	• Read about reducing waste **Skill** Make inferences	• Write about good advice **Skill** Use parallel structure	• Describe photos of hopes and dreams	**Pronunciation** • Study the sounds of new words

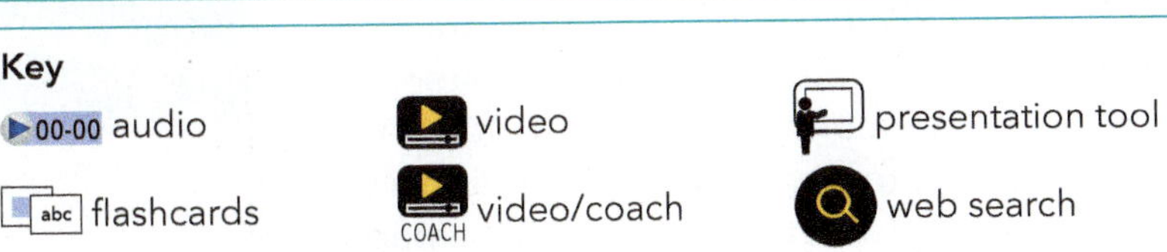

TO THE TEACHER

Welcome to StartUp

StartUp is an innovative eight-level, general American English course for adults and young adults who want to make their way in the world and need English to do it. The course takes students from CEFR A1 to C1 and enables teachers and students to track their progress in detail against the Global Scale of English (GSE) Learning Objectives.

StartUp Level	GSE Range	CEFR	Description
1	22-33	A1	Beginner
2	30-37	A2	High beginner
3	34-43	A2+	Low intermediate
4	41-51	B1	Intermediate

StartUp Level	GSE Range	CEFR	Description
5	49-58	B1+	High intermediate
6	56-66	B2	Upper intermediate
7	64-75	B2+	Low advanced
8	73-84	C1	Advanced

English for 21st century learners

StartUp helps your students develop the spoken and written language they need to communicate in their personal, academic, and work lives. In each lesson, you help students build the collaborative and critical thinking skills so essential for success in the 21st century. *StartUp* allows students to learn the language in ways that work for them: anytime anywhere. The Pearson Practice English App allows students to access their English practice on the go. Additionally, students have all the audio and video files at their fingertips in the app and on the Pearson English Portal.

Personalized, flexible teaching

The unit structure and the wealth of support materials give you options to personalize the class to best meet your students' needs. *StartUp* gives you the freedom to focus on different strands and skills; for example, you can spend more class time on listening and speaking. You can choose to teach traditionally or flip the learning. You can teach sections of the lesson in the order you prefer. And you can use the ideas in the Teacher's Edition to help you extend and differentiate instruction, particularly for mixed-ability and for large and small classes.

Motivating and relevant learning

StartUp creates an immersive learning experience with a rich blend of multimedia videos and interactive activities, including interactive flashcards for vocabulary practice; Grammar Coach and Pronunciation Coach videos; interactive grammar activities; podcasts, interviews, and other audio texts for listening practice; humorous, engaging videos with an international cast of characters for modeling conversations; high-interest video talks beginning at Level 5; media project videos in Levels 1-4 and presentation skills videos in Levels 5-8 for end-of-unit skills consolidation.

Access at your fingertips

StartUp provides students with everything they need to extend their learning to their mobile device. The app empowers students to take charge of their learning outside of class, allowing them to practice English whenever and wherever they want, online or offline. The app provides practice of vocabulary, grammar, listening, and conversation. Students can go to any lesson by scanning a QR code on their Student Book page or through the app menu. The app also provides students with access to all the audio and video files from the course.

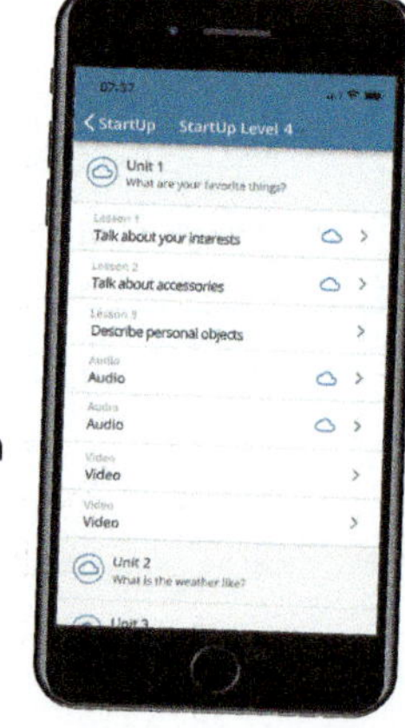

Components

For the Teacher

StartUp provides everything you need to plan, teach, monitor progress, and assess learning.

The ***StartUp* presentation tool** allows you to

- zoom in on the page to focus the class's attention
- launch the vocabulary flashcard decks from the page
- use tools, like a highlighter, to emphasize specific text
- play all the audio texts and videos from the page
- pop up interactive grammar activities
- move easily to and from any cross-referenced pages

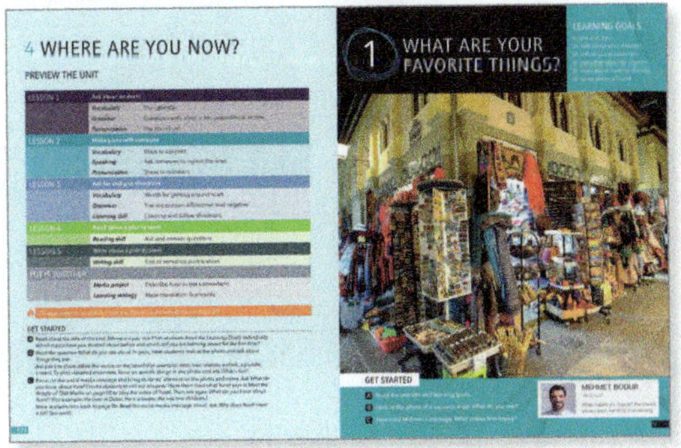

The interleaved **Teacher's Edition** includes

- an access code to the mobile app online resources
- language and culture notes
- teaching tips to help you improve your teaching practice
- *look for* notes to help assess students' performance
- answer keys on the facing page of the notes
- and more!

Teacher's online resources on the Teacher's Portal, include the following, plus video-conferencing integration with easy-to-use class scheduling:

- Teaching with StartUp videos
- Teaching StartUp online resources
- Teacher Methodology Handbook
- A unit walkthrough
- Test Generator assessment software
- Teacher's Edition notes
- Rubrics for speaking and writing
- Hundreds of reproducible worksheets
- Answer keys for all practice
- Audio and video scripts
- The GSE Teacher Mapping Booklet
- The GSE Toolkit

For the Student

StartUp Student's Book and eBook

The eBook enables students to complete grammar activities and play audio and videos directly from the page.

***StartUp* Mobile app** for anytime, anywhere on-the-go practice

- Vocabulary, grammar, and listening activities
- All audio and video files
- Access from the app menu or QR codes on the lesson page

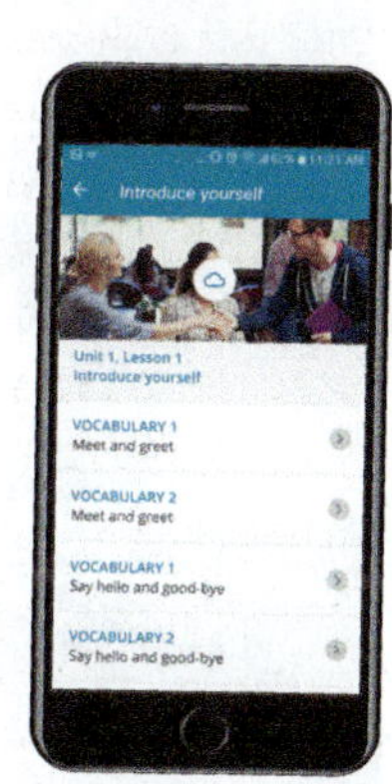

***StartUp* Online Practice** (optional) for more formal online practice

- Grammar practice and access to all Grammar Coach videos
- Vocabulary practice, including games and flashcards
- Feedback that guides students to the correct answer
- Speaking and pronunciation practice, with access to all Pronunciation Coach videos
- Summative assessments that measure students' mastery of all content
- A gradebook that records scores on practice and assessments and helps both teachers and students monitor progress and plan further practice

***StartUp* Workbook** (optional) for more formal traditional practice

- Practice of vocabulary, grammar, reading, and writing
- Self-assessments of grammar and vocabulary

WELCOME UNIT

1 IN THE CLASSROOM

A Get to know your classmates

Say your name and one thing about yourself. Repeat what your classmates said.

B Ask for help

▶00-01 Complete the conversations with sentences from the box. Then listen and check your answers.

~~What was that last part again~~?	Could you explain that a bit more?
Could you speak up, please?	How do you say "firma" in English?
What's the difference between"I want" and "I would like"?	
You're saying we should interview our partners and take notes?	

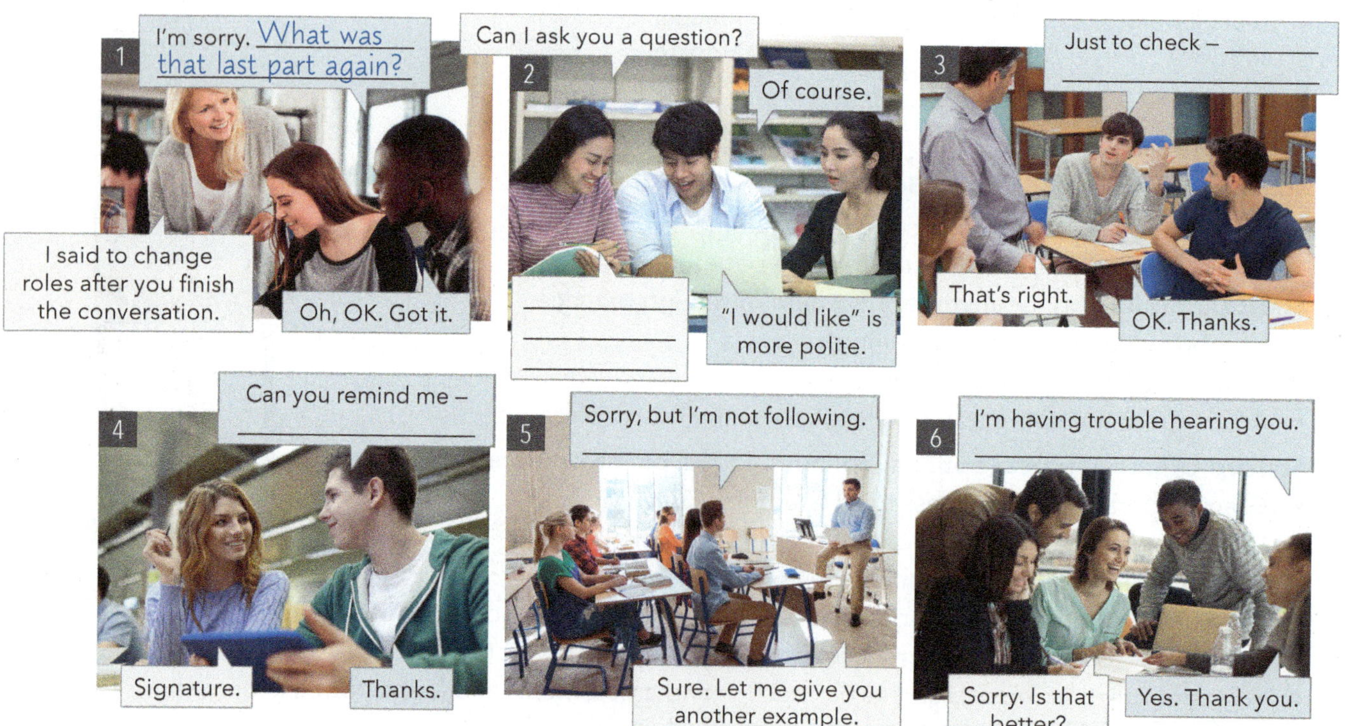

C ROLE PLAY Choose a conversation from 1B. Make your own conversation. Use different information.

2 LEARN ABOUT YOUR BOOK

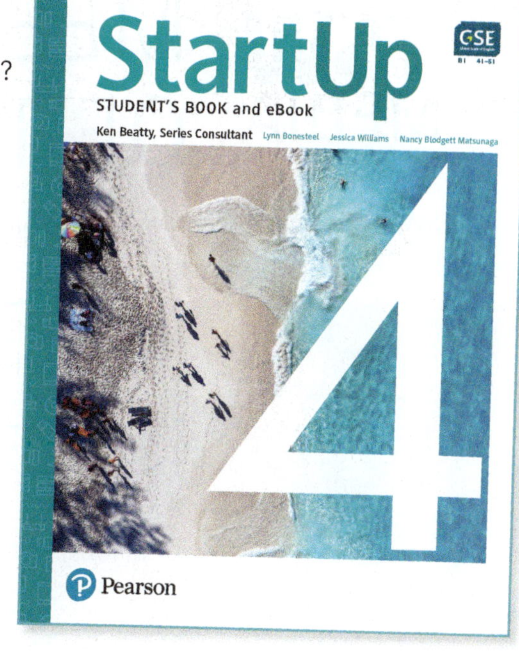

1. Look at pages iv–vii. What information is on those pages?
   ____

2. How many units are in the book? ______________
3. How many lessons are in each unit? ______________
4. Where is the grammar practice? ______________
5. Look at the QR code [QR code]. Find the icon on page 7. What does it mean? ______________
   ____
6. Look at the ■ I CAN STATEMENT. Find it on page 11. What does it tell you? ______________
   ____
7. Look at this icon [magnifying glass icon]. Find it on page 13. What does it mean?
   ____

3 LEARN ABOUT YOUR APP

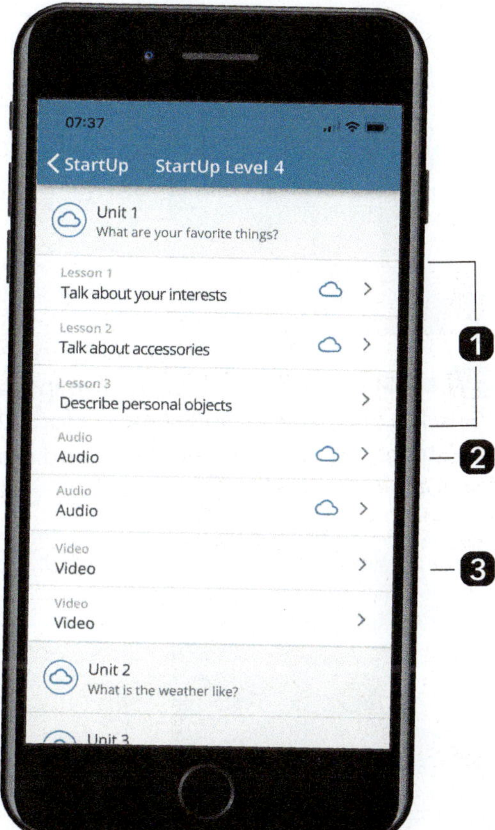

1. Look inside the front cover. Where can you go to download the Pearson Practice English app for StartUp? ______________
2. Where are the instructions for registering for the app? ______________
   ____
3. Look at the picture of the app. What do you see?
   ____
4. Look at the picture again. Fill in the blanks with the numbers 1-3.
   a. Number ______ shows the practice activities.
   b. Number ______ shows the video files.
   c. Number ______ shows the audio files.
5. Look at the picture again. What does this [cloud icon] mean? ______________
6. Look at the QR code on page 7 again. What happens when you scan the code? ______________
   ____

MEET THE PEOPLE OF TSW MEDIA

TSW Media is a big company with big ideas. It has offices all over the world. It works with international clients to help them market their products and services.

MEHMET BODUR
Graphic designer

▶00-02 Hey there. I'm Mehmet Bodur. I'm a graphic designer. In my free time, I like to cook and discover new foods.

SU-MIN KIM
Marketing intern

▶00-05 Hi everyone! I'm Su-min Kim. I'm from Seoul, South Korea, but I'm doing a marketing internship at the New York office. Every day I learn something new. It's really exciting!

LIZ FLORES
Social media

▶00-03 Hello. I'm Liz Flores. I live in Lima, Peru. I'm in charge of social media for TSW. I love traveling to unknown places and meeting the local people there.

JIM STEVENS
Copywriter

▶00-06 Hi! I'm Jim Stevens. I'm a copywriter. I live in New York. I enjoy writing and I love hearing people's stories. Tell me yours!

FLAVIO VEGA
Animator

▶00-04 Hola! My name is Flavio Vega. I live in Bogotá, Colombia with my wife Carmen. I'm an animator. I loved cartoons as a kid, and I still do!

DIANA OLVERA
Art director

▶00-07 Hi there! My name is Diana Olvera. I live in Santiago, Chile. I'm an art director and I love my job. I also enjoy visiting galleries and meeting new artists.

1 WHAT ARE YOUR FAVORITE THINGS?

LEARNING GOALS

In this unit, you

- talk about your interests
- talk about accessories
- describe personal objects
- read about making choices
- write about a friend

GET STARTED

A Read the unit title and learning goals.

B Look at the photo of a souvenir shop. What do you see?

C Now read Mehmet's message. What makes him happy?

MEHMET BODUR

@MehmetB

What makes you happy? For me it's always been traveling and cooking.

LESSON 1 TALK ABOUT YOUR INTERESTS

MEHMET BODUR

@MehmetB

Stayed up way too late watching soccer. What a game!

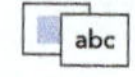

1 VOCABULARY Personal interests

A 01-01 Listen. Then listen and repeat.

B Make categories. Write a word or words that describe each list of words.

1. sports	2. ______	3. ______	4. ______
play soccer	go to the theater	enjoy hiking	do charity work
play baseball	go to a museum	enjoy traveling	discuss politics
play tennis	go to a gallery	enjoy cooking	do community service

C PAIRS Compare answers in 1B. Explain your categories.

COACH

2 GRAMMAR No article

Use no article before certain kinds of nouns

Abstract nouns	**Love** is blind.	Everyone has a right to **freedom**.
Languages	Millions of people speak **Spanish**.	**Chinese** is a difficult language to learn.
Fields of study	Do you like **politics**?	I'm going to study **law** when I graduate.
Sports and games	We sometimes play **chess**.	He's really good at **tennis**.

Notes

- Use *the* before a noun when
  - you know your listener is thinking about the same thing.
    *How do you like **the new Spanish teacher**?*
  - you have already mentioned an indefinite noun.
    *I'm going to a soccer game tomorrow. Do you want to go to **the game** with me?*
- Use *a* / *an* or *the* when the no-article noun is used as an adjective before a singular countable noun.
  *We went to **a history museum** last week.* *I can't believe **the soccer ball** costs $75!*
- Use *a* / *an* before a noun that is not specific.
  *Where can I buy **a travel book** about Guatemala?*

>> FOR PRACTICE, GO TO PAGE 125

3 PRONUNCIATION

COACH

A 01-03 **Listen. Notice the main stress. Then listen and repeat.**

A: I'm interested in **politics**.

B: Not **me**. I can't stand the **arguing**.

A: That's what I **like** about it!

Main stress

The main stress in a sentence is often on the last important word. The main stress usually highlights new or different information. We do not usually put the main stress on repeated words or on words like prepositions that do not carry a lot of meaning.

B 01-04 **Listen. Underline the word in each sentence that has the main stress. Then check your answers with a partner.**

1. A: I love going to museums.
   B: I like sports. Museums are too quiet for me.
2. A: I was up late watching the tennis match.
   B: Me, too. I was just talking to Sam about it.
3. A: I like cooking. I love trying new recipes.
   B: Me, too. But I never have time to cook.
4. A: I love going to the theater.
   B: Me, too. But tickets are too expensive.

C PAIRS **Practice the conversations in 3B. Then change some of the words with main stress to make new conversations.**

4 CONVERSATION

A 01-05 **Listen or watch. Check (✓) the correct boxes.**

	Su-min	Mehmet
1. likes soccer	☐	☐
2. likes traveling	☐	☐
3. likes politics	☐	☐

B 01-06 **Listen or watch. Complete the conversation.**

Su-min: I just had a great conversation with a colleague about soccer.

Mehmet: Oh yeah? I didn't know ________________ soccer.

Su-min: I love it!

Mehmet: Me, too! We have something in common.

Su-min: Yes, sounds like it. I wonder what else we both like.

Mehmet: I like politics.

Su-min: Not me. I ________________ politics!

CONVERSATION SKILL
Talk about your interests

To talk about what you're interested in, say:

I'm (really) into…
I love…
I can't stand…!
I'm interested in…

Listen to or watch the conversation in 4A again. Raise your hand when you hear the phrases above.

C 01-07 **Listen and repeat. Then practice with a partner.**

D PAIRS **Make new conversations. Use the words in 1A or your own ideas.**

5 TRY IT YOURSELF

A MAKE IT PERSONAL **Write three things you're interested in.**

________________ ________________ ________________

B PAIRS **Talk about your interests. Use** ***Not me*** **and** ***Me, too.***

A: I'm really into soccer.
B: Me, too. I'm also interested in…

☐ I CAN TALK ABOUT MY INTERESTS.

LESSON 2 TALK ABOUT ACCESSORIES

MEHMET BODUR

@MehmetB

Need a birthday gift for my sister. Any ideas?

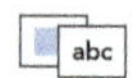

1 VOCABULARY Fashion accessories

A 01-08 Listen. Then listen and repeat.

B PAIRS What are your favorite fashion accessories from 1A?

I like watches. I wear a watch every day.

COACH

2 GRAMMAR Restrictive relative clauses

Restrictive relative clauses define the meaning of nouns. They provide information that is necessary to understand the sentence.

Relative pronoun	Used for	Example
who	people	I know the designer **who** made this jacket.
whom	people	Selena is the woman (**whom**) I met at the fashion show.
that	people and things	The man **that** owns the accessories store is sitting over there. It's one of the few pieces of jewelry (**that**) I wear.
Relative adverb		
when	time	I'll always remember the day **when** my husband gave me this ring.
where	place	The store **where** my cousin works is in London.

Notes

- The relative pronouns *who* and *that* can be the subject or the object of the relative clause.
  Subject: *I know the designer* ***who made*** *this jacket.* (S) (V)
  Object: *It's one of the few pieces of jewelry* ***that I wear****.* (obj) (S) (V)
- The relative pronoun can be deleted when it is the object of the relative clause.
  It's one of the few pieces of jewelry (***that***) *I wear.*

>> FOR PRACTICE, GO TO PAGE 126

3 PRONUNCIATION

COACH

A 01-10 **Listen. Notice the intonation. Then listen and repeat.**

That's a beautiful **necklace**. (I love the color.)

That's a beautiful **necklace**. (But it's too thin.)

That's a great **idea**. (Why didn't I think of that?)

That's a great **idea**. (But it won't work.)

Intonation in compliments

Sometimes *how* we say something is as important as *what* we say. When we give a compliment, the intonation jumps up high to emphasize the important words and then falls at the end of the sentence. If the intonation falls but then rises a little at the end, it can sound like we're going to add a negative idea beginning with a *but*.

B 01-11 **Listen. Notice the intonation. Circle the sentence that the speaker might say next.**

1. I like your sunglasses.
   a. They look great on you.
   b. But they're too big.
2. That's a really nice tie.
   a. It's very cool.
   b. But it doesn't look good with that shirt.
3. I like your ring.
   a. It looks really good on you.
   b. But I like your other ring better.
4. Your watch is very cool.
   a. I love it!
   b. But it's not my style.

4 CONVERSATION

A 01-12 **Listen or watch. Read the sentences. Circle *T* for *True* and *F* for *False*. If the statement is false, cross out the false information and correct it.**

1. Mehmet ~~hates~~ likes Su-min's bracelet. T (F)
2. The personal message on Su-min's bracelet is from her mother. T F
3. Mehmet thinks a gift like Su-min's bracelet is too personal and not a good idea. T F
4. Su-min wants to help Mehmet shop for his sister's birthday gift. T F

B 01-13 **Listen or watch. Complete the conversation.**

Mehmet: That's a ____________________ bracelet!

Su-min: Thanks. It's one of the few pieces of jewelry __________ I wear.

Mehmet: Well, I really like it.

Su-min: Thank you. By the way, that tie is very cool. Where did you get it?

Mehmet: I got it at a ____________________ my cousin works.

C 01-14 **Listen and repeat. Then practice with a partner.**

5 TRY IT YOURSELF

A MAKE IT PERSONAL **Think of a few items that are special to you, like Su-min's bracelet.**

B PAIRS **Talk about the items you thought about in 5A. Explain why they are special.**

☐ I CAN TALK ABOUT ACCESSORIES.

LESSON 3 DESCRIBE PERSONAL OBJECTS

MEHMET BODUR
@MehmetB
I found my father's old leather photo album with his childhood pictures.

1 VOCABULARY Adjectives for describing objects

A ▶01-15 Listen. Then listen and repeat.

B Put the vocabulary words in 1A into the correct categories.

Age	Physical quality (appearance and feel)	Shape	Material

C PAIRS Describe objects in the room with words from 1A.

There is a rectangular door. The window is made of glass.

2 GRAMMAR Sequence of adjectives

COACH

When more than one adjective is used before a noun, the adjectives generally occur in a certain order.

Opinion	Size	Physical quality	Age	Shape	Color	Origin	Material	Noun
		shiny					**metal**	keychain
		smooth		**rectangular**				tiles
			old	**round**				hatbox
beautiful							**silk**	top hat
	small				**black**	**Italian**		handbag

Note: Commas are often used to separate three or more adjectives. They may be left out in informal writing.

*I got this **small, black, Italian** handbag from my grandmother.*

>> FOR PRACTICE, GO TO PAGE 127

3 LISTENING

A ▶01-17 Listen to the radio show. Circle the correct answers.

1. What's the show about?
   a. childhood memories
   b. cleaning up your home
   c. special personal items
2. Where did the stories on the show come from?
   a. They are the host's personal stories.
   b. The listeners of the show sent them in.
   c. The writers of the show created the stories.
3. What do Larry's cards make him think of?
   a. college classes
   b. late night studying
   c. his old friends
4. What do all the stories have in common?
   a. They are about family and friends.
   b. They are about exciting events.
   c. They are about famous people.

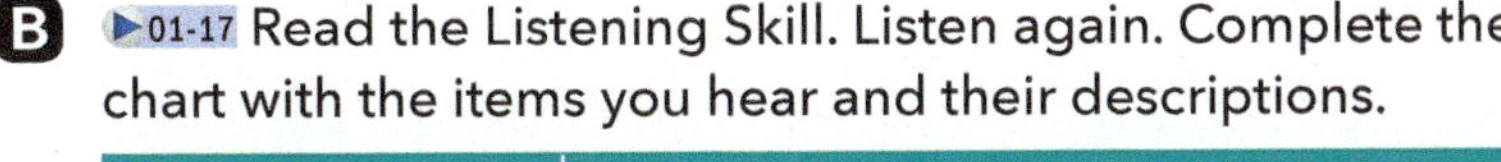

B ▶01-17 Read the Listening Skill. Listen again. Complete the chart with the items you hear and their descriptions.

Item	Description
keychain	shiny, metal

LISTENING SKILL
Visualize what you hear

When you listen to descriptions, try to create a mental image of what you hear. This will help you understand the information and remember it better.

C PAIRS Student A, use your notes from 3B to describe one of the items. Student B, try to identify the item your partner describes.

4 TRY IT YOURSELF

A MAKE IT PERSONAL Think of at least three items you would like to save for the future. Make notes.

Item	Description

B PAIRS Describe your items. Ask each other follow-up questions.

C WALK AROUND Ask three classmates to describe their items. Did anyone have the same item?

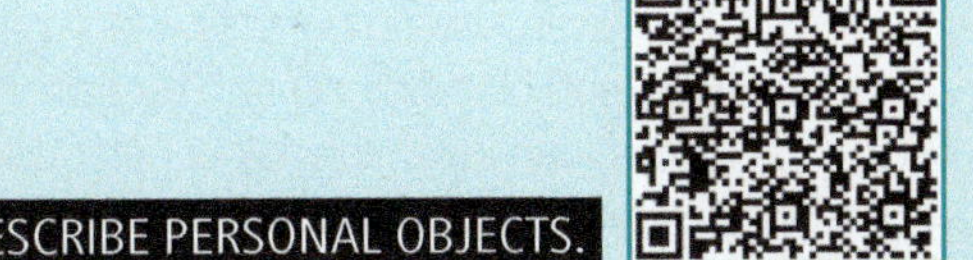

LESSON 4 READ ABOUT MAKING CHOICES

MEHMET BODUR
@MehmetB
You can CHOOSE to be happy!

1 BEFORE YOU READ

A PAIRS What is your favorite leisure activity?

I really enjoy Brazilian jujitsu.

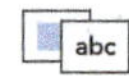

B ▶01-18 VOCABULARY Listen. Then listen and repeat.

last: to continue for a period of time
a possession: something that you own
joy: a feeling of happiness
eat out: to have a meal in a restaurant
temporary: happening for just a short time
significant: large or important
network: a group of people that are connected
immediate: happening right away or right after something else

>> FOR PRACTICE, GO TO PAGE 155

2 READ

A PREVIEW Read the title and look at the photo. Why do you think the people are happy?

B ▶01-19 Listen. Read the article.

ARE YOUR CHOICES MAKING YOU HAPPY?

Certainly, we've all felt pleasure when we buy something new. However, research shows that these good feelings don't actually last very long. For over two decades, Dr. Thomas Gilovich, a psychology professor at Cornell University, has studied the connection between happiness and the choices we make. His studies included over 1,200 people living in the U.S. ranging in ages from 21 to 69. According to Gilovich, it is experiences, and not possessions, that make people the happiest. People report the most joy when they participate in interesting activities. They feel happy when they go to concerts, eat out, learn a new skill, or enjoy a hobby.

When we buy something like a new phone, we gain a physical object that we can enjoy for a long time. Experiences are temporary and leave us with nothing but a memory. So why do they make us happier? Gilovich suggests that our new possessions make us happy at first. But we soon begin to take them for granted, or we just get tired of them when they become old. With experiences that make us happy, the opposite is true. After the experience is over, the memory of it continues to bring pleasure. In fact, we tend to remember events more positively as time passes.

These kinds of experiences also lead to more happiness because we usually share them with other people. We organize events with our friends, and enjoying these experiences together builds a sense of community. And these connections to other people make us happy. In fact, research shows that there is a significant connection between friendships and happiness. People with a good network of close friends and family members are generally happier and more successful in life.

Finally, leisure activities help you relax and reduce stress. Participants in one study reported feeling less stress and greater happiness after enjoying a hobby. Not only did the activities make the people feel better, but they also brought immediate and lasting health benefits. Many participants experienced a lower heart rate and reduced blood pressure. This calming effect lasted for hours. Over time, reducing stress can lower the risk of heart disease, weight gain, and depression. According to these studies, the health benefits of experiences are both emotional and physical.

3 CHECK YOUR UNDERSTANDING

A **Read the Reading Skill. Circle the correct answers.**

1. Which phrase best describes the topic of the article?
   a. the relationship between choices and stress
   b. the relationship between choices and happiness
   c. the relationship between happiness and experiences
2. What point is the writer making about this topic?
   a. Experiences can bring long-lasting pleasure.
   b. People should not buy possessions.
   c. Being happy can help you stay healthy.

READING SKILL Find the main idea

The main idea has two parts: (1) the topic and (2) the point that the writer wants to make about that topic. When you read, ask yourself: "What is this text about?" and then, "What point is the writer making about this topic?"

B DETAILS **Check (✓) the ideas that are true based on the reading.**

☐ 1. Pleasure from possessions ends quickly.
☐ 2. Experiences are often social.
☐ 3. Experiences are less expensive than possessions.
☐ 4. People who have experiences are less likely to get sick.
☐ 5. Experiences are good for physical health.
☐ 6. Possessions can't make people happy.
☐ 7. Experiences with others often lead to more happiness.
☐ 8. Experiences are good for mental health.
☐ 9. The number of possessions people buy is increasing.
☐ 10. Pleasure from experiences lasts.

C FOCUS ON LANGUAGE **Reread lines 8–15 in the article. Think about the phrases *take them for granted* and *sense of community*. Circle the correct answers.**

1. The expression *take them for granted* means ___.
   a. to get used to something and think about it less
   b. to stop using something
   c. to take a long time using something
2. The expression *sense of community* means ___.
   a. a wish to stay together
   b. a feeling that you are part of a larger group
   c. a place where people can gather

D PAIRS **What is the article about? Retell the most important ideas in the article. Use your own words.**

The article explains that experiences are...

Find out about other things that make people happy. Are they similar to what makes you happy? 

4 MAKE IT PERSONAL

A **Think about the questions below. Take notes.**

Which do you get more pleasure from, possessions or experiences? Give examples and say why.

B PAIRS **Discuss your answers in 4A.**

I get more pleasure from experiences, such as cycling, because...

☐ I CAN READ ABOUT MAKING CHOICES.

LESSON 5 WRITE ABOUT A FRIEND

MEHMET BODUR
@MehmetB
My conversation with Su-min this morning got me thinking about friendship…

1 BEFORE YOU WRITE

A Think about a good friend. What makes that person a good friend?

B Read Mehmet's post. What are some things he does together with his friend Callum?

Blog | About | Contact

Search

My Best Friend

Posted on September 19

I have a lot of friends, but I have only a few friends who I feel very close with. My best friend is Callum. Callum and I met three years ago, at a design conference. We started talking about a presentation that we both liked. Then we found out that we have a lot of the same interests in our personal lives. Both of us like sports, especially soccer and tennis. We also both like traveling. Callum has been to some really interesting places, like Nepal and South Africa.

As designers, Callum and I both have very busy lives, but we always make time to see each other. We play tennis together almost every weekend. Afterwards, we have lunch and talk about a lot of different things. We often talk about the projects we are working on. Sometimes it's nice to get an outside opinion. We also discuss politics. We don't always agree with each other, but Callum always has interesting points to make. I like that he introduces new ideas to me.

It's not every day you find someone that you get along with so well. I really enjoy spending time with Callum.

Leave a Reply

Enter your comment here…

About
RSS Feed
Social Media
Recent Posts
Archives
Email

C Read the post again. Complete the chart.

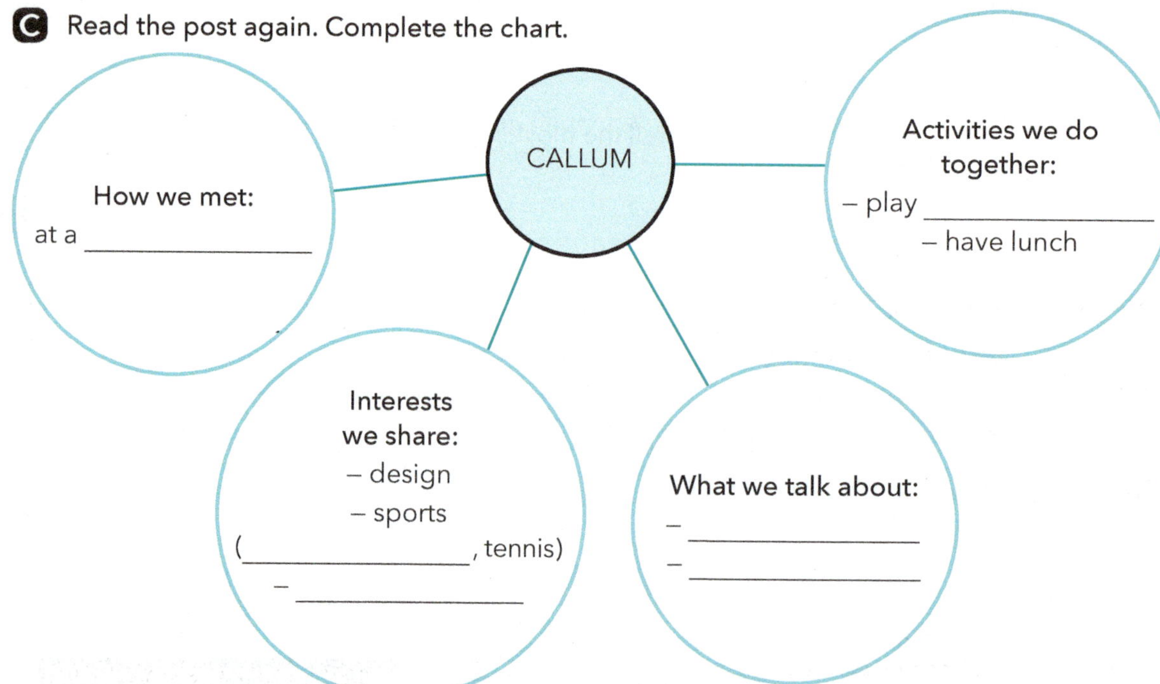

2 FOCUS ON WRITING

Read the Writing Skill. Then reread Mehmet's post. Circle the main idea sentence. Underline the supporting details.

WRITING SKILL Use a main idea and supporting details

To write in an organized way, include a **main idea** sentence to state your main point. Then give **supporting details**. Supporting details are examples which further explain the main idea.

3 PLAN YOUR WRITING

A Think about a friend you enjoy spending time with. Complete the chart to help plan your writing.

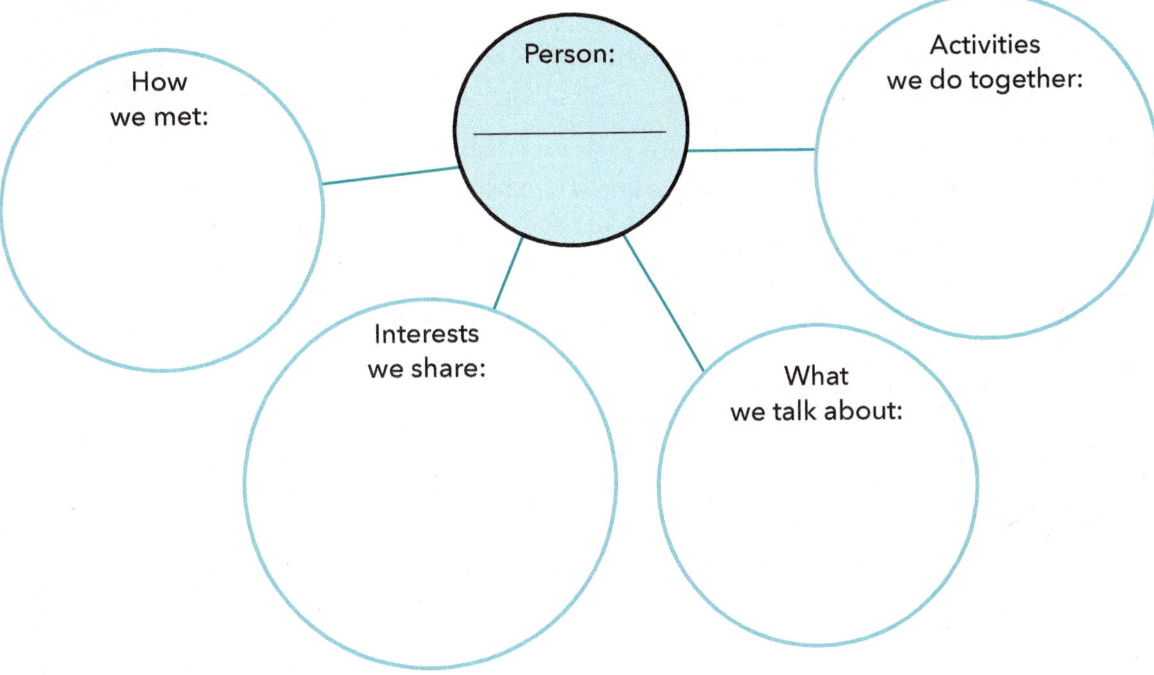

B PAIRS Talk about the friend you enjoy spending time with.

I enjoy spending time with my friend Ella. We like to go to concerts...

4 WRITE

Write a post about a good friend using your details in 3A. Remember to include a main idea sentence and clear supporting details. Use the post in 1B as a model.

5 REVISE YOUR WRITING

A PAIRS Exchange and read each other's posts.

1. Circle the main idea sentence and underline all of the supporting details.
2. Did your partner's supporting details help you understand why he or she enjoys spending time with this friend? Why or why not?

B PAIRS Can your classmate improve his or her post? Make suggestions.

6 PROOFREAD

Read your post again. Can you improve your writing?

Check your
- spelling
- punctuation
- capitalization

☐ I CAN WRITE ABOUT A FRIEND.

PUT IT TOGETHER

1 MEDIA PROJECT

A ▶01-20 **Listen or watch. What does Keiko talk about?**

B ▶01-20 **Listen or watch again. Answer the questions.**

1. What items does Keiko describe?
____
2. Where did she get these items?
____
3. Why are these items important to her?
____

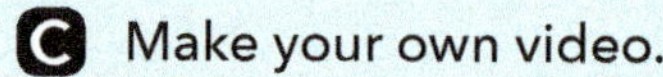

C **Make your own video.**

Step 1 Think of 1 or 2 items that are important to you. Where did you get them? What memories or stories do you have about them?

Step 2 Make a 30-second video. Describe each of your items. Tell why the item is special.

Step 3 Share your video. Answer questions and get feedback.

2 LEARNING STRATEGY

USE GOOD EXAMPLES TO MAKE NEW SENTENCES

Study new grammar by making new sentences from a good example sentence. Use the good example to make some fill-in-the-blank sentences. Fill in the blanks with your own words. Say the sentences aloud for speaking practice with the grammar.

I'm studying _______.
Chinese
engineering
law

Review the grammar from the unit. Find some good example sentences. Use these to make fill-in-the-blank practice sentences. Write five new sentences and say them for practice.

3 REFLECT AND PLAN

A **Look back through the unit. Check (✓) the things you learned. Highlight the things you need to learn.**

Speaking objectives
- ☐ Talk about my interests
- ☐ Talk about accessories
- ☐ Describe personal objects

Vocabulary
- ☐ Personal interests
- ☐ Fashion accessories
- ☐ Adjectives for describing objects

Pronunciation
- ☐ Main stress
- ☐ Intonation in compliments

Grammar
- ☐ No article
- ☐ Restrictive relative clauses
- ☐ Sequence of adjectives

Reading
- ☐ Find the main idea

Writing
- ☐ Use a main idea and supporting details

B **What will you do to learn the things you highlighted? For example, use your app, review your Student Book, or do other practice. Make a plan.**

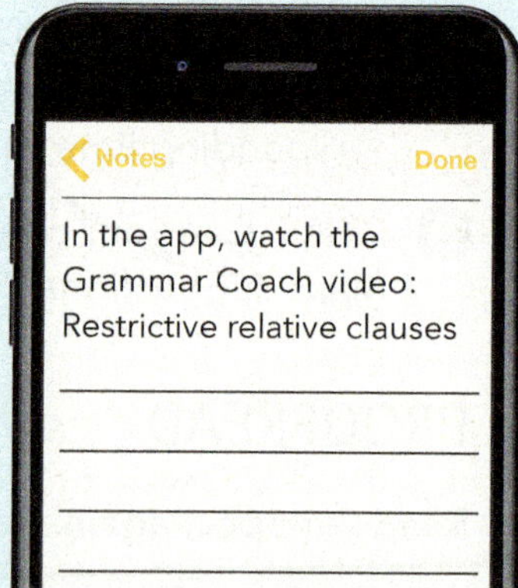

2 WHAT IS THE WEATHER LIKE?

LEARNING GOALS

In this unit, you

- talk about the weather
- report dangerous weather
- discuss the effects of weather
- read about extreme weather
- write about a weather event

GET STARTED

A Read the unit title and learning goals.

B Look at the photo. What do you see?

C Now read Diana's message. What is she worried about?

DIANA OLVERA

@DianaO

I hope we don't have a bad storm this week!

LESSON 1 TALK ABOUT THE WEATHER

DIANA OLVERA
@DianaO
I wonder if I need my umbrella today…

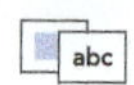

1 VOCABULARY Weather conditions

A ▶02-01 Listen. Then listen and repeat.

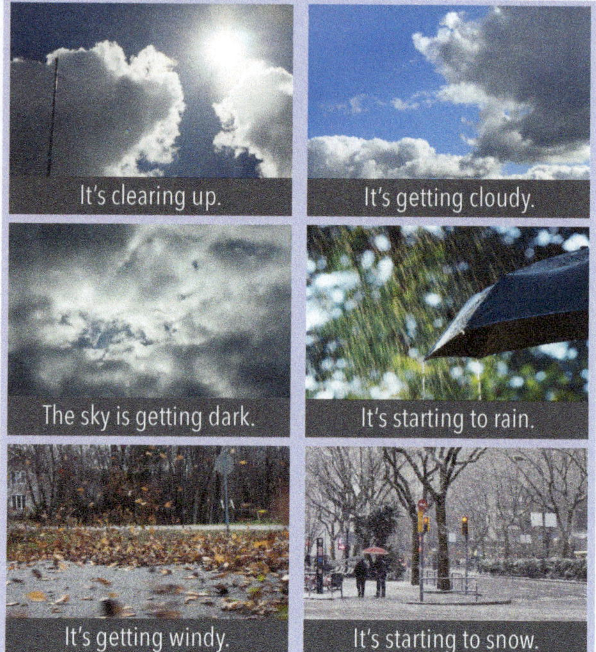

B ▶02-02 Listen. Write the weather condition that each speaker talks about.

1. ______________________
2. ______________________
3. ______________________
4. ______________________
5. ______________________
6. ______________________

COACH

2 GRAMMAR *Must / may / might / could* for conclusions

Use modals to draw conclusions about present situations based on facts. The modal shows varying degrees of certainty.

Fact	Conclusion				
	Subject	**Modal (*not*)**		**Base form of verb**	
The sky is getting dark.	The storm	**must**	very certain	be	close.
	You	**may**		need	a raincoat.
	The game	**might**		start	late.
	They	**could**	least certain	cancel	the picnic.
The sky is clearing up.	The storm	**couldn't**	very certain	be	close.
	The storm	**must not**		be coming	this way.
	You	**may not**		need	a raincoat.
	They	**might not**	least certain	be	late.

Note: Affirmative and negative modals show different degrees of certainty.

>> FOR PRACTICE, GO TO PAGE 128

3 PRONUNCIATION

COACH

A 02-04 Listen. Notice the two pronunciations of *th*. Then listen and repeat.

/ð/	/θ/
they, there, weather	thanks, three, fourth

Pronouncing *th*

There are two *th* sounds in English. For both *th* sounds, put your tongue between your teeth. Push air out between your tongue and top teeth. To say the voiced *th* sound in *they*, use your voice. To say the voiceless *th* sound in *thanks*, do not use your voice.

B 02-05 Write each word with *th* in the correct box in 3A. Then listen and check your answers.

1. Was that thunder?
2. It's this Thursday.
3. Where's the theater?
4. I think so.
5. When is your brother's birthday?
6. It's on Third Avenue.

C PAIRS Match the questions and answers in 3B to make two-line conversations.

4 CONVERSATION

A 02-06 Listen or watch. Circle the correct answers.

1. Why do Jim and Diana think a storm is coming?
   a. They see lightning. b. It's starting to rain. c. It's getting windy.
2. How is the weather at the end of the day?
   a. It clears up. b. The sky gets darker. c. It rains more.

B 02-07 Listen or watch. Complete the conversation.

Diana: Did you hear that?
Jim: Yeah. Sounds like thunder.
Diana: The sky is getting dark. There ______________ a storm coming.
Jim: I don't think I'll go out for lunch today.
Diana: Good idea. You don't want to be out in this weather.

C 02-08 Listen and repeat. Then practice with a partner.

D PAIRS Make new conversations. Use these words or your own ideas.

it's starting to rain | it's getting cloudy | thunderstorm

5 TRY IT YOURSELF

ROLE PLAY You are planning an outdoor event today. Choose a picture. Take turns describing the weather conditions. Make conclusions about the weather and what you may need to do.

Picture 1 A: Look. The sky is getting dark.
B: It might rain. We may need to...

I CAN TALK ABOUT THE WEATHER.

LESSON 2 REPORT DANGEROUS WEATHER

DIANA OLVERA

@DianaO

I just heard we're going to get another storm! I need to listen to the weather report.

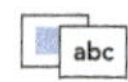 1 VOCABULARY Dangerous weather

A  02-09 Listen. Then listen and repeat.

Weather events

a tornado

a hurricane

a blizzard

a drought

a wildfire

a landslide

an earthquake

Weather conditions

heavy rain

heavy snow

strong winds

freezing temperatures

icy roads

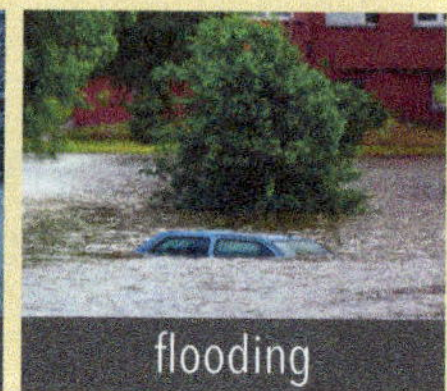
flooding

B Circle the word that doesn't belong to each weather event.

1. **a tornado**	strong winds	icy roads	heavy rain
2. **a blizzard**	flooding	icy roads	heavy snow
3. **a wildfire**	heavy rain	strong winds	a drought
4. **a landslide**	heavy rain	flooding	freezing temperatures

C PAIRS Describe a dangerous weather event from 1A. Your partner guesses the word.

A: There are freezing temperatures and heavy snow.
B: It's a blizzard.

 COACH 2 GRAMMAR Present perfect and present perfect continuous

Use contractions in spoken English and informal writing, such as *I've*, *I haven't*, *she's*, *she hasn't*.

Present perfect				Present perfect continuous				
Subject	*Have / has*	Past participle		Subject	*Have / has*	*Been*	Present participle	
I	**have**	**watched**	the news.	I	**have**		**watching**	the news all day.
The fire	**has**	**destroyed**	ten homes.	The fire	**has**	**been**	**burning**	for two days.
They	**have**	**issued**	warnings.	They	**have**		**issuing**	warnings since 5:00.

Notes

- The present perfect shows
  - a completed action at some point in the past
  - how much, how many

  *The fire **has destroyed** 60 homes.*
- The present perfect continuous shows
  - a continuing action
  - how long

  *The fire **has been burning** for five days.*
- With some verbs such as *live*, *study*, and *work*, there is little difference between the two tenses.

  *I **have lived** here since 2014.* *I **have been living** here since 2014.*

>> FOR PRACTICE, GO TO PAGE 129

3 PRONUNCIATION

COACH

A 02-11 **Listen. Notice the stressed words. Then listen and repeat.**

1. **Snow** has been **falling** for **hours**.
2. The **roads** have been **icy**.
3. I **haven't left** the **house**.
4. Have you **checked** the **weather**?
5. **Yes**, I **have**.
6. **No**, I **haven't**.

Stressed and unstressed words

We stress the important words in a sentence. We usually stress words that have a clear meaning, like nouns, adjectives, and main verbs. We do not usually stress helping verbs like *has*, *have*, or *been*. They are stressed only at the end of a sentence or in negative contractions.

B 02-12 **Underline the stressed words. Then listen and check your answers.**

1. I've lived in a place with hurricanes.
2. I've driven on icy roads.
3. I haven't seen a tornado.
4. I've been watching the news a lot.
5. It hasn't rained in a month.
6. The weather has been colder.

C PAIRS **Practice the sentences in 3A and B.**

4 LISTENING

A 02-13 **Listen to the radio news reports. Circle the correct answers.**

1. What is the purpose of the reports?
   a. to warn people about dangerous weather
   b. to explain how a tornado starts
   c. to give tips on how to predict the weather
2. How is the weather news organized?
   a. by type of weather b. by area or city c. by time and day

LISTENING SKILL

Listen for organization

When you listen, notice how the speaker organizes his or her ideas. Understanding how the information is grouped together will help you get the information you need

B 02-13 **Read the Listening Skill. Listen again. Complete the notes about weather events.**

Place	What has been happening?	What has happened?
The Midwest	Dangerous ______ have been moving through the area.	20,000 ______ in western Texas have reported loss of power.
Montreal	______ have been falling all week.	A ______ has dropped ten inches of snow on the city.
Santiago	Chile has been experiencing a severe ______.	The wildfire has burned more than ______.

5 TRY IT YOURSELF

A MAKE IT PERSONAL **Imagine you are reporting a dangerous weather event. Complete the chart.**

Weather event	Place	What has been happening?	What has happened?

B ROLE PLAY **Report the dangerous weather event to your classmate. Take notes.**

☐ I CAN REPORT DANGEROUS WEATHER.

LESSON 3 DISCUSS THE EFFECTS OF WEATHER

DIANA OLVERA
@DianaO
It's been raining the entire week. Is this normal here?

 1 VOCABULARY Effects of dangerous weather

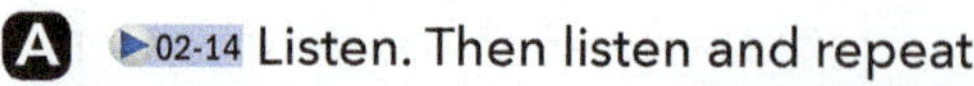

A 02-14 Listen. Then listen and repeat.

We had to evacuate.

We lost power.

The streets were flooded.

Trees fell down.

The roads were closed.

The roads were icy.

Stores were closed.

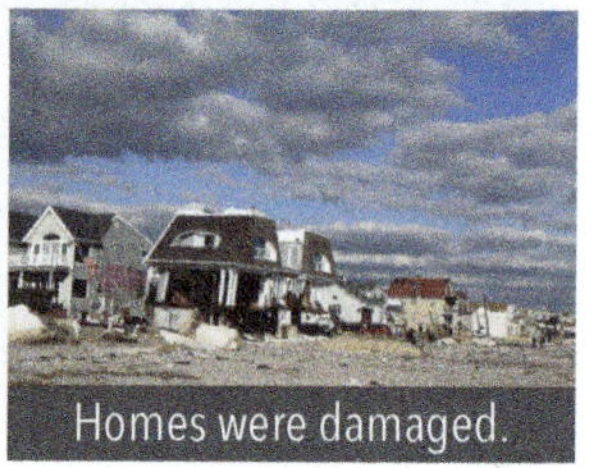
Homes were damaged.

B Match weather events in Lesson 2 with the effects below. There can be more than one answer.

We had to evacuate.	We lost power.	The streets were flooded.	Trees fell down.
The roads were closed.	**The roads were icy.**	**Stores were closed.**	**Homes were damaged.**

C PAIRS Compare your answers in 1B.

2 GRAMMAR Expressing cause and effect with *so / such…that*

COACH

Subject	Verb	*So* + adjective	*That* clause
I	was	**so** scared	**that** I ran from the thunder.
It	is	**so** cold	**that** I can't feel my fingers.
The roads	were	**so** dangerous	**that** people stayed home.
Subject	**Verb**	***So* + adverb**	***That* clause**
He	drove	**so** carefully	**that** we arrived safely.
We	have prepared	**so** well	**that** we are ready for the storm.
The fires	are spreading	**so** quickly	**that** people can't get out.
Subject	**Verb**	***Such* + adjective + noun**	***That* clause**
She	was	**such** a brave firefighter	**that** she won an award.
The tornado	caused	**such** terrible damage	**that** it will take years to rebuild.
The countries	experienced	**such** a long drought	**that** people had no food.

>> FOR PRACTICE, GO TO PAGE 130

3 CONVERSATION

A ▶02-16 **Listen or watch. Check (✓) all the effects of the hurricane.**

- ☐ The streets flooded.
- ☐ People had to evacuate.
- ☐ Jim's sister's house flooded.
- ☐ Trees fell down.
- ☐ Jim's sister's house lost power.
- ☐ Stores were closed.
- ☐ Roads were closed.
- ☐ Jim's sister lived near the water, so her house was damaged.
- ☐ People lost their homes and cars.

B ▶02-17 **Listen or watch. Complete the conversation.**

Diana: Have you ever been in a hurricane?
Jim: Yeah. I have.
Diana: Really? What happened?
Jim: It rained so hard that streets were flooded.
Diana: Oh no!
Jim: And the wind was ______________________ trees fell down.
Diana: Sounds like it was dangerous!
Jim: It was. A lot of homes were damaged.

CONVERSATION SKILL
Express relief

To express relief, say:
That's a relief.
I'm glad to hear that.
Phew!
Thank goodness!

Listen to or watch the conversation in 3A again. Raise your hand when you hear the phrases above.

C ▶02-18 **Listen and repeat. Then practice with a partner.**

D PAIRS **Make new conversations. Use these words or your own ideas.**

roads were closed | we lost power | We had to evacuate.

4 TRY IT YOURSELF

A MAKE IT PERSONAL **Have a conversation about the effects of dangerous weather. Use words from 1A.**

A: Have you ever been in an earthquake?
B: Yes. We lost power. But we were OK.
A: I'm glad to hear that.

B WALK AROUND **Talk to three other classmates about their experiences with dangerous weather. Take notes.**

☐ I CAN DISCUSS THE EFFECTS OF WEATHER.

LESSON 4 READ ABOUT EXTREME WEATHER

DIANA OLVERA
@DianaO
Watched Sharknado 5 on TV during my workout. My life will never be the same 😉

1 BEFORE YOU READ

A PAIRS **What is the strangest weather you have ever seen?**

Once, during a storm, I saw a rainbow in a complete circle. It's called a glory.

B ▶02-19 VOCABULARY **Listen. Then listen and repeat.**

a creature: an animal
frequent: happening often
logical: based on clear thinking
extreme: very unusual or very bad
a body of water: a lake, a pond, or an ocean
inspire: to give someone the idea to do something
attack: to try to hurt someone

>> FOR PRACTICE, GO TO PAGE 155

2 READ

A PREVIEW **Read the title and headers and look at the image. What is strange about the rain?**

B ▶02-20 **Listen. Read the article.**

STRANGE RAIN

What's falling from the sky?

Not long ago, a man in a village in Serbia looked up and saw a strange, dark cloud in the sky. Suddenly, hundreds of frogs were falling from the cloud onto the road. A similar event occurred in Hungary five years later, when falling frogs surprised shoppers during a storm. The same year, hundreds of small fish fell on the tiny town of Lajamanu, Australia.

Since early times, there have been reports of frogs, fish, worms, and other creatures falling from the sky. In 200 BCE, a Greek historian reported that it "often rained fishes" near his home. In Yoro, Honduras, the rain of fish was at one time so frequent that the town celebrates *The Festival of Rain of Fishes* every year. Strange rain is not limited to living creatures; in 1969, people in Punta Gorda, Florida, reported a sudden storm of golf balls.

Where does this strange rain come from?

A writer named Charles Fort was fascinated by these reports. In the early 1900s, he collected more than 60,000 newspaper articles about different forms of strange rain. Although most people who hear about strange rain assume these are just stories, Fort disagreed. He felt there had to be a scientific explanation, yet his own explanations were not particularly scientific! He suggested that an ocean in the clouds might be the cause of the rain. In another idea, he suggested that perhaps the frogs were from a spaceship that had exploded far above the earth.

Most people can agree that Fort's explanations are probably not correct; however, the reports have been frequent enough that experts believe there must be some logical explanation. Today, scientists believe that this strange rain is the result of extreme weather. When powerful winds, especially tornadoes, move over a lake or river, they may pick up the water—and everything in it—including fish and frogs. The strong winds then move across land, often for very long distances. The town of Lajamanu, Australia, for example, is more than 300 miles or 482 kilometers away from a body of water. When the wind becomes weaker, everything falls to the ground, resulting in strange rain.

Strange rain goes to Hollywood

These reports of strange rain have inspired books, television programs, and movies. The *Sharknado* movies are probably the most well-known movies about creatures that fall from the sky. In these movies, a powerful tornado picks up shark-filled water from the ocean. It drops the water, along with the sharks, across the city of Los Angeles. As they fall through the air, the sharks attack hundreds of people. No one takes these movies seriously, but they are extremely popular. Strange rain makes a good story!

3 CHECK YOUR UNDERSTANDING

A Which statement best describes the main idea of the article?

a. Strange rain has no logical explanation.
b. Extreme weather can bring strange forms of rain.
c. Strange rain has a long history.

B Read the Reading Skill. What examples support the ideas in each section? Complete the chart.

Idea	Examples
What's falling from the sky?	1. frogs 2. 3. 4.
Where does this strange rain come from?	1. ocean in the clouds 2. 3.
Strange rain goes to Hollywood	1.

READING SKILL
Identify examples as supporting details

Writers often use examples to support their ideas. Identifying these examples can help you understand what the writer is trying to tell you.

C FOCUS ON LANGUAGE Reread lines 8-9 and 25-27 in the article. Think about the phrases *at one time* and *take seriously*. Circle the correct answers.

1. The expression *at one time* means that ___.
   a. it happened once
   b. it happened at a time in the past
   c. it happened a long time ago
2. The expression *take something seriously* means ___.
   a. to think something is real and important
   b. to think something is dangerous
   c. to want to buy something

D PAIRS What is the article about? Retell the most important ideas in the article. Use your own words.

The article is about an unusual kind of rain...

Find other news reports on strange rain.

4 MAKE IT PERSONAL

A Have you ever experienced strange rain or other kinds of strange weather? Complete the chart about a strange weather experience that you had.

What did you see?	Who were you with?	What did you do?

B PAIRS Share your weather experience. Use your notes in 4A.

When I was eleven years old, my family...

☐ I CAN READ ABOUT EXTREME WEATHER.

LESSON 5 WRITE ABOUT A WEATHER EVENT

DIANA OLVERA

@DianaO

Busy emailing everyone back home. Want them to know everything is okay here!

1 BEFORE YOU WRITE

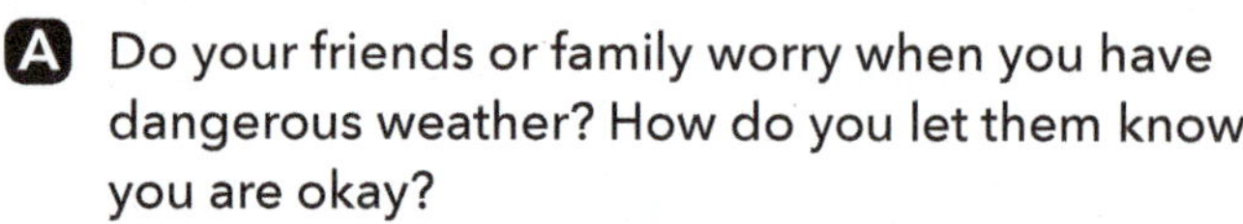

A Do your friends or family worry when you have dangerous weather? How do you let them know you are okay?

B Read Diana's email. What weather event is she writing about?

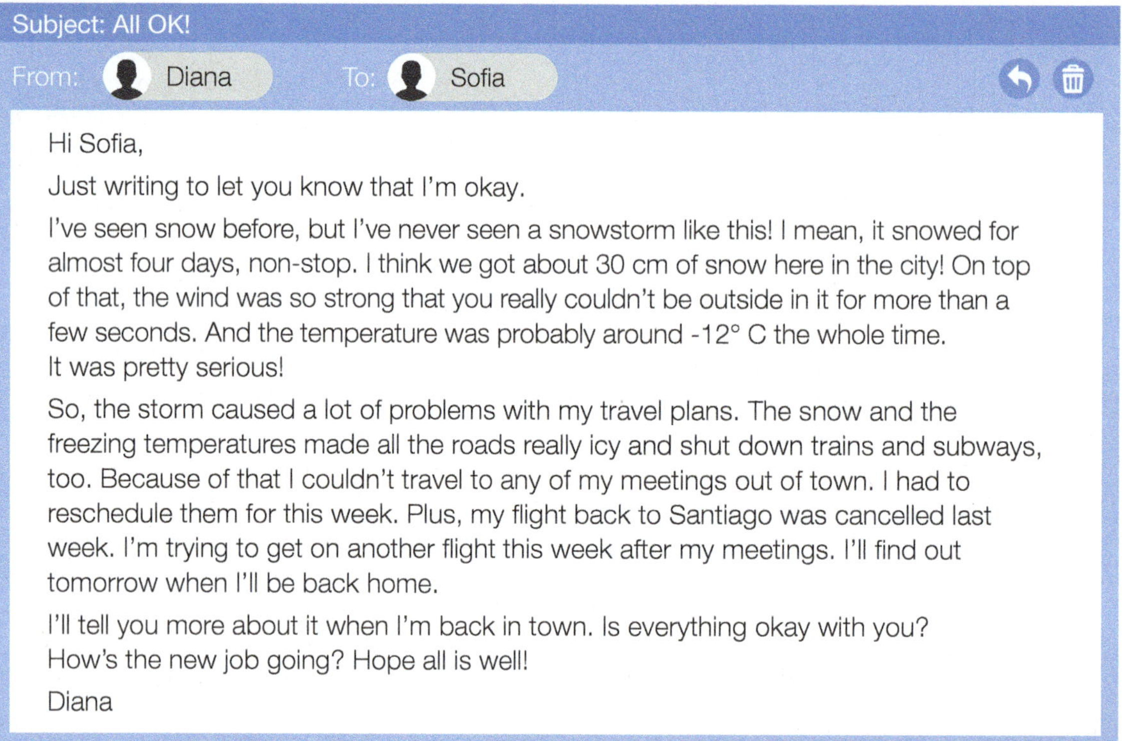

Subject: All OK!

From: Diana To: Sofia

Hi Sofia,

Just writing to let you know that I'm okay.

I've seen snow before, but I've never seen a snowstorm like this! I mean, it snowed for almost four days, non-stop. I think we got about 30 cm of snow here in the city! On top of that, the wind was so strong that you really couldn't be outside in it for more than a few seconds. And the temperature was probably around -12° C the whole time. It was pretty serious!

So, the storm caused a lot of problems with my travel plans. The snow and the freezing temperatures made all the roads really icy and shut down trains and subways, too. Because of that I couldn't travel to any of my meetings out of town. I had to reschedule them for this week. Plus, my flight back to Santiago was cancelled last week. I'm trying to get on another flight this week after my meetings. I'll find out tomorrow when I'll be back home.

I'll tell you more about it when I'm back in town. Is everything okay with you? How's the new job going? Hope all is well!

Diana

2 FOCUS ON WRITING

Read the Writing Skill. Then reread Diana's email. Take notes in the chart.

WRITING SKILL Organize one idea per paragraph

To make your writing clear, describe only one idea in each paragraph. This will make both your informal writing, such as emails, and formal writing, such as essays, clear.

Opening (greeting, reason for writing)
- Greeting: Hi Sofia
- Reason for writing: Just letting you know that I'm okay.

Details about the weather
- Snowed for four days non-stop
- ______________________
- Strong winds made it difficult to be outside
- ______________________

How weather affected plans
- Shut down trains and subways
- ______________________
- Flight to Santiago cancelled last week
- ______________________

Closing (ask about friend, sign off)
- Ask about friend: ______________________
- Sign off: ______________________

3 PLAN YOUR WRITING

A Think about a bad weather event you experienced. Imagine you are writing an email to someone about the event. Complete the chart to help plan your email.

Opening (greeting, reason for writing)
- Greeting: ______________________
- Reason for writing: ______________________

Details about the weather
- ______________________
- ______________________
- ______________________
- ______________________

How weather affected plans
- ______________________
- ______________________
- ______________________
- ______________________

Closing (ask about friend, sign off)
- Ask about friend: ______________________
- Sign off: ______________________

B PAIRS Talk about the weather event in your email.

I was in a hurricane last year. It rained so much...

4 WRITE

Write an email about the weather event using your ideas from 3A. Remember to use one idea per paragraph for each point you want to make. Use the email in 1B as a model.

5 REVISE YOUR WRITING

A PAIRS Exchange and read each other's emails.

1. Did your partner organize one idea per paragraph?
2. Did your partner include clear supporting details?

B PAIRS Can your classmate improve his or her email? Make suggestions.

6 PROOFREAD

Read your email again. Can you improve your writing?

Check your
- spelling
- punctuation
- capitalization

☐ I CAN WRITE ABOUT A WEATHER EVENT.

PUT IT TOGETHER

1 MEDIA PROJECT

A ▶02-21 **Listen or watch. What does Lucas talk about?**

B ▶02-21 **Listen or watch again. Answer the questions.**

1. What weather conditions does Lucas talk about?
____
2. What did he do?
____
3. What does he predict for tomorrow's weather?
____

C **Show your own photos.**

Step 1 Think about a time when weather changed your plans and how it changed them. Choose 3–5 photos to show the weather.

Step 2 Show the photos to the class. Describe the weather and what happened to your plans.

Step 3 Answer questions and get feedback.

2 LEARNING STRATEGY

MAKE A VOCABULARY WORD WEB

Make a word web to help you learn vocabulary. Word webs show how words in a group are related to each other. When you study words that are connected, it is easier to remember them.

BLIZZARD – freezing temperatures; heavy snow – strong winds; icy roads – dangerous conditions

Review the vocabulary from the unit. What words do you need to study? Make two or more word webs of related words. Review the word webs twice a week.

3 REFLECT AND PLAN

A **Look back through the unit. Check (✓) the things you learned. Highlight the things you need to learn.**

Speaking objectives
- ☐ Talk about the weather
- ☐ Report dangerous weather
- ☐ Discuss the effects of weather

Vocabulary
- ☐ Weather conditions
- ☐ Dangerous weather
- ☐ Effects of dangerous weather

Pronunciation
- ☐ Pronouncing *th*
- ☐ Stressed and unstressed words

Grammar
- ☐ *Must / may / might / could* for conclusions
- ☐ Present perfect and present perfect continuous
- ☐ Expressing cause and effect with *so / such…that*

Reading
- ☐ Identify examples as supporting details

Writing
- ☐ Organize one idea per paragraph

B **What will you do to learn the things you highlighted? For example, use your app, review your Student Book, or do other practice. Make a plan.**

3 HOW WELL DO YOU WORK TOGETHER?

LEARNING GOALS

In this unit, you

- discuss problems at work
- talk about avoiding problems
- talk about a misunderstanding
- read about creative thinking
- write about communication skills

GET STARTED

A Read the unit title and learning goals.

B Look at the photo of a meeting. What do you see?

C Now read Liz's message. Why does she talk about communication?

LIZ FLORES

@LizF

Communication is key in working with others.

LESSON 1 DISCUSS PROBLEMS AT WORK

LIZ FLORES
@LizF
Check out the new brochure design on our website. It wasn't easy, but we did it!

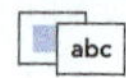

1 VOCABULARY When things go wrong

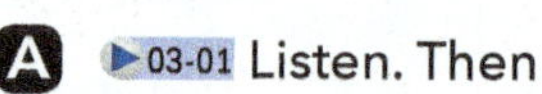

A 03-01 Listen. Then listen and repeat.

Negative feelings
embarrassed: feeling ashamed
frustrated: feeling upset because something is preventing you from doing something
mad: feeling angry
tense: feeling nervous or anxious

Ways to work successfully
communicate clearly: to talk about or explain things in a clear way
follow instructions: to do what you are supposed to do
have experience: to know how to do something well because you have done it before
meet deadlines: to finish something on time

B 03-02 Listen to four conversations. Match the words and phrases with each conversation.

Conversation 1	embarrassed	didn't meet deadlines
Conversation 2	frustrated	didn't follow instructions
Conversation 3	mad	doesn't have experience
Conversation 4	tense	didn't communicate clearly

C PAIRS Make four sentences, each one using one negative feeling and one action in 1A.
I was embarrassed because...

COACH

2 GRAMMAR Object complements

An object complement is a noun or adjective that comes after a direct object and renames or describes the direct object.

Subject	Verb	Direct object	Complement
I	find	the project	**interesting**.
She	painted	her office	**blue**.
It	makes	me	**uncomfortable**.
We	elected	Rosa	**president of the company**.
They	made	the presentation	**easy to understand**.

Notes
- Object complements are commonly used with certain verbs, such as *call*, *consider*, *elect*, *find*, and *make*.
- The complement can be a noun phrase (e.g., *president of the company*) or an adjective phrase (e.g., *easy to understand*).

>> FOR PRACTICE, GO TO PAGE 131

3 PRONUNCIATION

COACH

Stress with word endings

In words with more than one syllable, one syllable is stressed: communicate. When we add an ending like *-er*, *-ed*, or *-ly* to a word, usually the stress does not change: communicated. But with some endings, like *-tion*, the stress moves to the syllable just before the ending: communication.

A 03-04 **Listen. Notice the stressed syllables. Then listen and repeat.**

communicate	They didn't communicate clearly.
communicated	We communicated by email.
communication	Communication was a problem.

B 03-05 **Underline the stressed syllable in each word. Then listen and check your answers.**

1. design — designer
2. embarrassed — embarrassing
3. graduate — graduation
4. frustrated — frustrating
5. effective — effectively
6. organized — organization

C PAIRS **Student A, say a word in 3B. Student B, say the other word in the pair.**

4 CONVERSATION

A 03-06 **Listen or watch. Circle the correct answers.**

1. What was good about the printing company?
   a. They had a lot of experience. b. Their work was good. c. They met deadlines.
2. The printing company didn't __________.
   a. use the right paper b. return phone calls c. use the right color
3. Will Liz and Diana use the printing company again?
   a. Yes. b. No. c. They don't know yet.

B 03-07 **Listen or watch. Complete the conversation.**

Diana: So what went wrong?
Liz: Well first, they didn't communicate clearly.
Diana: I agree. They didn't respond to emails very well.
Liz: And they didn't follow instructions.
Diana: Yes! That ____________________ so frustrated!
Liz: Yeah, I found that __________ to understand.

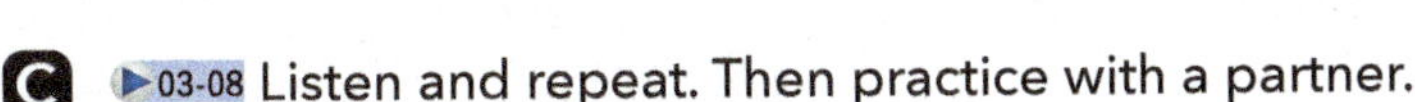

C 03-08 **Listen and repeat. Then practice with a partner.**

D PAIRS **Make new conversations. Use the words in 1A or your own ideas.**

5 TRY IT YOURSELF

A MAKE IT PERSONAL **Think of a problem you've had at work. Complete the chart.**

Who was involved?	What was the problem?	How did it make you feel?
project team member	didn't meet deadlines	mad

B PAIRS **Talk about the problems you've had.**

A: *My project team member made me so mad.*
B: *Why? What happened?*

☐ I CAN DISCUSS PROBLEMS AT WORK.

LESSON 2 TALK ABOUT AVOIDING PROBLEMS

LIZ FLORES
@LizF
Lesson for today: If you never make mistakes, you never learn!

1 VOCABULARY Ways to avoid problems

A ▶03-09 Listen. Then listen and repeat.

brainstorm ideas: to come up with ideas (usually with other people)
offer suggestions: to tell someone what you think he/she could or should do
set up a meeting: to arrange a time and place to come together to discuss something
set clear goals: to carefully plan what you want to achieve
stay on schedule: to do your work on time
give feedback: to tell people how well they did something, and how they can do it better
create an agenda: to think of a list of topics to discuss at a meeting

B When do you do the activities in 1A? Check (✓) the boxes. Some actions can happen multiple times.

	Before starting a project	During a project	After the project
1. brainstorm ideas	☐	☐	☐
2. offer suggestions	☐	☐	☐
3. set up a meeting	☐	☐	☐
4. set clear goals	☐	☐	☐
5. stay on schedule	☐	☐	☐
6. give feedback	☐	☐	☐
7. create an agenda	☐	☐	☐

C PAIRS Compare your answers in 1B.

2 GRAMMAR Making suggestions

COACH

	Subject	Base form of verb	
What if **Why don't** **How about**	I we	give	them feedback?

	Verb + *-ing*	
How about	setting	some goals?

Subject 1 + *suggest*	*(that)*	Subject 2	Base form of verb	
I **suggest** She **suggests**	(that)	she we	set up	a meeting.

Notes
- With *suggest that*, the verb in the second clause is always in the base form.
- You can use *Let's* and *could* to make suggestions.
  ***Let's** talk to them about it.* *We **could** send them an email.*

We often use questions to make suggestions as a way of softening them, or making them more polite.

>> FOR PRACTICE, GO TO PAGE 132

3 CONVERSATION

A ▶03-11 Listen or watch. Read the sentences. Circle *T* for *True* and *F* for *False*. If the statement is false, cross out the false information and correct it.

1. Liz and Diana have decided not to use the printing company again. T F
2. They will give the printing company feedback with specific examples. T F
3. They will set clear goals to communicate better. T F
4. They will ask the printing company for daily reports. T F

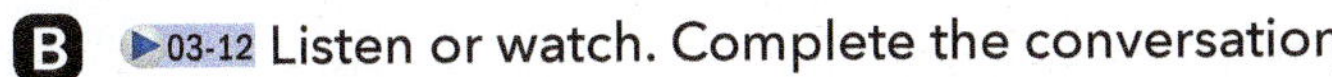

B ▶03-12 Listen or watch. Complete the conversation.

Liz: ____________________ we offer suggestions on how to work together more effectively?

Diana: That's a great idea! What did you have in mind?

Liz: Well, for one, we __________ set up weekly meetings.

Diana: I couldn't agree more! That will give us a specific time to discuss problems that come up.

Liz: Exactly!

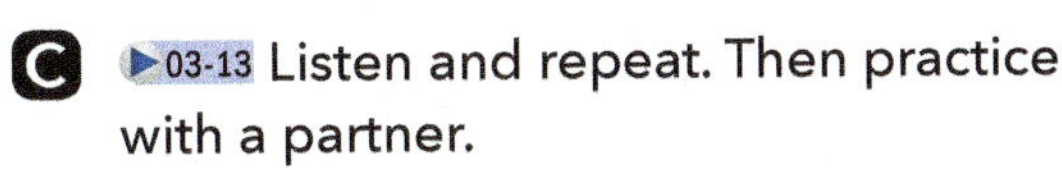

C ▶03-13 Listen and repeat. Then practice with a partner.

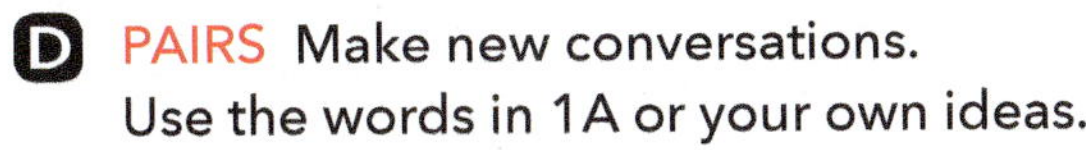

D PAIRS Make new conversations. Use the words in 1A or your own ideas.

CONVERSATION SKILL Show agreement

To show that you agree with something, say:

Right. I agree.
That sounds good / great.
I couldn't agree more.
That's a great / good idea.
Exactly!

Listen to or watch the conversation in 3A again. Underline the phrases that you hear above.

4 TRY IT YOURSELF

ROLE PLAY Imagine that you work for TSW Media. Choose one of these situations and then have a meeting. Brainstorm ways to avoid a similar problem in the future.

Situation 1	Situation 2
Your project was late by a month.	A project costs 25% more than you planned.

A: I can't believe our project was late by a month.
B: What can we do next time?

☐ I CAN TALK ABOUT AVOIDING PROBLEMS.

LESSON 3 TALK ABOUT A MISUNDERSTANDING

LIZ FLORES

@LizF

Just listened to a couple of hilarious stories on the podcast *Daily Trouble*. Still laughing!

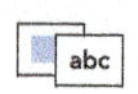

1 VOCABULARY Words related to understanding

A ▶03-14 Listen. Then listen and repeat.

be confused: to not understand something clearly
clarify: to try and make something easier to understand
figure out: to understand or solve something
misunderstand: to understand something in the wrong way
assume: to think that something is true even though you don't have proof
realize: to finally understand something that you did not know before

B Complete the sentences. Use words from 1A.

1. It's easy to ______________ the question, so listen carefully.
2. I am totally ______________. Can you explain that again?
3. I don't know where Bora is, but I ______________ she is still coming.
4. We have to ______________ how to solve this problem together.
5. I didn't ______________ how difficult this class was going to be until I failed my first test.
6. Pictures can help ______________ written instructions.

C PAIRS Write a sentence with each of the verbs in 1A that are true for you. Tell your classmate.

Yesterday, I finally figured out the meaning of "brainstorm ideas."

2 GRAMMAR Imperatives in reported speech

COACH

Use *said*, *told*, and *asked* with an infinitive to report past orders and requests.

Direct speech				Reported speech				
Subject	Verb	Object	Imperative	Subject	Verb	Object	(Not) infinitive	
I You	said,	–	"Arrive on time." "Don't be late."	I You	**said**	–	**to arrive** **not to be**	on time. late.
She	told	him,		She	**told** **asked**	him us		

Notes
- Never use a noun or pronoun as an object with *said*.
- Always use a noun or pronoun as an object with *told* and *asked*.
- Never use *ask* with imperatives in direct speech.
- Always use a comma before the imperative in direct speech.

>> FOR PRACTICE, GO TO PAGE 133

COACH

3 PRONUNCIATION

A ▶03-16 **Listen. Notice the way the stress moves in these numbers. Then listen and repeat.**

Turn to page fifteen. I read fifteen pages.

She's twenty-five. Let's meet in twenty-five minutes.

B ▶03-17 **Listen. Circle the number you hear. Then listen and repeat.**

1. There were 13 / 30 students in the class.
2. They've been married for 14 / 40 years.
3. The book cost 18 / 80 dollars.
4. The meeting took about 15 / 50 minutes.

Numbers and moving stress

We always stress the first syllable of numbers ending in *-ty*: fifty.

But in -teen numbers (like *fifteen*) and numbers with two parts (like *twenty-five*), the stress can move. We stress the last part of these numbers when we say them alone or at the end of a sentence: *fifteen*. But we often stress the first part of the number when another word follows: *fifteen pages*.

4 LISTENING

LISTENING SKILL

Listen for cause and effect

Understanding cause and effect relationships can help you identify the important ideas in a listening. For example, stories often start with a problem. That is the *cause*. The *effect* is what happens because of the problem.

A ▶03-18 **Listen to the two stories. Circle the correct answers.**

1. What was the problem in the first story?
   a. Tony's mom didn't understand what a vegetarian was.
   b. Tony didn't want his mother to cook.
   c. Tony's mother didn't know Tony had a girlfriend.
2. What was the problem in the second story?
   a. Greg didn't know how to set up the meeting room.
   b. Greg set up the meeting for the wrong number of people.
   c. Greg didn't know where to order the sandwiches.

B ▶03-18 **Read the Listening Skill. Listen again. Complete the chart.**

	Story 1	Story 2
Who	Tony and his mother	Greg and his boss
Effect of the misunderstanding	First, mom asked Tony if she could make ______ (1) Then she wanted to make ______ (2)	Greg reserved a ______ (3) that was too small. Greg didn't order enough ______ (4)

C PAIRS **Student A, retell the first story. Student B, retell the second story.**

5 TRY IT YOURSELF

A MAKE IT PERSONAL **Complete the chart with information about a misunderstanding. It can be something that happened to you or to someone you know.**

Who	
Why it happened	
What was the effect	

B PAIRS **Tell your stories. Ask follow-up questions.**

☐ I CAN TALK ABOUT A MISUNDERSTANDING.

LESSON 4 READ ABOUT CREATIVE THINKING

LIZ FLORES
@LizF
Do you know what helps me think of original ideas? Riddles and puzzles—they're a great brain exercise!

1 BEFORE YOU READ

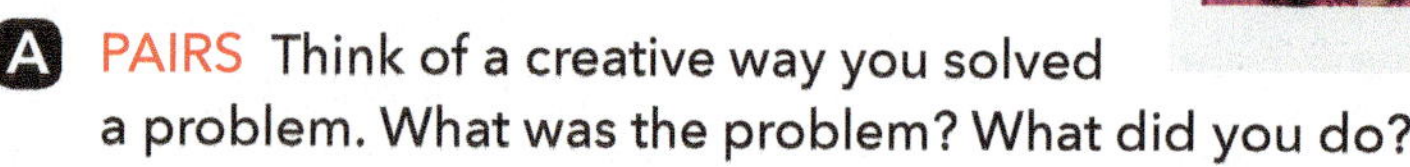

A PAIRS Think of a creative way you solved a problem. What was the problem? What did you do?

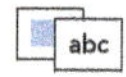

B 03-19 VOCABULARY Listen. Then listen and repeat.

flexible: able to change easily
an assumption: something you think is probably true but don't know for sure
relevant: related to what you are doing or talking about
obvious: easy to notice or understand
a criminal: a person who is involved in illegal activities or has been proven guilty of a crime
arrest: to take a person to the police station because the person has done something illegal

>> FOR PRACTICE, GO TO PAGE 156

2 READ

A PREVIEW Read the title. What do you think the dots in the article are?

B 03-20 Listen. Read the article.

LATERAL THINKING

Sometimes no matter how much I think about a problem, I just can't solve it. Solving problems is important for my job, so when a colleague mentioned lateral thinking, I was ready to listen. Lateral thinking means thinking in an indirect and creative way and looking at the problem in a new and unusual way. This can help you become more flexible when you try to solve a problem. Lateral thinking is different from how I thought about problems. I was being too logical. I was thinking about each problem in a very direct, step-by-step way and making too many assumptions. You've probably heard the expression, "thinking outside of the box." It actually comes from a famous problem called the nine-dot puzzle. To solve the puzzle, you have to connect all nine dots with four straight lines, but you can't take your pen off the page. HINT: To complete this task successfully, you must go "outside the box." Solving this puzzle is an example of lateral thinking.

Nine-dot puzzle

Situation puzzles are other examples of practicing lateral thinking. To solve situation puzzles, you may ask only yes/no questions, which have three possible answers: "yes," "no," or "the information isn't relevant." There's not only one answer to problems like these, but one answer is usually the best. That answer usually seems obvious after you know it.

Here is an example:

Someone calls the police to tell them that a criminal named Jim Price is playing cards in the apartment next door. The police know Price is dangerous, but they don't know what he looks like. They go into the apartment and they see three people playing cards: two truck drivers and a firefighter. They don't say a word, but they immediately arrest the firefighter. How do the police know he is Jim Price?

Here is one way that *yes/no* questions could help you find the solution:

Did any of the players say anything? No
Did the firefighter try to run away? No
Did the policemen know any of the players? No
Did the firefighter look different from the truck drivers? Yes
Was the firefighter wearing a hat? Not relevant
Was the firefighter's hairstyle different from the truck drivers'? Yes

Price looked different from the truck drivers and had a different hairstyle from them because Price was a man and the truck drivers were women. Many people begin with the assumption that truck drivers are always men.

Lateral thinking is already helping me at my job in market research. After practicing this type of thinking, I suggested a whole new group of customers for our products to my boss. Try it! It just might work for you!

3 CHECK YOUR UNDERSTANDING

A **Which statement best describes the main idea of the article?**

a. Lateral thinking is the best way to solve a problem.
b. Lateral thinking helps you make assumptions.
c. Lateral thinking might help you to solve problems.

B **Read the Reading Skill. Circle the correct answer.**

1. Where is the definition of lateral thinking?
   a. Lines 4–6 b. Lines 7–8 c. Lines 16–18
2. Where does the writer explain how lateral thinking is different from other ways of thinking?
   a. Lines 6–8 b. Lines 7–11 c. Lines 24–26
3. Where is an example of lateral thinking?
   a. Lines 11–16 b. Lines 19–23 c. Lines 28–46

READING SKILL Understand extended definitions

Writers often provide extended definitions to explain important or difficult ideas. They can do this by providing:

- dictionary definitions
- differences from other ideas
- examples

C **Read the Reading Skill again. Circle the correct answer.**

1. What does lateral thinking mean?
   a. thinking in a creative way
   b. taking a direct approach to problems
   c. asking questions about a situation
2. Lateral thinking is different from ___.
   a. problem solving
   b. logical, step-by-step thinking
   c. thinking outside the box
3. What is an example of lateral thinking?
   a. making an assumption
   b. solving a situation puzzle
   c. asking a yes / no question
4. Why are situation puzzles difficult?
   a. People think the solution is too obvious.
   b. People add their own information.
   c. People don't understand the problem.

D FOCUS ON LANGUAGE **Reread lines 9–11 in the article. Think about the phrase *step-by-step*. Circle the correct answer.**

The expression *step-by-step* means ___.

a. a way that helps you finish quickly
b. a new and different way
c. a way of doing something in a certain order

E PAIRS **What is the article about? Retell the most important ideas in the article. Use your own words.**

Lateral thinking is a different way to solve problems...

Find out about lateral thinking. What other puzzles use lateral thinking? 

4 MAKE IT PERSONAL

A **Read the situation puzzle. Write *yes / no* questions like the ones in the article to solve it.**

A man is dressed in black. He is wearing a black mask. There are no streetlights. There is no moon. A car is coming toward him. It has no lights. Then the driver turns away. How was the driver able to see the man in black?

B PAIRS **Share your *yes / no* questions with your classmate. Decide who will ask the questions and try to solve the puzzle, and who will provide the answer.**

Did the man say something to the driver?

It was daytime so it was light.

☐ I CAN READ ABOUT CREATIVE THINKING.

LESSON 5 WRITE ABOUT COMMUNICATION SKILLS

LIZ FLORES
@LizF
Good communication is so important! I've been thinking about how to communicate better...

1 BEFORE YOU WRITE

A What are some good communication skills?

B Read Liz's blog post. What communication skill is she writing about?

Blog | About | Destinations | Contact

Search

About
RSS Feed
Social Media
Recent Posts
Archives
Email

The secret to good communication

A famous Greek philosopher once said, "We have two ears and one mouth so that we can listen twice as much as we speak." I couldn't agree more. It is so important to listen well in order to communicate well.

Listening is especially important when you disagree with people. If you want to solve the disagreement, you first have to listen and understand how they are feeling. Are they frustrated, angry, disappointed? If they feel like you are trying to understand them, they will be more open to you. Also, if you understand how they are feeling, it's easier to come up with solutions that you can both agree on.

Listening is also important because it can help you succeed at work. The most successful business leaders are good listeners. They are always paying attention to what others are saying so that they can hear new or different ideas. Listening to new ideas like this can help you think of a better way to do something.

Of course it's important to learn how to speak well and communicate your point clearly. But it doesn't matter how clear you are if you can't hear what other people are saying. I think listening is probably the most important communication skill.

Leave a Reply

Enter your comment here...

C Read the post again. Complete the chart.

Argument: Listening is the most important communication skill.

Supporting argument 1: Listening well makes it easier to solve disagreements.

Reason: When you understand someone's feelings, they will be more open to you

Reason: When you understand someone's feelings, you can find solutions you both like.

Supporting argument 2: Listening well helps you succeed at work.

Reason: You can hear new ideas if you listen well.

Reason: You can think of a better way to do something.

sâg ciol

2 FOCUS ON WRITING

Read the Writing Skill. Then reread Liz's post. Underline the two supporting arguments. Circle the reasons given for each one.

WRITING SKILL Develop an argument

When writing your opinion about a topic, provide **supporting arguments.** These arguments should include details which further explain and support your main idea. You can give reasons for your opinion, or you can provide specific examples that help to support your point.

3 PLAN YOUR WRITING

A The Greek philosopher Plato said, "Wise men speak because they have something to say; fools speak because they have to say something." What do you think this means? Do you agree or disagree? Develop your argument with supporting reasons and examples. Complete the chart to help plan your writing.

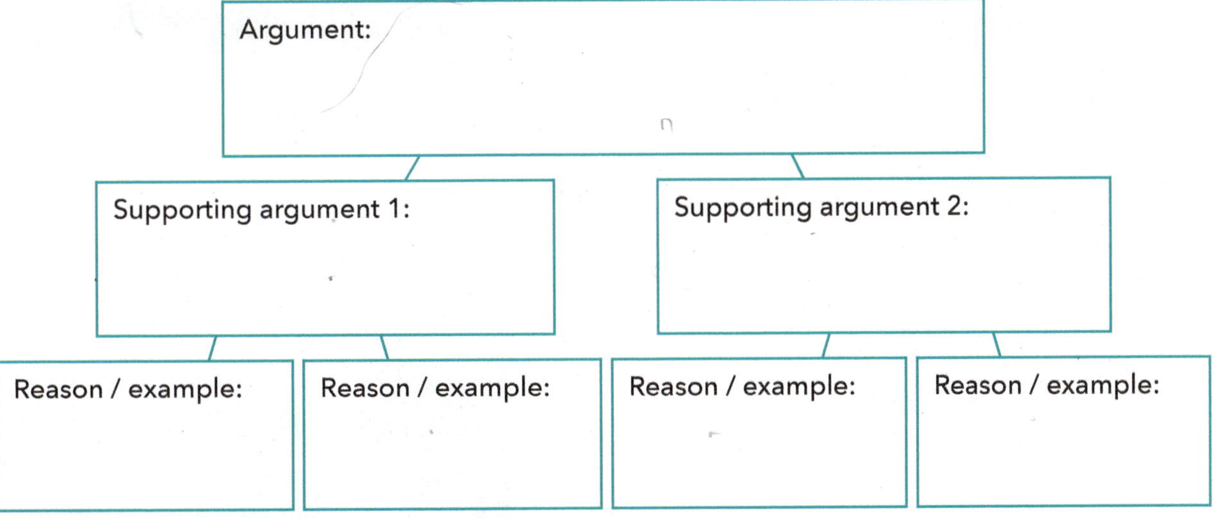

B PAIRS Share your opinion and supporting arguments.

I agree with the quote. I think it means that...

4 WRITE

Write a post giving your opinion about the quote using your details from 3A. Remember to give supporting arguments with reasons and examples. Use the post in 1B as a model.

5 REVISE YOUR WRITING

A PAIRS Exchange and read each other's posts.

1. Underline the supporting arguments.
2. Circle all the reasons or examples given.
3. Did your partner's reasons and examples help to develop their argument in a clear and persuasive way? Why or why not?

B PAIRS Can your classmate improve his or her post? Make suggestions.

6 PROOFREAD

Read your post again. Can you improve your writing?

Check your
- spelling
- punctuation
- capitalization

☐ I CAN WRITE ABOUT COMMUNICATION SKILLS.

PUT IT TOGETHER

1 MEDIA PROJECT

A ▶03-21 **Listen or watch. Who does Rafi talk about?**

B ▶03-21 **Listen or watch again. Answer the questions.**

1. What does Rafi do with Malik?
   ____
2. Why is Rafi happy to know Yanni?
   ____
3. How does Tariq help Rafi?
   ____

C **Show your own photos.**

Step 1 Take photos of 2–3 co-workers or friends. What do you do with them? How do they help you?

Step 2 Show the photos to the class. Talk about each person.

Step 3 Answer questions and get feedback.

2 LEARNING STRATEGY

How about we offer suggestions?

LISTEN, READ, AND SAY

To improve your pronunciation, listen to audio while reading. For example, listen to audio while reading the script from your book. Read aloud along with the video for practice.

Review the audio / video from the unit. Listen to the Conversation audio while reading along with the script on the page. Listen again. This time read aloud. Try to match the pronunciation. Review the audio / video at least twice.

3 REFLECT AND PLAN

A **Look back through the unit. Check (✓) the things you learned. Highlight the things you need to learn.**

Speaking objectives
- ☐ Discuss problems at work
- ☐ Talk about avoiding problems
- ☐ Talk about a misunderstanding

Vocabulary
- ☐ When things go wrong
- ☐ Ways to avoid problems
- ☐ Words related to understanding

Pronunciation
- ☐ Stress with word endings
- ☐ Numbers and moving stress

Grammar
- ☐ Object complements
- ☐ Making suggestions
- ☐ Imperatives in reported speech

Reading
- ☐ Understand extended definitions

Writing
- ☐ Develop an argument

B **What will you do to learn the things you highlighted? For example, use your app, review your Student Book, or do other practice. Make a plan.**

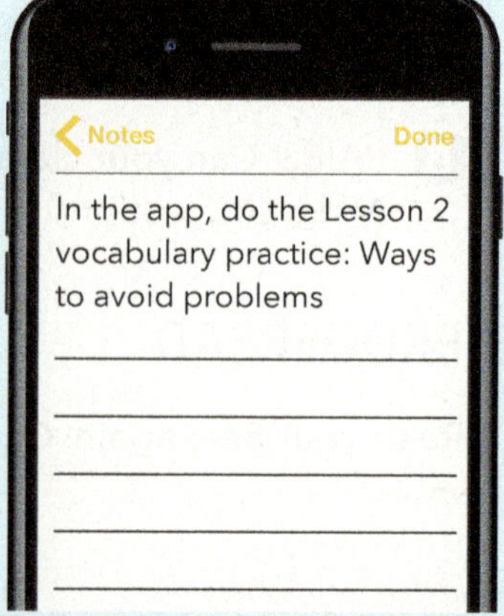

4 HOW DO YOU RELAX?

LEARNING GOALS

In this unit, you

- talk about how life has changed
- talk about what you like
- talk about a movie review
- read an interview with a location scout
- write a movie review

GET STARTED

A Read the unit title and learning goals.

B Look at the photo of a concert. What do you see?

C Now read Flavio's message. What did he do last night?

FLAVIO VEGA

@FlavioV

Went to a great concert last night with my best friends!

LESSON 1 TALK ABOUT HOW LIFE HAS CHANGED

FLAVIO VEGA
@FlavioV
Forgot my cell phone—feeling a little lost! Email me!!!

1 VOCABULARY Ways to connect

A ▶04-01 Listen. Then listen and repeat.

stay in touch

meet in person

connect online

shop online

post on social media

write a blog

video chat

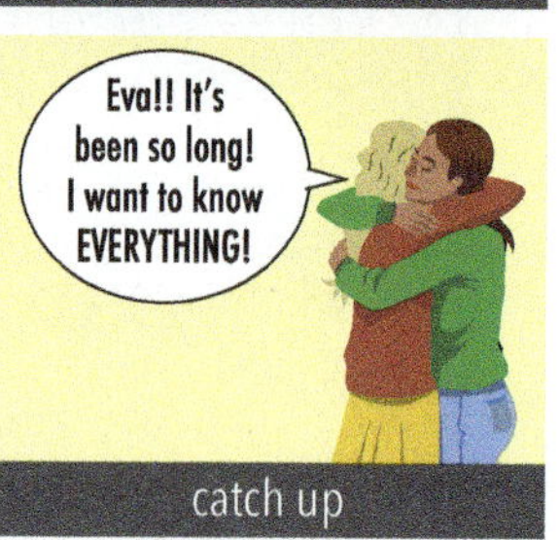

catch up

B PAIRS Choose one of the ways to connect in 1A and describe what you do, how often, and other details.

I post on social media every day...

2 GRAMMAR *Used to* and *would*

Use *used to* or *would* for past habits or situations that don't happen or are not true anymore.

Statements

Subject	*Used to / Would*	Base form of verb	
He They	**used to / would**	live write	in Chile. letters in the past.

Subject	*Didn't*	*Use to*	Base form of verb	
I	didn't	**use to**	study	hard.

Notes
- Use *used to* (not *would*) with past situations: *He **used to** live in Chile.*
- Do not use *would* unless it follows a clear reference to past time: *When I was a child, I **would** play a lot of video games.*
- In negative statements, *never used to* is more common than *didn't use to*: *I **never used to** study hard.*

Questions

Wh- word	*Did*	Subject	*Use to*	Base form of verb	
Where	did	you	**use to**	work?	
	Did	you	**use to**	have	a blog?
	Didn't	he	**use to**	play	guitar?

Notes
- Do not use *would* with questions.
- In questions, the simple past is more common than *did use to*: ***Did** you **have** a blog then?*

>> FOR PRACTICE, GO TO PAGE 134

3 PRONUNCIATION

COACH

Blended pronunciation of *used to* ("useta")

The verb *use* is normally pronounced /yuz/ (past *used* /yuzd/). But when we use *used to* or *use to* to talk about past habits, we blend the two words together and say "useta" /yustə/.

A 04-03 Listen. Notice the blended pronunciation of *used to* and *use to*. Then listen and repeat.

/yustə/	/yuzd/
I used to hate shopping.	I used a credit card.
He didn't use to see his friends.	She used an app to pay.

B 04-04 Listen. Circle "yes" if the sentence uses the blended pronunciation "useta" /yustə/. Circle "no" if it doesn't. Then check your answers with a partner.

1. yes / no 2. yes / no 3. yes / no 4. yes / no 5. yes / no 6. yes / no

C PAIRS Talk about things you used to do or like and how that has changed. Try to find a change that you have in common.

A: I used to play soccer, but I don't have time anymore.
B: Not me. I never played soccer.

4 CONVERSATION

A 04-05 Listen or watch. Who does each statement refer to? Write *Jim* or *Flavio*.

______ 1. He forgot his phone today.
______ 2. He hates shopping in stores.
______ 3. He stays in touch with his friends more easily now.
______ 4. He video chats with his niece in Taipei.

B 04-06 Listen or watch. Complete the conversation.

Flavio: I was thinking about what we ______ do before all this technology.
Jim: What do you mean?
Flavio: Well, before social media, I ______ stay in touch with my friends much less frequently.
Jim: What do you do now?
Flavio: Now I message them all the time.

CONVERSATION SKILL
Ask for clarification

To ask someone to clarify his or her meaning, say:
What do you mean?
Can you explain that a little bit?
Why's that?

Listen to or watch the conversation in 4A again. Underline the phrases that you hear above.

C 04-07 Listen and repeat. Then practice with a partner.

D PAIRS Make new conversations. Use the words in 1A or your own ideas.

5 TRY IT YOURSELF

A MAKE IT PERSONAL Think about how technology shapes your social life. Think about what your parents and grandparents used to do before modern technology. Take notes.

B PAIRS Use your notes to talk about how social life has changed.

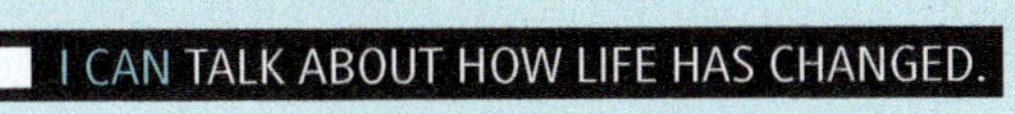

I CAN TALK ABOUT HOW LIFE HAS CHANGED.

LESSON 2 TALK ABOUT WHAT YOU LIKE

FLAVIO VEGA
@FlavioV
I miss playing with my band. Time to dust off my old guitar!

1 VOCABULARY Entertainment

A 04-08 Listen. Then listen and repeat.

B PAIRS Student A, describe a word from 1A. Student B, guess the word. Take turns.

A: You need a camera to do this. B: Photography!

2 GRAMMAR *So, neither, too,* and *either* with simple present action verbs

COACH

Use *so, neither, too,* and *either* to show similarity or agreement.

Statement	Response	
Affirmative	***So***	***do / does* + subject**
Sara loves rock. I enjoy taking photos.	So	does John. do I.
Negative	***Neither***	***do / does* + subject**
Jake doesn't watch suspense movies. We don't like dancing.	Neither	does Amy. do we.

Statement	Response	
Affirmative	**Subject**	***do / does* + *too***
She takes hip-hop classes. I love painting.	Sam I	does, too. do, too.
Negative	**Subject**	***doesn't / don't* + *either***
Karl doesn't paint well. They don't like comedies.	Yoko We	doesn't, either. don't, either.

Note: In informal speech, we often use *me, too* and *me, neither*.

A: *I love pop music.*
B: *Me, too.*

A: *I don't like comedies.*
B: *Me, neither.*

>> FOR PRACTICE, GO TO PAGE 135

3 PRONUNCIATION

A 04-10 **Listen. Notice the rhythm. Then listen and repeat.**

●••	●•●•	•●•●
modern dance So do I.	science fiction I don't, either.	play the guitar Neither do I.

Sentence rhythm

Every language has its own rhythm, or beat. The pattern of stressed and unstressed syllables gives English its rhythm. Words, phrases, and sentences can have the same rhythm. For example, the word *introduce* has the same rhythm as the sentence *What's your name*?

B 04-11 **Write each sentence in the correct column in 3A. Then listen and repeat.**

1. I do, too.
2. Where are you from?
3. We can do it.
4. How did you do?
5. How's it going?
6. What about you?

4 CONVERSATION

A 04-12 **Listen or watch. Circle the correct answers.**

1. What do Flavio and Jim both like?
   a. action / adventure movies
   b. photography
   c. playing jazz guitar
2. What will Flavio and Jim do on Saturday?
   a. go to a movie
   b. go to a photography show
   c. go to a music festival

B 04-13 **Listen or watch. Complete the conversation.**

Flavio: What kind of movies do you like?
Jim: All kinds. But I don't like suspense movies too much.
Flavio: Yeah. I ____________________. I like science fiction.
Jim: ____________________! A good sci-fi movie can really make you think.
Flavio: I agree.

C 04-14 **Listen and repeat. Then practice with a partner.**

D PAIRS **Make new conversations. Use the words in 1A or your own ideas.**

5 TRY IT YOURSELF

A MAKE IT PERSONAL **Write two or three things from 1A that you like and one thing you don't like.**

B WALK AROUND **Find someone who has similar likes and dislikes. Then report to the class.**

Monica loves jazz, and so do I.
I don't like pop music, and neither does she.

LESSON 3 TALK ABOUT A MOVIE REVIEW

FLAVIO VEGA
@FlavioV
Get Out of Town! is in theaters this week. Do you think it's worth watching?

1 VOCABULARY Movies

A 04-15 Listen. Then listen and repeat.

release: to make a movie available for the public to see
direct: to give instructions to the actors in a movie about how to perform
play: to act as a character in a movie
adapt: to change something and be able to use it in a different way
a plot: the details of a story
acting: the way an actor performs in a movie
a role: a character in a movie
a blockbuster: a movie that is a big success

B Complete the sentences. Use words from 1A.

1. Actors need to be good at ________________, and directors need to ________________ well.
2. The movie made millions of dollars. It was a ________________.
3. They will ________________ the movie next summer, but only in a few cities.
4. My favorite actors ________________ the main characters in the movie.
5. Valerie Vaine will play the ________________ of Jessica in the new movie.
6. The ________________ of the movie includes suspense, comedy, and action/adventure.
7. The writers will ________________ the story of a famous novel to turn it into a movie.

C PAIRS Compare your answers in 1B.

2 GRAMMAR Simple present and simple past passives

Use the passive when it is not known or not important who performs an action.

Simple present passive				
Subject	***Be***	**(*Not*)**	**Past participle**	
I The movie Blockbusters	**am** **is** **are**	(not)	**employed** **adapted** **released**	as a director. from a book every day.
Simple past passive				
Subject	***Be***	**(*Not*)**	**Past participle**	
The movie The actors	**was** **were**	(not)	**filmed** **known**	last year. in Hollywood.

Notes

- In passive sentences, the focus shifts from the agent to the object.
  Active: *People invited the writer.* Passive: *The writer was invited.*
- Use *by* when it *is* important to know who performs an action:
  The role is played **by** *award-winning actor Henry Davis.*
- In questions, the verb *be* comes before the subject:
  Are you *employed now?* *Where* ***were you*** *employed last year?*

>> FOR PRACTICE, GO TO PAGE 136

3 LISTENING

A ▶04-17 Listen to the movie review. Circle the correct answers.

1. *Get Out of Town!* is a(n) _________ movie.
   a. action/adventure b. suspense/thriller c. science fiction
2. The plot in *Get Out of Town!* is _________.
   a. confusing b. wonderful c. mysterious
3. In *Get Out of Town!*, Patrick Solaro brings out the best in _________.
   a. the actors b. the action c. the story

B ▶04-17 Read the Listening Skill. Listen again. How many stars do you think Brad Johnson would give the director, actors, and plot? Circle the correct answers.

2h 12min
Directed by: Patrick Solaro
Written by: Kathleen Doherty, based on a novel by Melissa Bridges
Stars: Belle Winter, Henry Davis, Susan Robinson…

Get Out of Town!

Great acting. Confusing story. ★★★☆☆

Author: bjohnson2410

9 October

Patrick Solaro's new movie was expected to be a big hit. After all, he is last year's winner of the Academy Award… …More

Was this review helpful? Yes 87 No 2

★★★★★ = Excellent ★★★☆☆ = Good ★☆☆☆☆ = Bad

1. Director
   a. ★★★★★ b. ★★★☆☆ c. ★☆☆☆☆
2. Actors
   a. ★★★★★ b. ★★★☆☆ c. ★☆☆☆☆
3. Plot
   a. ★★★★★ b. ★★★☆☆ c. ★☆☆☆☆

LISTENING SKILL
Draw inferences
An inference is a conclusion based on the information you hear. It is not said directly, but the listener can understand it from the context.

C PAIRS Compare your answers in 3B. Explain your choices.

4 TRY IT YOURSELF

A MAKE IT PERSONAL Take notes on a movie you want to review using the chart.

Movie title	Actors and director	Characters	Story	What I liked	What I disliked	Number of stars

B PAIRS Student A, talk about your movie. Student B, guess how many stars Student A gave it.
The movie is called Jumping Jack. It was directed by Thomas England…

☐ I CAN TALK ABOUT A MOVIE REVIEW.

LESSON 4 READ AN INTERVIEW WITH A LOCATION SCOUT

FLAVIO VEGA
@FlavioV
I wish they made more movies like *The Lord of the Rings*. The scenery was breathtaking!

1 BEFORE YOU READ

A PAIRS What are some of your favorite movie locations?

I loved the jungle scenes in King Kong.

B ▶04-18 VOCABULARY Listen. Then listen and repeat.

an industry: all the business of similar kind
shoot: to make a movie
authentic: made or done in the traditional way
remote: far away from other places
a scene: one part of a movie
a bonus: a good thing you did not expect

>> FOR PRACTICE, GO TO PAGE 156

2 READ

READING SKILL **Make predictions based on text features**

Before you start reading, look at the title, any headings, and text in bold or italics. These features can help you predict the type of text and what it is about.

A Read the Reading Skill. Answer the questions.

1. What kind of article do you think this will be?
____
2. What do you think Sam Dinh will talk about?
____

B ▶04-19 Listen. Read the interview.

A SCOUT'S STORY

As a writer for *On the Move*, I get the chance to share some of the fascinating behind-the-scenes details about making movies and to talk to people working in the film industry. I recently met Sam Dinh, a location scout for the new blockbuster, *Our Time in the Sun*.

Sam, you grew up near Los Angeles, but you moved to Vietnam about ten years ago. Now you are a top movie location scout in the industry. How did that happen?

Actually, I moved to Hanoi to be near my family. Then, one day I was talking to a friend who works for a movie director. The director was shooting a film in Vietnam and wanted a location in the jungle. I found the perfect location and things just continued from there.

What exactly do location scouts do?

We have to find the right locations for every scene in the movie, but we also make sure that all the details on the set look and sound authentic.

So, when you look for that perfect location, what are some of the things you have to think about?

The main thing is to find a location that looks right, but there are other things to consider as well. For one film, I found an old house in a remote village. The director said it was exactly what she had in mind. And it looked perfect, but…

What was the problem?

There was no electricity or running water in the village. We had to bring our own generators to produce electricity.

Wow! What about really unusual or unexpected tasks? Can you tell us about some of them?

I once had to set up a scene where a village was attacked by a tiger. There was a professional animal trainer and we had an emergency plan in place so there was no real danger. But so many things can go wrong with wild animals.

I can imagine! We don't think about all the details that make each scene authentic.

That's true, especially for historical movies. For example, *Our Time in the Sun* takes place in Hanoi in the 1950s. Of course, I knew that satellite dishes and other modern technology had to be removed, but those white lines on the streets? They had to go, too. They weren't there in the 1950s.

So, what's the best part of your job?

Well, one great bonus is that I sometimes get to play small roles—usually just in crowd scenes—but never with any tigers!

3 CHECK YOUR UNDERSTANDING

A What do location scouts do? Circle three answers.

a. They help the director make changes after the filming is finished.
b. They help set up the scenes.
c. They find the best locations for every scene in a movie.
d. They make changes in the location if it is not perfect.
e. They help the actors to look authentic.

B Circle the correct answer.

1. What was the problem with the house in a remote village?
   a. There were wild animals.
   b. It needed a lot of changes to make it authentic.
   c. There was no power for the equipment.
2. What kind of unexpected job has Sam had?
   a. finding remote locations
   b. building roads
   c. working with wild animals
3. What is one thing Sam had to do to make a scene authentic?
   a. remove modern technology
   b. find a professional animal trainer
   c. do historical research
4. What makes a scout's job challenging?
   a. attention to lots of details
   b. the need for emergency plans
   c. living far from home

C FOCUS ON LANGUAGE Reread lines 21-23 and 29-31 in the interview. Think about the phrases *had in mind* and *in place*. Circle the correct answers.

1. The expression *had in mind* means to have ____.
   a. an opinion about something b. a plan or intention c. an original idea
2. The expression *in place* means ____.
   a. organized and ready for use b. in a specific location c. close to you

D PAIRS What is the article about? Retell the most important ideas. Use your own words.

The reading is an interview with a location scout. He...

Look for information about location scouts. How can someone find a job as a location scout?

4 MAKE IT PERSONAL

A Think about a location that would be interesting for a movie. Describe the location and say what kind of movie you imagine.

Location	Description	Movie type

B PAIRS Talk about the locations you chose for each movie type and why you chose them.

☐ I CAN READ AN INTERVIEW WITH A LOCATION SCOUT.

LESSON 5 WRITE A MOVIE REVIEW

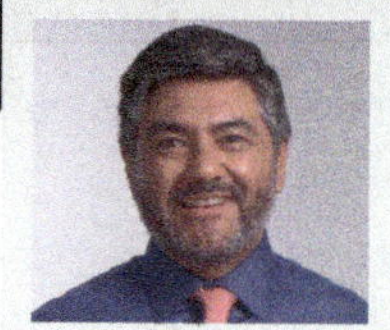

FLAVIO VEGA

@FlavioV

I saw a new movie this weekend. Check out my review before you go to see it.

1 BEFORE YOU WRITE

A What are your favorite kinds of movies? Why do you like those movies?

B Read Flavio's online movie review. How did he feel about the movie?

1h 49 min

Directed by: Oscar Lombard

Written by: Kate Reynolds

Stars: Pia Andrade, Britt Malcolm, Jan Jansen...

***Hunted* Review** Critic Review | **Audience Reviews**

Flavio V  

I went to see *Hunted* this weekend, and I thought it was awful! I felt like I wasted two hours and twelve dollars.

First of all, the plot sounds exciting, but it is actually very predictable. Carla, an ordinary woman—a high school teacher—is chased by a group of bad men. We don't know who they are, and we don't know why they are chasing her. As the movie goes on, you find out more and more about Carla's past, and how she is connected to these men. Of course, it turns out that she isn't so ordinary after all. By the time the movie reveals the "surprise", it isn't much of a surprise. I knew exactly what was going to happen in the end.

The star of the movie is Pia Andrade, an actress I usually like a lot. Her acting in this movie is good—she is the reason I gave the movie two stars instead of just one. While the role she plays in this movie is very silly, Andrade makes the character realistic. Still, with her talent, I think she should play more serious roles.

This is the second movie that was directed by Oscar Lombard. I loved his first movie, *Awaken*. It had an interesting, surprising plot, and the acting was great. In contrast, *Hunted* is a real disappointment. Let's hope his next movie is better!

C Read the review again. Complete the chart. Indicate positive (+) and negative (-) opinions.

Feature	Summary	+ or -	Why?
Plot	An ________ is chased by a group of bad men. You learn about ________ throughout the movie. It turns out she is connected to the men in some way.		The plot sounds ________ but is predictable.
________	The ________ is Pia Andrade.		While the role is silly, Andrade makes the character ________.
Director	The director is Oscar Lombard. This is his ________ movie.		In contrast to his first movie, *Hunted* is a ________.

2 FOCUS ON WRITING

Read the Writing Skill. Then read Flavio's review again. Underline the words and sentences that show a contrast to what he expected.

WRITING SKILL Use contrast to express your opinion

Sometimes, when you express your opinion, you can make it stronger by saying how it is different from what you expected. Use **contrast words** like *but*, *however*, *while*, *although*, *in contrast*, *on the other hand*, and *despite* to express these contrasts.

3 PLAN YOUR WRITING

A Think of a movie you want to review. Complete the chart to help plan your review.

Feature	Summary	+ or -	Why?

B PAIRS Share your opinions about the movie.

I saw the movie *Inception* and really liked it. It's about...

4 WRITE

Write a movie review using your details from 3A. Remember to use contrasts to express your opinion. Use the review in 1B as a model.

5 REVISE YOUR WRITING

A PAIRS Exchange and read each other's reviews.

1. Underline the sentences your partner used to express his or her opinion using contrasts.
2. Did these sentences make your partner's opinion stronger? Why or why not?

B PAIRS Can your classmate improve his or her review? Make suggestions.

6 PROOFREAD

Read your review again. Can you improve your writing?

Check your
- spelling
- punctuation
- capitalization

☐ I CAN WRITE A MOVIE REVIEW.

PUT IT TOGETHER

1 MEDIA PROJECT

A ▶04-20 **Listen or watch. What type of music does Sofia like?**

B ▶04-20 **Listen or watch again. Answer the questions.**

1. Who is Sofia's favorite band?

   ____

2. What does she like about the band?

   ____

3. How does she describe their music and videos?

   ____

C **Show your own photos.**

Step 1 Think about your favorite band, book, or movie. Choose 3–5 photos to show what you like about it.

Step 2 Show the photos to the class. Talk about what you like. Describe the music, story, characters, or actors.

Step 3 Answer questions and get feedback.

2 LEARNING STRATEGY

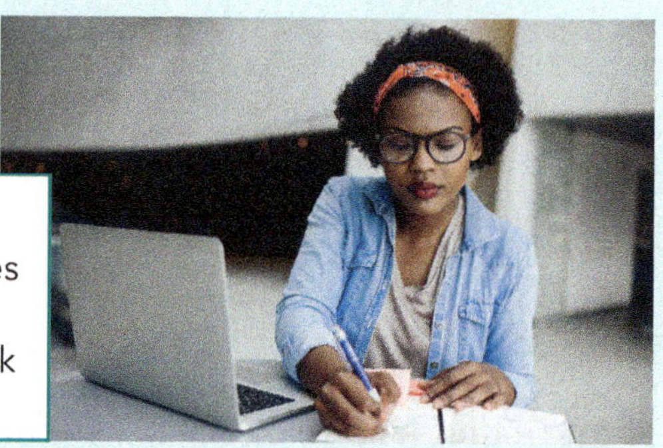

FIND GRAMMAR EXAMPLES IN REAL-LIFE ENGLISH

When you learn a new grammar form, look for examples of it in places other than your textbook. Write down examples you find to study later. You can also bookmark or save what you find on an app or computer.

Review the grammar from the unit. Look or listen for the grammar on the internet, in movies, or in other classes. Make note of the examples. Review the grammar examples at least once a week.

3 REFLECT AND PLAN

A **Look back through the unit. Check (✓) the things you learned. Highlight the things you need to learn.**

Speaking objectives
- ☐ Talk about how life has changed
- ☐ Talk about what I like
- ☐ Talk about a movie review

Vocabulary
- ☐ Ways to connect
- ☐ Entertainment
- ☐ Movies

Pronunciation
- ☐ Blended pronunciation of *used to* ("useta")
- ☐ Sentence rhythm

Grammar
- ☐ *Used to* and *would*
- ☐ *So, neither, too,* and *either* with simple present action verbs
- ☐ Simple present and simple past passives

Reading
- ☐ Make predictions based on text features

Writing
- ☐ Use contrast to express your opinion

B **What will you do to learn the things you highlighted? For example, use your app, review your Student Book, or do other practice. Make a plan.**

Notes　Done

In the app, watch the Lesson 1 conversation: Talk about how life has changed

____

____

____

____

5 WHAT ARE WE EATING?

LEARNING GOALS

In this unit, you

- discuss restaurant experiences
- talk about food preferences
- tell a story about a party
- read a restaurant review
- write a food blog

GET STARTED

A Read the unit title and learning goals.

B Look at the photo of a restaurant. What do you see?

C Now read Mehmet's message. Why is he excited?

MEHMET BODUR

@MehmetB

Can't wait to share my favorite restaurants with Liz during her visit!

LESSON 1 DISCUSS RESTAURANT EXPERIENCES

MEHMET BODUR

@MehmetB

Going to an awesome restaurant for lunch. So much good food and so little time!

1 VOCABULARY Restaurant experiences

A  05-01 Listen. Then listen and repeat.

Taste

Atmosphere

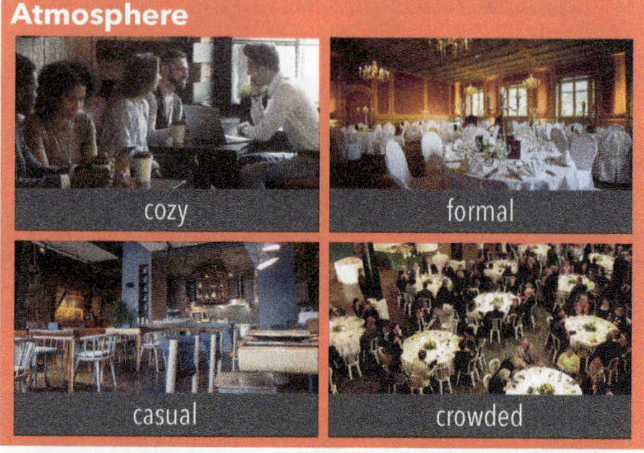

Service

B PAIRS Write the words from 1A in the chart. Discuss your answers.

Positive (good things)	Negative (bad things)	Neutral (not good or bad)

COACH

2 GRAMMAR Tag questions

We use tag questions to confirm the information we have.

Affirmative sentence	Negative tag	Negative sentence	Affirmative tag
The atmosphere is great,	**isn't** it?	You aren't coming,	**are** you?
You have eaten here many times,	**haven't** you?	She didn't bring the menu,	**did** she?
He owns this restaurant,	**doesn't** he?	We can't walk there,	**can** we?

Real questions

In tag questions, our *voice rises* at the end when we are *not sure* if our statement is true. We are asking a real question and expect the listener to *give us information*.

A: *You don't like sushi, do you?* **B:** *Yes, I do! I like it a lot!*

Questions expecting agreement

Our *voice falls* at the end when we are *sure* our statement is true. We expect the listener to *agree*.

A: *The food here is terrible, isn't it?* **B:** *Yes, it really is.*

>> FOR PRACTICE, GO TO PAGE 137

COACH

3 PRONUNCIATION

A ▶05-04 Listen. Notice the sound of the underlined consonants. Then listen and repeat.

/ʃ/	/ʒ/	/ʧ/	/ʤ/
fresh	casual	chicken	juice

B ▶05-05 Circle the word that has a different consonant sound than the first word in the line. Then listen and check your answers.

1. **fresh** efficient service delicious rushed
2. **casual** usually Asian Russian television
3. **chicken** chef question chowder adventure
4. **juice** beverage dangerous greasy orange

The sounds /ʃ/, /ʒ/, /ʧ/, and /ʤ/

The sounds /ʃ/, /ʒ/, /ʧ/, and /dʒ/ have the following usual spellings, but note that they also have other spellings.

Sound	Example	Usual spelling
/ʃ/	fresh	sh
/ʒ/	casual	s
/ʧ/	chicken	ch
/dʒ/	juice	j or g

C PAIRS Create three sentences. Each sentence should include at least two words with the consonant sounds /ʃ/, /ʒ/, /ʧ/, or /ʤ/. Use words from 3A or 3B, or your own ideas.

I usually eat fish chowder for lunch.

4 CONVERSATION

A ▶05-06 Listen or watch. Circle the correct answers.

1. The restaurant is ***formal / cozy / crowded***.
2. The service is ***efficient / slow / poor***.
3. The restaurant has fresh ***bread / vegetables / sandwiches***.

B ▶05-07 Listen or watch. Complete the conversation.

Mehmet: You ____________ been here before, ____________?

Liz: No. It's my first time. The atmosphere is great, casual, not too crowded. And I love the modern style.

Mehmet: Yeah, it's a nice place. And just wait until you taste the food!

C ▶05-08 Listen and repeat. Then practice with a partner.

D PAIRS Make new conversations. Use these words or your own ideas. service efficient rushed

5 TRY IT YOURSELF

A PAIRS Make up a restaurant. Complete the chart.

Restaurant name	Kind of food	Atmosphere	Quality of service

B ROLE PLAY You're at the restaurant. Have a conversation about food, service, or atmosphere. Use tag questions to check on whether you agree.

☐ I CAN DISCUSS RESTAURANT EXPERIENCES.

LESSON 2 TALK ABOUT FOOD PREFERENCES

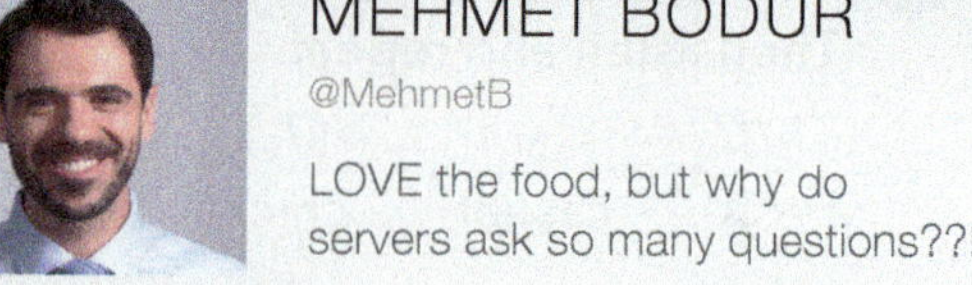

1 VOCABULARY Categories on a menu

A ▶05-09 Listen. Then listen and repeat.

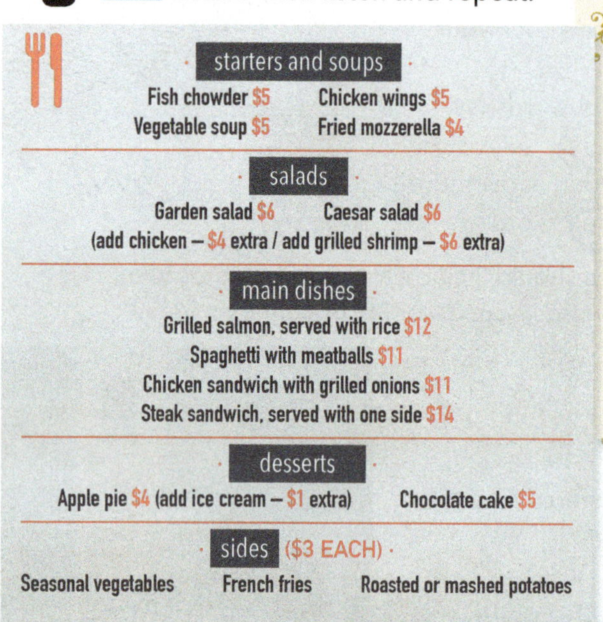

Dessert
Cheesecake $6
Lemon meringue pie $6

beverages
Sodas $2
Fresh fruit juice (orange, apple, cranberry) $3
Coffee / Tea $2

B Complete the chart with the category names from the menus in 1A. Some categories can have two names.

Beverages	Desserts	Appetizers	Main	Side
water milk	cookies pie	nachos shrimp cocktail	fish and chips spaghetti	rice onion rings

C PAIRS Discuss which parts of the meal you usually have when you eat at a restaurant.
When we eat in a restaurant, we usually have a main dish and one or two sides.

2 GRAMMAR Expressing preference with *would rather* and *would prefer*

COACH

Subject	*Would rather*	(*Not*)	Base form of verb	
I He	**would rather**	(not)	**have** **eat**	the steak. Italian food tonight.
Subject	***Would prefer***	**(*Not*)**	**Infinitive**	
We They	**would prefer**	(not)	**to sit** **to order**	outside. appetizers.

Notes
- Use the contraction form of *would* (*'d*) with subjects in spoken English and informal writing: *I'd, You'd, He'd, They'd.*
- To form questions, place *would* before the subject.
  Would *you* ***prefer*** *to eat at 7:00?* *What time* ***would*** *you* ***prefer*** *to eat?*

>> FOR PRACTICE, GO TO PAGE 138

3 PRONUNCIATION

COACH

A ▶05-11 **Listen. Notice that the spellings for all three vowel sounds usually include the letter *u* or *o*. Then listen and repeat.**

1. /u/	2. /ʊ/	3. /ʌ/
mood	book	lunch
blue	sugar	love

The sounds /u/, /ʊ/, and /ʌ/

Notice how we say the following sounds:

sound	example	description	how to say it
/u/	*blue*	a long sound	push your lips into a circle.
/ʊ/	*book*	a shorter sound	make your lips less round.
/ʌ/	*lunch*	a relaxed sound	open your mouth just a little.

B ▶05-12 **Listen. Do the underlined letters have the vowel sound 1. /u/, 2. /ʊ/, or 3. /ʌ/? Write the numbers in the spaces. Then listen and repeat.**

1. fruit ___ 2. juice ___ 3. good ___ 4. food ___ 5. onion ___ 6. soup ___

C PAIRS **Write five sentences. Include two words with vowel sounds in 3A in each sentence.**

The onion soup looks wonderful!

4 CONVERSATION

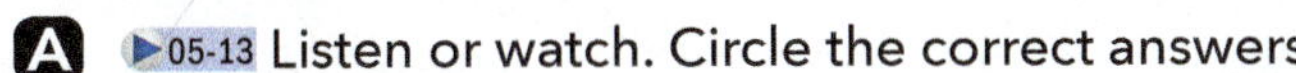

A ▶05-13 **Listen or watch. Circle the correct answers.**

1. What does Mehmet order?
   a. fish b. a garden salad c. a steak sandwich
2. What would Mehemt rather have than potatoes?
   a. vegetables b. a salad c. a soup
3. What does Liz find funny?
   a. the waiter's questions
   b. Mehmet's choices
   c. the menu options

B ▶05-14 **Listen or watch. Complete the conversation.**

Mehmet: So, ____________________?
Liz: The salmon looks good, but I had it last night. ____________________ try something else.
Mehmet: Well, how about the salad with grilled shrimp?
Liz: Perfect! So, what are you having?
Mehmet: I usually order fish, but I'm not ________________ today. Maybe the steak sandwich?
Liz: The steak sandwich looks good.

CONVERSATION SKILL
Talk about preferences

Here are some useful expressions you can use when talking about preferences.
What do you feel like?
I feel like Italian food.
What are you in the mood for?
I'm in the mood for a steak
Listen to or watch the conversation in 4A again. Raise your hand when you hear the phrases above.

C ▶05-15 **Listen and repeat. Then practice with a partner.**

D PAIRS **Make new conversations. Use these words or your own ideas.**

fish chowder caesar salad with chicken pasta fried chicken

5 TRY IT YOURSELF

A MAKE IT PERSONAL **Look at the menus in 1A. Check (✓) the food you prefer.**

B PAIRS **Talk about your choices in 5A.**

☐ I CAN TALK ABOUT FOOD PREFERENCES.

LESSON 3 TELL A STORY ABOUT A PARTY

MEHMET BODUR

@MehmetB

Went to a great party on Saturday! Good job, Sis!

1 VOCABULARY Party food

A ▶05-16 Listen. Then listen and repeat.

chips and salsa

guacamole

cheese and crackers

pretzels

hummus

chili

donuts

cheesecake

B Put the words from 1A in the chart.

Foods I have tried	Foods I haven't tried

C PAIRS Discuss your answers in 1B. Are any of these foods served in restaurants and cafés near you? What other party foods do you like?

A **count noun** can be counted: *I ate a cookie. There are twenty cookies.*

A **non-count noun** cannot be counted: *Food is important for survival.*

Some categories of non-count nouns

- **Abstract nouns:** time, happiness, love
- **Sports and activities:** soccer, chess, baseball
- **Food and drink:** bread, pasta, rice, milk, coffee
- **Materials:** wood, paper, plastic, metal
- **Groups of similar things:** homework, furniture, money

2 GRAMMAR Quantifiers

COACH

	Count nouns	Non-count nouns
Affirmative	I have **many / a lot of** friends. She has **some** pies. We have **a few** notebooks. They have **enough** chairs.	I have **a lot of** time. She has **some** food. We have **a little** paper. They have **enough** furniture.
Negative	I don't have **many / a lot of** friends. You don't have **any** notebooks.	We don't have **much / a lot of** time. He doesn't have **any** food.
Question	Do we have **any** pies? Do we have **enough** chairs?	Do they have **any** furniture? Do we have **enough** paper?

Notes

- Be careful: *a few* and *few* and *a little* and *little* have different meanings.
  a few = several *a little = some*
  few = not enough *little = not enough*
- *Much* is formal and less common. Use *a lot of / lots of* instead of *much* in spoken English.
- Use phrases that show quantity to make non-count nouns plural:
  a bottle of (water), two pieces of (paper), a game of (chess)

>> FOR PRACTICE, GO TO PAGE 139

3 LISTENING

A ▶05-18 Listen to the radio show. What went wrong at the party?

a. Katy didn't share a secret, so her sister got upset.
b. People left because there was hardly any food.
c. The dog ate almost everything that Katy had prepared.

B ▶05-18 Read the Listening Skill. Listen again. Put the events from the story in the correct order. Write the numbers in the boxes.

LISTENING SKILL

Listen for time words

Pay attention to time words such as *when*, *after*, *before*, *at first*, *at that moment*, and *later*. They will help you understand the order of the events in a story.

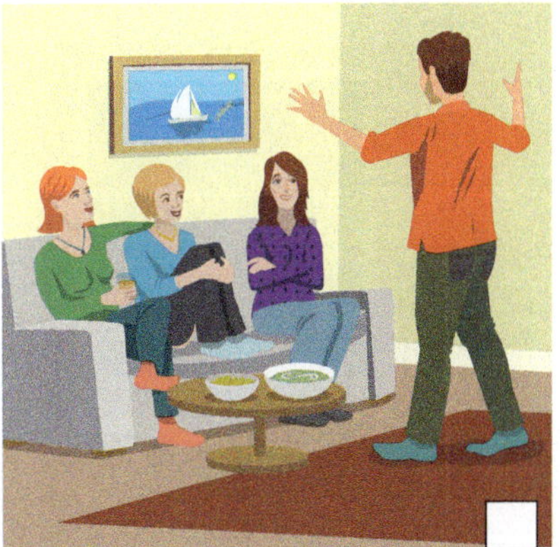

C PAIRS Retell the story you just heard. Take turns.

4 TRY IT YOURSELF

A GROUPS Work in a group of 3–4. Choose one of the sets of words from the chart. Make up a story about a party. Use all of the words in the set, as well as your own ideas.

Set 1	not enough	cheesecake, chips	later	rushed
Set 2	a little bit	chili, donuts	at that moment	stale
Set 3	a few	hummus, pretzels	before	greasy

B CLASS Tell your story to the class. One student in the group starts the story, then the next student speaks, and so on.

☐ I CAN TELL A STORY ABOUT A PARTY.

LESSON 4 READ A RESTAURANT REVIEW

MEHMET BODUR
@MehmetB
I tried some unusual food yesterday. And it was definitely worth it!

1 BEFORE YOU READ

A PAIRS Do you read or write restaurant reviews?

I write restaurant reviews all the time, especially when…

B ▶05-19 VOCABULARY Listen. Then listen and repeat.

superb: excellent
to order: according to a customer's request
an option: something that you can choose
tender: easy to cut and eat
skip: not do something that you would usually do
intimate: suggesting warmth or privacy
tough: difficult to cut or eat

>> FOR PRACTICE, GO TO PAGE 156

2 READ

A PREVIEW Read the title and look at the photo. Are the reviews positive or negative?

B ▶05-20 Listen. Read the reviews.

Churrasco
New York City-Midtown
$$$ Brazilian/Steak

Review for Churrasco

Cristina M. Mexico City ★★★★★

If you're a meat lover, you're going to love Churrasco. Churrasco is my favorite Brazilian steakhouse, where the meat is the star of the show, but there's also seafood and a great salad bar. It's an all-you-can-eat restaurant but Churrasco offers more than quantity. The quality of all the food is also very high and the service is superb. They come to your table with a selection of meat, and then your choice is cooked to order.

Churrasco is a great choice if you're dining out with a big group of friends because there are lots of options—beef, lamb, or chicken—and each piece is perfectly prepared—juicy and tender. I agree it's a little expensive. But for top-quality food, I think the price is fair. My advice is to skip lunch before you go so you're really hungry for dinner. Then you can really get your money's worth. I think I gain about two kilos every time I go!

Marco C. New York City ★☆☆☆☆

I cannot recommend this place. We expected a choice of different kinds of meat, but when the waiter finally arrived, he only offered us lamb. Then we had to wait 40 minutes to get steaks. Much too salty and almost raw, they were definitely not worth the wait. I'd heard that their salad bar is very good, but again, there were hardly any choices—just a lot of different kinds of lettuce and a few tomatoes. And guess what? Dessert is not included in the price. It's a separate menu, at an additional price. Finally, I expected a quiet, intimate atmosphere, but there were kids running around the tables, and the music was much too loud.

Joan F. San Francisco ★★★☆☆

I tried Churrasco for the first time last week when my friends and I went there for my birthday. I have to say that I was a bit disappointed with the food. I thought the steaks were rather tough; on the other hand, I loved the garlic mashed potatoes and the bread, which they bake fresh every morning. At the end of the meal, the waiters brought me a big slice of chocolate cake and they all sang, "Happy Birthday" to me. They were very sweet.

3 CHECK YOUR UNDERSTANDING

A What can readers learn from the three reviews of Churrasco? Circle the correct answer.

a. Most people like it so it is probably a good choice.
b. People have had very different experiences there.
c. It's only good for meat lovers.

B Read the statements made by the three reviewers. Who do you think made each statement? Write *C* for Cristina, *M* for Marco, or *J* for Joan.

1. "I'll never go back." ___
2. "I always eat too much when I go there." ___
3. "The additional cost of dessert makes the restaurant quite expensive." ___
4. "I think the service was better than the food." ___
5. "In the end, we all had a good time at Churrasco." ___
6. "There are so many choices." ___

C FOCUS ON LANGUAGE **Reread lines 2-4 and 10-11 in the reviews. Think about the phrases *star of the show* and *get your money's worth*. Circle the correct answers.**

1. The expression *star of the show* means ___.
   a. very high quality b. the best thing c. the most expensive thing
2. The expression *get your money's worth* means ___.
   a. get as much as possible for what you paid
   b. receive something very expensive
   c. not pay too much for something

READING SKILL

Identify author's opinion with key words

Writers can express their opinion with negative or positive words; for example, *wonderful*, *terrible*, *too hot* and *too expensive*. Look for these kinds of words in texts to identify the writer's opinion.

D Read the Reading Skill. Write each phrase in the correct place in the chart.

Cris

too salty	lots of options	helpful waiters
perfectly prepared	hardly any choices	too loud
steaks were tough	a great salad bar	

	Positive	Negative
Cristina	lots of options, a great salad bar	
Marco		Too saltty, Too loud
Joan		

E PAIRS **What information do the reviews provide? Retell the most important ideas in the reviews. Use your own words.**

Each review is different...

Find reviews of your favorite restaurant or a restaurant you know well. Are the reviewers' opinions similar to yours?

4 MAKE IT PERSONAL

A Think about a restaurant you know well. What's good and bad about it? Why do people go there? Take notes.

1. What is your opinion of the food there? Give some specific details about your experience.
2. What about the service and atmosphere? What is good or bad about it?

B PAIRS **Discuss your answers from 4A.**

The best thing about this restaurant is...

☐ I CAN READ A RESTAURANT REVIEW.

LESSON 5 WRITE A FOOD BLOG

MEHMET BODUR

@MehmetB

My top two Korean dishes this week: kal-gook-soo and seafood pa-jeon.

1 BEFORE YOU WRITE

A What are some of your favorite foods? What do you like about them?

B Read Mehmet's food blog. What foods does he write about?

Food of the week: Korean

April 2 by Mehmet Bodur–15 comments

Korean food is one of my favorites, and there are several great Korean restaurants in my neighborhood. I wanted to share with you a couple of new dishes I discovered.

The first dish is kal-gook-soo. This is a noodle soup that comes in a variety of flavors. The noodles are what make the dish so special. They are long, thick noodles, similar to the width and thickness of fettuccini noodles in Italian cooking. Kal-gook-soo noodles taste best when they're fresh, so most restaurants make their own noodles. That's what makes them so good! The broth is made of vegetable, seafood, or chicken broth, depending on which flavor you choose. My favorite is the spicy chicken. Eating a bowl of spicy chicken kal-gook-soo makes any cold winter day feel warm and cozy.

Another dish I recently discovered is seafood pa-jeon. *Pa* in Korean means scallion, and *jeon* is a kind of pancake, but with meats and vegetables in it. Instead of pancake batter, pa-jeon uses a flour mix. And instead of breakfast, this is usually served as an appetizer. The seafood pa-jeon includes a variety of seafoods and scallions mixed into the flour mix. The batter is then fried in vegetable oil until the outside is slightly crispy. Delicious!

Try these two dishes the next time you're at a Korean restaurant. You'll thank me!

C PAIRS Based on Mehmet's descriptions, would you try these two dishes? Why or why not?

2 FOCUS ON WRITING

Read the Writing Skill. Then read Mehmet's food blog again. Take notes in the chart.

WRITING SKILL Use specific details

When you use **specific, clear details** in your writing, you can create mental images in the minds of your readers. Ask yourself questions such as: *What did this look like? Feel like? Taste like?* And add these kinds of details to your writing.

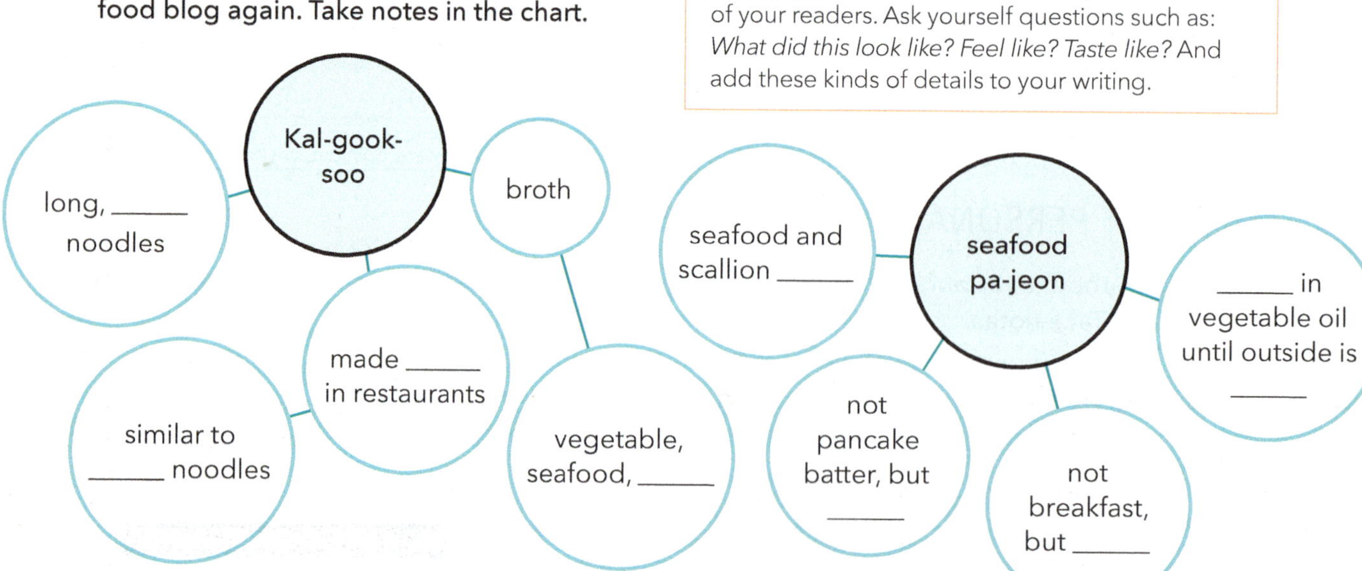

3 PLAN YOUR WRITING

A Think of your favorite foods. Complete the chart to help plan your blog post.

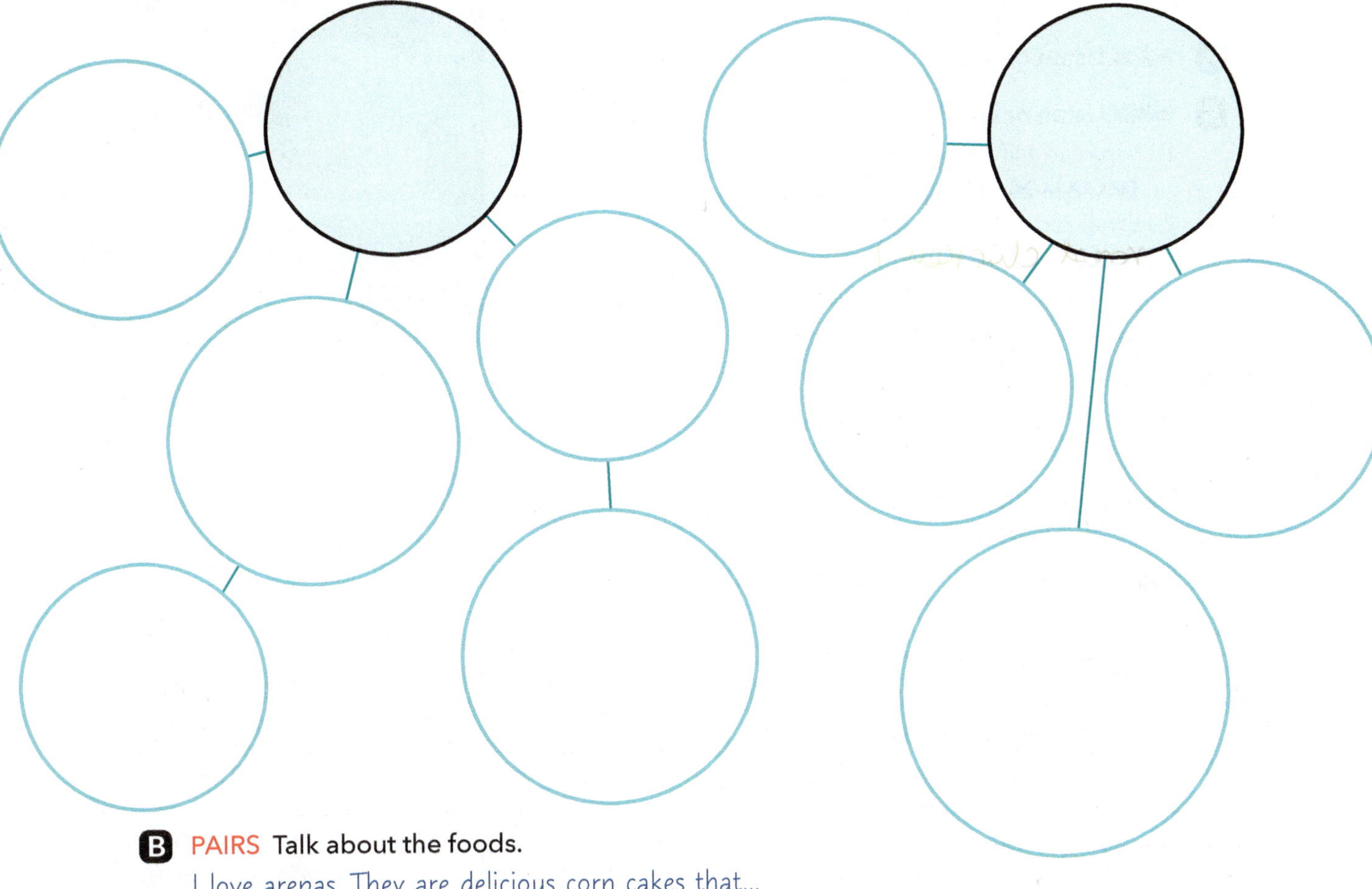

B PAIRS Talk about the foods.

I love arepas. They are delicious corn cakes that...

4 WRITE

Write a post using your information from 3A. Remember to give specific, clear details. Use the post in 1B as a model.

5 REVISE YOUR WRITING

A PAIRS Exchange and read each other's reviews.

1. Underline the specific details.
2. Did your partner's specific details help to give you a clear mental image of the foods? Why or why not?

B PAIRS Can your classmate improve his or her post? Make suggestions.

6 PROOFREAD

Read your review again. Can you improve your writing?

Check your
- spelling
- punctuation
- capitalization

☐ I CAN WRITE A FOOD BLOG.

PUT IT TOGETHER

1 MEDIA PROJECT

A ▶05-21 Listen or watch. What does Elif talk about?

B ▶05-21 Listen or watch again. Answer the questions.

1. Why did Elif choose this restaurant?
   because is fast and efficient
2. What did she eat?
   roast chicken)
3. What did she enjoy most about her meal?
   ____

C Show your own photos.

Step 1 Choose a meal that you want to talk about. It can be prepared at home or ordered at a restaurant. Take 3–5 photos to talk about.

Step 2 Show the photos to the class. Why did you choose this meal? Describe the food. What do you like most about the meal?

Step 3 Answer questions and get feedback.

2 LEARNING STRATEGY

USE NEW VOCABULARY IN DAILY LIFE

When you learn new vocabulary, practice by making your own sentences that use the new words. Try to use the new words in conversation or in your writing each week.

Review the vocabulary from the unit. What words do you need to study? Write at least five sentences with new vocabulary.

3 REFLECT AND PLAN

A Look back through the unit. Check (✓) the things you learned. Highlight the things you need to learn.

Speaking objectives
- ☐ Discuss restaurant experiences
- ☐ Talk about food preferences
- ☐ Tell a story about a party

Vocabulary
- ☐ Restaurant experiences
- ☐ Categories on a menu
- ☐ Party food

Pronunciation
- ☐ The sounds /ʃ/, /ʒ/, /ʧ/, and /ʤ/
- ☐ The sounds /u/, /ʊ/, and /ʌ/

Grammar
- ☐ Tag questions
- ☐ Expressing preference with *would rather* and *would prefer*
- ☐ Quantifiers

Reading
- ☐ Identify author's opinion with key words

Writing
- ☐ Use specific details

B What will you do to learn the things you highlighted? For example, use your app, review your Student Book, or do other practice. Make a plan.

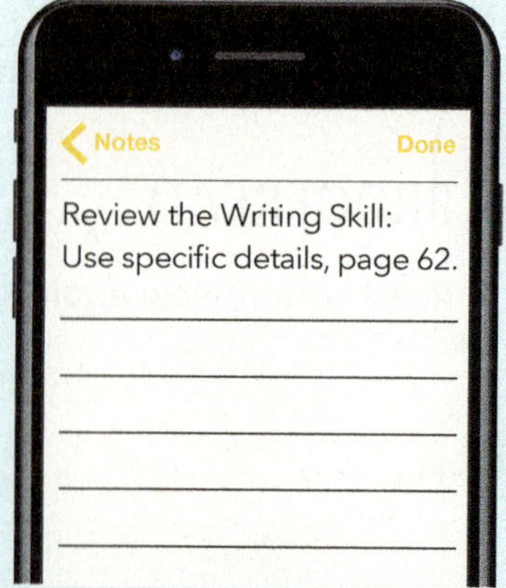

6 HOW DO YOU STAY HEALTHY?

LEARNING GOALS

In this unit, you

- talk about fitness activities
- talk about managing stress
- give advice on staying healthy
- read about fitness apps
- write about health and fitness

GET STARTED

A Read the unit title and learning goals.

B Look at the photo. What do you see?

C Now read Su-min's message. Why is she feeling good?

SU-MIN KIM

@Su-minK

Feeling great after last night's run! Nothing clears up your head like a little exercise!

LESSON 1 TALK ABOUT FITNESS ACTIVITIES

SU-MIN KIM

@Su-minK

Good meetings today, but too much sitting around! Can't wait to get to the gym and MOVE!

1 VOCABULARY Fitness activities

A ▶06-01 Listen. Then listen and repeat.

weight training

spinning

cycling

rock climbing

jogging

running a marathon

kickboxing

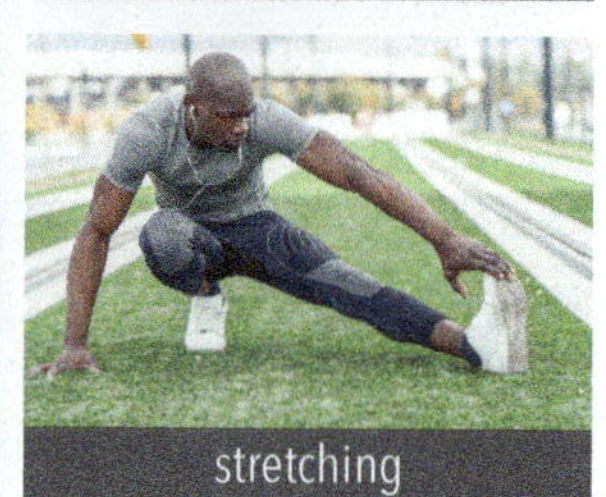
stretching

B Put the activities from 1A in the chart.

Done indoors	Done both indoors and outdoors	Done outdoors
weight training		

C PAIRS Compare your answers in 1B. Do you do any of the activities in 1A?

COACH

2 GRAMMAR Gerunds as subjects and objects

Gerunds are *-ing* verb forms used as nouns.

Gerund as subject			Gerund as object		
Subject	**Verb**		**Subject**	**Verb**	**Object**
Weight training	makes	you strong.	I	enjoy	**hiking** outdoors.
Kickboxing	is	fun.	She	suggested	**working out** every day.

Gerund as object of a preposition		
	Preposition	**Object**
You should stretch	before	**running**.
He asked the coach	about	**joining** the team.

Notes

- Use *not* + *gerund* to form the negative. ***Not running*** *will help your foot feel better.*
- Do not confuse the gerund with the continuous verb or adjective.
  *He **loves hiking**.* (gerund) *He **is hiking** now.* (verb) *He has new **hiking boots**.* (adjective)

>> FOR PRACTICE, GO TO PAGE 140

3 PRONUNCIATION

COACH

A ▶06-03 **Listen. Notice the way we link the consonant sounds. Then listen and repeat.**

weight training   rock climbing   a dangerous sport

B ▶06-04 **Draw a line to show where we link two identical consonant sounds. Listen and check your answers.**

1. Do you like kickboxing?
2. Do you drink coffee?
3. Have you ever gone ice skating?
4. What makes you feel less stressed?

Linking identical consonants

When one word ends in a consonant sound and the next word begins with the same consonant sound, we usually link the two sounds together to make one long consonant sound, for example, phone number.

4 CONVERSATION

A ▶06-05 **Listen or watch. Circle the correct answers.**

1. Why do Flavio and Su-min start talking about exercise?
   a. Flavio is upset because the weather is bad and he can't go cycling.
   b. Flavio would like to go to the gym with Su-min.
   c. Su-min tells Flavio that she's on her way to the gym.
2. Both Flavio and Su-min ___.
   a. hate running alone.
   b. are interested in marathons.
   c. are training for a marathon.
3. Su-min thinks that Flavio ___.
   a. doesn't want to run with her. b. is going to the laundromat. c. doesn't like to exercise.

B ▶06-06 **Listen or watch. Complete the conversation.**

Su-min: __________ in shape can be tough when you're really busy. Do you do any kind of exercise?

Flavio: I like __________ things outdoors, like __________ or cycling.

Su-min: You do? That's cool.

Flavio: How about you?

Su-min: I'm really into running these days.

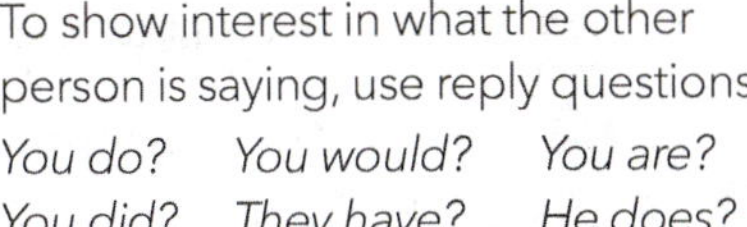

CONVERSATION SKILL

Reply questions

To show interest in what the other person is saying, use reply questions.

You do? *You would?* *You are?*
You did? *They have?* *He does?*

Listen to or watch the conversation in 4A again. Underline the reply questions that you hear above.

C ▶06-07 **Listen and repeat. Then practice with a partner.**

D PAIRS **Make new conversations. Use these words or your own ideas.**

rock climbing
weight training

5 TRY IT YOURSELF

A ROLE PLAY **Student A is really into rock climbing. Student B is into weight training. Explain why your classmate should try your fitness activity.**

You should try rock climbing. It is great because...

B WALK AROUND **Find a new partner. Repeat the role play, but choose two different activities from 1A or your own ideas. Ask follow-up questions.**

☐ I CAN TALK ABOUT FITNESS ACTIVITIES.

LESSON 2 TALK ABOUT MANAGING STRESS

SU-MIN KIM
@Su-minK
Flavio's the best—like a big brother! He always makes me feel better.

1 VOCABULARY Managing stress

A ▶06-08 Listen. Then listen and repeat.

make time for yourself: to take the time to do the things that make you feel relaxed and happy
reduce your stress: to worry less about things in your work or personal life
keep a work-life balance: to have time for work, your family and friends, and yourself
set realistic goals: to make plans that are likely to be successful
take a break: to make time for a short rest
go offline: to stop using the internet for a period of time
take time off: to take a break from work or school for a period of time
burn out: to do an activity so often and for so long that you don't want to do it anymore

B **Complete the sentences with the phrases from 1A. More than one answer may be possible. Use each phrase only one time.**

1. Thinking positively and talking to trusted friends and family are good ways to ________.
2. You're working too hard. You need to ________. Why don't you stop and get some coffee?
3. He works all the time and he's never home. He doesn't know how to ________.
4. You always promise to do too much, and then you can't finish on time. You need to ________.
5. If you don't take breaks, you're going to ________.

C PAIRS **Which of the things in 1A do you find difficult to do? Explain.**

2 GRAMMAR Past form of *be* + *going to* for past intentions

Use *was* / *were* + *going to* to talk about something you intended, or planned, to do, but didn't.

Subject	*Was / Were*	*Going to*	Base form of verb		*But*	
I	**was**	**going to**	go	to yoga class,	but	I didn't.
He			take	time off,		he was too busy.
They	**were**		run	after work,		they were too tired.

Notes

- When we talk about past intentions, we often explain why we did or didn't do something.
- Use *wasn't* and *weren't* to form the negative:
  *I **wasn't going to** exercise after work, but I changed my mind.*
- Use *was* / *were* + *going to* + verb to form questions.
  ***Was** he **going to** meet us at 7:00?* ***Were** you **going to** train for the marathon?*

>> FOR PRACTICE, GO TO PAGE 141

3 PRONUNCIATION

COACH

A 06-10 **Listen. Notice the blended pronunciations. Then listen and repeat.**

I was going to go hiking, but I had to study.
sounds like: I was *gonna* go hiking, but I *hadta* study.

I want to travel, but I have to finish school first.
sounds like: I *wanna* travel, but I *hafta* finish school first.

I've got to leave now.
sounds like: I've *gotta* leave now.

> **Blended pronunciation with *to***
>
> The phrases *want to*, *have to* (and *had to*), *got to*, and *going to* are very common in conversation. When we speak quickly, we often reduce these phrases. We make the pronunciation of *to* very weak and blend the two words together so that they sound like one word.

B 06-11 **Listen. Complete the conversation. Write full words, not the blended pronunciations you hear. Then read the conversation in pairs.**

1. A: I thought ____________________ stay home today.
   B: ____________________ come in for a meeting.
2. A: ____________________ go to the gym?
   B: Now? ____________________ make some phone calls.
   A: Well, ____________________ take a break and move around.

4 CONVERSATION

A 06-12 **Listen or watch. Circle the correct answers.**

1. Su-min is upset because she didn't finish ***her goals / her workout / a marketing plan***.
2. At home, Flavio and his wife ***don't watch television / turn off their phones / work just a little bit***.
3. Flavio is trying to help Su-min ***keep a work-life balance / train for the marathon / work faster***.

B 06-13 **Listen or watch. Complete the conversation.**

Flavio: Hey, you need to take a break or ____________________ burn out!
Su-min: I know. I ____________________ make more time for myself, but…
Flavio: I know it's hard. But it's not healthy for you to work like this.

C 06-14 **Listen and repeat. Then practice with a partner.**

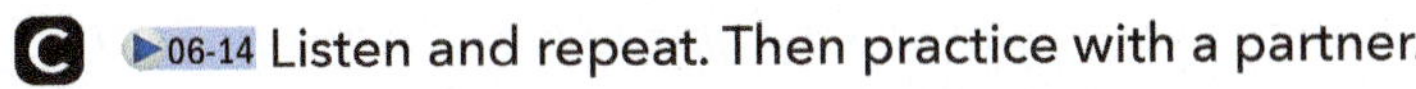

D PAIRS **Make new conversations. Use these words or your own ideas.**

reduce your stress
take some time off

5 TRY IT YOURSELF

A MAKE IT PERSONAL **Think about a situation when you were going to reduce stress in your life, but something stopped you.**

I was going to ____________________, but ____________________.

B PAIRS **Student A, tell Student B about your past intention to manage your stress. Explain. Student B, ask follow-up questions.**

☐ I CAN TALK ABOUT MANAGING STRESS.

LESSON 3 GIVE ADVICE ON STAYING HEALTHY

SU-MIN KIM
@Su-minK
Love the podcast *A Fitter You*—some great ideas for getting and staying healthy. Check it out!

1 VOCABULARY Staying healthy

A ▶06-15 Listen. Then listen and repeat.

intense: describes an activity that requires a lot of effort
moderate: describes an activity that requires some effort
fit: healthy and strong because you exercise regularly
build strength: to do exercises to become physically stronger, usually by growing muscles
burn calories: to use energy, usually by doing physical activities, to lose some of the calories you get from food
be out of shape: to be in a bad physical condition
stay in shape: to exercise or do other healthy activities to keep in good physical condition

B Complete the sentences with words and phrases from 1A. Use the correct form. More than one answer may be possible.

1. When you're ______________, you can do ______________ exercises without problems.
2. When you ______________, you can't do even ______________ exercises.
3. When you exercise, you ______________ and ______________.
4. Exercise helps you ______________.

C PAIRS Talk about yourself or someone you know. Use the words from 1A.
My sister is out of shape. She doesn't like to exercise at all.

2 GRAMMAR Prepositions of time

Preposition	Meaning or use	Examples
after	later than something	*I usually run* ***after*** *work.*
at	used with specific times	*Let's have dinner* ***at*** *7:30.*
before	earlier than something	*Sal goes to the gym* ***before*** *breakfast.*
between... and...	somewhere in the middle of two times	*Kim usually gets to work* ***between*** *9:00* ***and*** *9:30.*
by	before a certain time in the future	*We'll be done* ***by*** *8:00 P.M.*
during	used to show a period of time	*They prefer to work out* ***during*** *the day.*
for	used to show a length of time	*My legs have been sore* ***for*** *three days.*
from...to...	used to show a start and end time	*Let's take a break* ***from*** *12:30* ***to*** *1:00.*
in	used with months, years, and lengths of time	*I usually take a vacation* ***in*** *July.*
on	used with days and dates	*Are you going to the gym* ***on*** *Saturday?*
since	from a point in time in the past	*They have been running* ***since*** *early this morning.*
until	up to a certain time	*Spinning class lasts* ***until*** *6:00 P.M.*

>> FOR PRACTICE, GO TO PAGE 142

3 LISTENING

A  **06-17 Listen to the podcast. Circle the correct answers.**

1. What is the main idea?
   a. There's too much information on getting fit, and it confuses people.
   b. Exercising intensely for a short time, followed by a short time to rest, is the best way to stay fit.
   c. If you want to get fit, there are several simple things to start doing immediately.
2. What is the third idea that the speaker talks about?
   a. Add small amounts of exercise to your everyday life.
   b. Repeat the fast/slow cycle five times.
   c. Stand up whenever you can.

LISTENING SKILL

Listen for enumeration

Speakers often tell you how many ideas they are going to talk about at the beginning of a speech or presentation. Then they begin each idea with a number or the words "next," "another," and "finally."

B **06-17 Read the Listening Skill. Listen again. Put a check (✓) next to the picture that matches the speaker's suggestions.**

1

2

3

4 TRY IT YOURSELF

A MAKE IT PERSONAL **Think of reasons why staying healthy can be difficult. Discuss the reasons with your partner. Then give each other advice. Use the vocabulary in 1A or your own ideas plus these prepositions:** ***at*****,** ***on*****,** ***in*****,** ***before*****,** ***during*****, and** ***after*****.**

A: I don't have time to exercise during the day.
B: How about exercising in the morning?

B WALK AROUND **Talk to four other classmates. Give and get advice about staying healthy.**

☐ I CAN GIVE ADVICE ON STAYING HEALTHY.

READ ABOUT FITNESS APPS

SU-MIN KIM
@Su-minK
Just reached 10 miles on my app with great time, and still going!

1 BEFORE YOU READ

A PAIRS How do you like to exercise?

I go swimming with friends twice a week.

B ▶06-18 VOCABULARY Listen. Then listen and repeat.

encouragement: things that you say to make someone feel more hopeful or confident
rate: to give something a score to show how good or bad it is
adjust: change something a little bit to make it better
keep track of: to record the development of something over time
a diet: the kind of food you eat every day
a feature: an important or typical part of something
a barcode: a row of black lines on products that can be scanned to get information
an incentive: something that makes you want to work harder

>> FOR PRACTICE, GO TO PAGE 157

2 READ

A PREVIEW Read the title and look at the photo. What do you think the text will be about?

B ▶06-19 Listen. Read the review.

THIS YEAR'S BEST FITNESS APPS

Today, with all the fitness apps available, staying fit and eating right are a lot easier than before. But that's also the problem. There are so many apps that it's hard to know which one is right for you. I've reviewed some of the most popular fitness apps out there today. I hope this information helps you find an app that works for you.

Before you download an app, you need to ask yourself what kind of fitness program you like best. Do you prefer working out by yourself? Do you want data? How about some music? For some people, a little more encouragement—maybe from a coach or friends on social media—helps push them to the next level. For others, there is nothing like a little competition.

One of my favorite apps is *FitVeu*. It's free to download, but there is a small monthly fee to use it. I like it because it lets you choose whether you want to exercise on your own, get help from a coach, or share your workouts on social media. After your first workout, you can rate the difficulty of each part of the workout and the app adjusts the workout to your fitness level. It also keeps track of how much and how fast you run, bike, etc. Its exercise programs are great, but it doesn't keep track of your diet.

FitterNow is another great choice. Compared to *FitVeu*, *FitterNow* is more expensive, but I think it's worth it. *FitterNow* does everything *FitVeu* does, but unlike *FitVeu*, it has a diet feature that helps you keep track of your food. It can read a product's barcode and then calculate the number of calories it has. It has a few other features that *FitVeu* doesn't have. One feature lets you and your friends set goals and compete. For example, you enter how many miles you'll run and your friend enters how many miles she'll bike. But this is the fun part: You use money as an incentive. You say how much money your goal is worth. The app checks your progress and if you don't meet your goal, your friend gets your money.

This year's best free app is *YouGoPal*. With just a few features, it is much easier to use than the other two. Some people just want to know how far and how fast they run, which is exactly what *YouGoPal* gives you. This one is a good choice if you prefer to exercise alone and you don't need features like exercising with friends, a coach, or social media. And the best part? It's completely free.

3 CHECK YOUR UNDERSTANDING

A What is the main idea of the review? Circle the correct answer.

a. *FitterNow* is probably the best among the three apps.
b. Competition and financial incentives are most likely to make you exercise.
c. The best app choice depends on how you like to exercise.

B Read the chart with some features of the fitness apps from the review. Write (✓) if the app has the feature and (X) if it doesn't.

Features	*FitVeu*	*FitterNow*	*YouGoPal*
Free			
Provides a fitness coach			
Connects to social media			
Adjusts workout to fitness level			
Keeps track of - speed			
- distance			
- diet			
Lets you compete with friends			

C FOCUS ON LANGUAGE Reread lines 8–10 in the review. Think about the phrases *push them to the next level* and *there's nothing like a little competition*. Circle the correct answers.

1. The expression *push to the next level* means ___.
   a. to work harder b. to encourage one's friends c. to gain social media followers
2. The expression *there's nothing like a little competition* means ___.
   a. people don't like competition
   b. people don't compete anymore
   c. competition is a good incentive to exercise

D Read the Reading Skill.

1. Circle the two things that are compared or contrasted in the sentences below.
   a. "Compared to *FitVeu*, *FitterNow* is more expensive, but I think it's worth it."
   b. "*FitterNow* does everything *FitVeu* does, but unlike *FitVeu*, it has a diet feature that helps you keep track of your food."
2. Write the two signal words from the sentences in 1a and 1b.

____

READING SKILL Identify comparison and contrast

Writers often compare or contrast two or more things, people, or situations. Look for signals of comparison, such as *like*, *similar*, *compared to*, and *just as*. Signals of contrast include *unlike*, *in contrast*, and *whereas*.

E PAIRS What information did the review provide? Retell the most important ideas in the review. Use your own words.

The review compares three different...

Find some reviews of fitness apps online. Which ones have a high rating? Why?

4 MAKE IT PERSONAL

A Think about what you want in a fitness app. Take some notes.

B PAIRS Discuss your ideas in 4A.

For me, a great fitness app has to have...

☐ I CAN READ ABOUT FITNESS APPS.

LESSON 5 WRITE ABOUT HEALTH AND FITNESS

SU-MIN KIM

@Su-minK

I love being strong and healthy! My post today is all about how I do that.

1 BEFORE YOU WRITE

A What are some of your healthy habits?

B Read Su-min's post. What two healthy habits does she mention?

Su-min Kim

Oct 25, 5:45 P.M.

What's my secret to staying healthy and in shape? Well, I actually have two secrets: running and meditation.

Everyone knows that exercising regularly is a great way to get and stay healthy. And running is a great exercise because it strengthens your whole body. You use all the muscles in your body when you run, so it works out your legs, stomach, and your upper body. Running is also a great way to exercise because it's so easy to do! You can do it anywhere, anytime, and you don't even need to go to the gym! A lot of people think you need to do long, hard workouts. That's not true! All you need to do is do something active regularly. And because running is so easy to do, it's a ***great*** way to stay active regularly.

I also think it's really important to meditate every morning. One effect of meditation is that I feel calm even when work gets stressful. Another effect is that I can concentrate really well. I am able to stay focused on the task for a long time. Finally, I believe that meditation makes me more creative. I can come up with new and different ideas because my mind is relaxed.

What are *your* favorite ways to stay healthy?

C PAIRS Do you agree that it's important to keep both your body and your mind healthy? What are some other ways you can do this?

2 FOCUS ON WRITING

WRITING SKILL Show cause and effect

Use signal words to help organize **causes and effects** in your writing:
so, because, as a result, one/another, effect of, and *makes/helps.*

A Read the Writing Skill. Then reread Su-min's post. Underline all of the cause and effect signal words.

B Complete the chart with the causes and effects Su-min discusses in her post.

Cause		Effects
Running	→	• It strengthens her whole ______. • It works out her ______, ______ and upper body. • It's so ______ to do.
______	→	• It helps her feel ______. • It helps her concentrate well. • It makes her more ______.

3 PLAN YOUR WRITING

A How do you stay healthy and in shape? Think of two ways and the effects each one has on your health. Complete the chart.

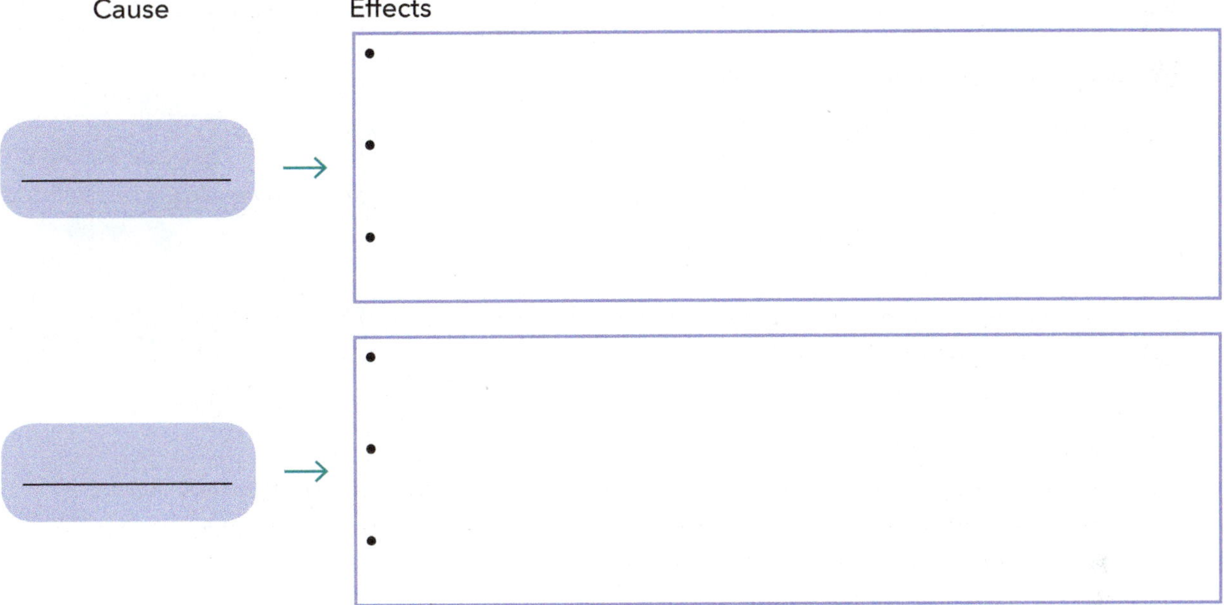

B PAIRS Talk about the ways you stay healthy and in shape.

To keep healthy, I like to swim because...

4 WRITE

Write a post about staying healthy and in shape using your information from 3A. Remember to use signal words to show cause and effect. Use the post in 1B as a model.

5 REVISE YOUR WRITING

A PAIRS Exchange and read each other's post.

1. Circle the signal words that show the causes and effects.
2. What two healthy habits did your partner write about? What effects does each habit have on his or her health?
3. Did your partner's causes and effects clearly explain how he or she stays healthy?

B PAIRS Can your classmate improve his or her post? Make suggestions.

6 PROOFREAD

Read your review again. Can you improve your writing?

Check your
- spelling
- punctuation
- capitalization

☐ I CAN WRITE ABOUT HEALTH AND FITNESS.

PUT IT TOGETHER

1 MEDIA PROJECT

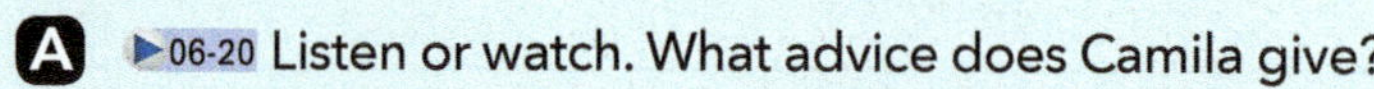

A ▶06-20 **Listen or watch. What advice does Camila give?**

B ▶06-20 **Listen or watch again. Answer the questions.**

1. What does Camila do when she feels stressed?
   ____
2. Can anyone do the moves she shows us?
   ____
3. How does she feel after the exercise?
   ____

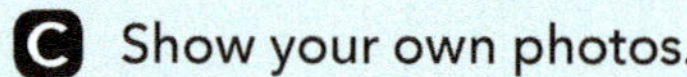

C **Show your own photos.**

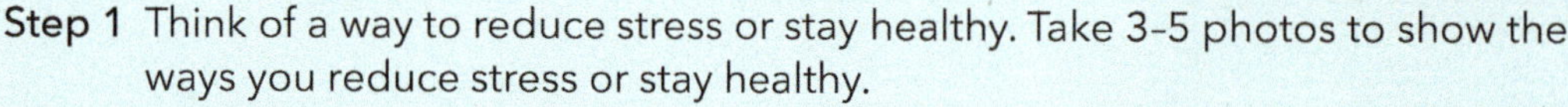

Step 1 Think of a way to reduce stress or stay healthy. Take 3–5 photos to show the ways you reduce stress or stay healthy.

Step 2 Show the photos to the class. Talk about how to stay healthy or reduce stress even when you are busy.

Step 3 Answer questions and get feedback.

2 LEARNING STRATEGY

GROUP WORDS

Grouping words that are related can help you remember new vocabulary. There are many different ways to do this. For example, when you learn new sports, you can group them into indoor and outdoor sports. Or you can group the sports by those played on a team or individually.

Individual sports	Team sports
cycling	basketball
weight lifting	soccer

Review the vocabulary from the unit. Try grouping the same list of words in two different ways. Read the words aloud to remember them better. Try to learn a new group of words once a week.

3 REFLECT AND PLAN

A **Look back through the unit. Check (✓) the things you learned. Highlight the things you need to learn.**

Speaking objectives
- ☐ Talk about fitness activities
- ☐ Talk about managing stress
- ☐ Give advice on staying healthy

Vocabulary
- ☐ Fitness activities
- ☐ Managing stress
- ☐ Staying healthy

Pronunciation
- ☐ Linking identical consonants
- ☐ Blended pronunciations with *to*

Grammar
- ☐ Gerunds as subjects and objects
- ☐ Past form of *be* + *going to* for the past intentions
- ☐ Prepositions of time

Reading
- ☐ Identify comparison and contrast

Writing
- ☐ Identify cause and effect

B **What will you do to learn the things you highlighted? For example, use your app, review your Student Book, or do other practice. Make a plan.**

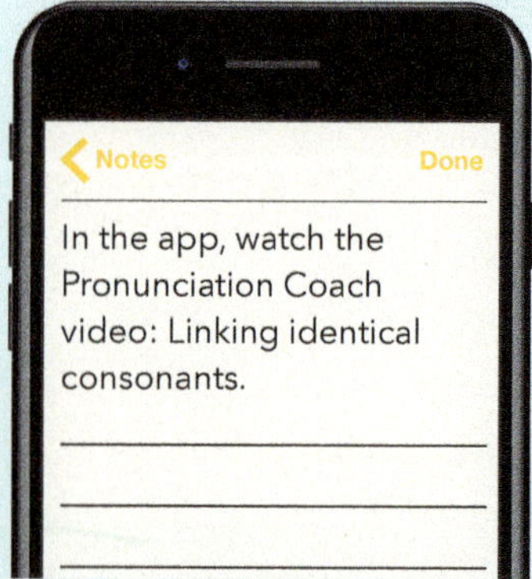

7 HOW DO YOU DO THIS?

LEARNING GOALS

In this unit, you

- ask about how to do something
- talk about expectations
- give instructions
- read about good work habits
- write about how people learn

GET STARTED

A Read the unit title and learning goals.

B Look at the photo of an office. What do you see?

C Now read Jim's message. How do you think he feels? Why?

JIM STEVENS

@JimS

Finally finishing up the North Pole campaign. It's taken a while, but we're almost there!

LESSON 1 ASK ABOUT HOW TO DO SOMETHING

JIM STEVENS
@JimS
It's going to be a busy day. Send some energy my way—I'm going to need it!

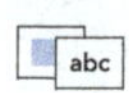 1 VOCABULARY Technology verbs

A ▶07-01 Listen. Then listen and repeat.

scroll	forward	delete	download	upload	copy
paste	attach	access	click	browse	install

B What can you do with a file (*F*), an email (*E*), or on an Internet site (*I*)? Write the correct letters *I*, *F*, or *E*, next to the words. Some words can have more than one letter.

1. scroll I, F, E
2. forward ________
3. delete ________
4. download ________
5. upload ________
6. copy ________
7. attach ________
8. access ________
9. click ________
10. browse ________

C PAIRS When do you do the things in 1A?

When I write emails to my friends, I often attach some photos.

 COACH 2 GRAMMAR Embedded *wh-* questions

Embedded questions are questions inside other statements or questions. Embedded questions are more polite than direct questions.

Direct *wh*-questions				Embedded questions			
***Wh-* word**	**Auxiliary verb**	**Subject**	**Main verb**		***Wh-* word**	**Subject**	**Verb**
What	**is**	the password?		Do you know	what	the password	**is?**
Where	**can**	I	**find** it?	Can you tell me	where	I	**can find** it?
When	**are**	we	**meeting?**	I don't know	when	we	**are meeting.**
How	**does**	this software	**work?**	I'm not sure	how	this software	**works.**

Notes

- Embedded questions often appear after introductory phrases, such as *Do you know*, *Can you tell me*, *I don't know*, *I'm not sure*, *I'd like to know*, or *Would you mind explaining*.
- Use statement word order in embedded questions. The subject always comes before the verb.
- The auxiliary verbs *do*, *does*, and *did* do not appear in the embedded question.

>> FOR PRACTICE, GO TO PAGE 143

3 CONVERSATION

  ▶07-03 Listen or watch. Circle the correct answers.

1. Su-min asks where the ___ is.
   a. email list
   b. North Pole file
   c. marketing meeting
2. Su-min wants to know when the ___ meeting is.
   a. marketing
   b. software
   c. lunch
3. Jim explains why ___.
   a. Su-min didn't get a pop-up window
   b. there was a mistake on the calendar
   c. Su-min needs to stop asking him questions

  **B** ▶07-04 Listen or watch. Complete the conversation.

Su-min:	Can you explain _________ install the Image View software?
Jim:	Sure. Open up the link and look for version 5.1 of the file.
Su-min:	Just a sec. OK, I'm there.
Jim:	Now click on direct download next to the file and wait for the pop-up window.
Su-min:	Got it. Thanks!
Jim:	_________.

CONVERSATION SKILL

Respond to "thank you"

Here are some ways to respond when someone thanks you for helping them:

It was no big deal.
Don't worry about it.
No problem.
Don't mention it.

Listen to or watch the conversation in 3A again. Underline the expressions that you hear above.

C ▶07-05 Listen and repeat. Then practice with a partner.

D PAIRS Make new conversations. Use these words or your own ideas.

access download

4 TRY IT YOURSELF

A ROLE PLAY Ask your classmate to explain how to do things on your cell phone. Use the ideas below or your own ideas. Take turns asking and explaining.

delete an app	upload photos into a text or email
download pictures	copy and paste a text or an image

Do you know how to delete this app?

B WALK AROUND Find someone who can answer the questions your partner couldn't answer. If your partner answered all of your questions, ask another question, or answer someone's question.

☐ I CAN ASK ABOUT HOW TO DO SOMETHING.

LESSON 2 TALK ABOUT EXPECTATIONS

JIM STEVENS
@JimS
A shout out to Diana for finding the best interns in the business!

1 VOCABULARY Describe work and co-workers

A ▶07-06 Listen. Then listen and repeat.

experienced: having skills or knowledge because you have done something often
intimidating: making you feel worried or frightened
laid-back: relaxed and not seeming to worry about anything
supportive: giving help or encouragement
confident: sure that you can do something well
challenging: difficult in an interesting way

B Circle the correct answers.

1. I don't like to be bored at work. I like ***laid-back*** / ***challenging*** projects.
2. When I have a problem, I talk with my best friend. He's very ***supportive*** / ***experienced***.
3. My boss is always relaxed. She is the most ***laid-back*** / ***intimidating*** person I know.
4. They have done this many times before. They are very ***experienced*** / ***challenging***.
5. He makes me feel nervous when I'm around him. He is ***confident*** / ***intimidating***.
6. I know that I'm going to do well because I'm ***supportive*** / ***confident*** in my experience.

C PAIRS For the sentences in 1B, say if this is true for you. If not, make a true statement.
This is true for me. I don't like to be bored at work. I like challenging projects.

2 GRAMMAR Comparisons with *as...as*

COACH

Use *as* + adjective + *as* to show similarities or differences between two people or things.

almost as = similar, *not as* = different, *not nearly as* = completely different

To show similarities					
	Just	***As***	**Adjective**	***As***	
The work is	–	as	**challenging**	as	I thought.
We are	just		**busy**		they are.
To show differences					
	Almost, not, not nearly	***As***	**Adjective**	***As***	
Jun is	almost	as	**experienced**	as	Carmen.
Yuri is	not		**laid-back**		May is.
These designs are	not nearly		**creative**		the last ones.

Notes

- Use *just* to make the comparison stronger.
- If the verb in the first and second part of the comparison are the same, you can leave it out in the second part. *Yuri **is** not as laid-back as May (is).*
- You can leave out the second part of the comparison when the meaning is clear because it's already been mentioned.
  *A: Sue **has a lot of meetings today**.* *B: Ask Sam. **He isn't as busy** (as Sue is).*

>> FOR PRACTICE, GO TO PAGE 144

3 PRONUNCIATION

COACH

Stress and linking in comparisons with *as…as*

In comparisons with *as*, we stress the adjective and words like *just*, *almost*, or *nearly*. The word *as* is usually unstressed and pronounced /əz/, with the short, weak vowel /ə/. We link *as* to the words around it.

A 07-08 **Listen. Notice the stress and linking. Then listen and repeat.**

The job isn't as easy as I expected.

She's just as experienced as her co-workers.

B 07-09 **Listen. Write the missing words.**

1. My friends ______________________ I am.
2. I'm ______________________ I seem.
3. English ______________________ some other languages.
4. Cell phones ______________________ laptops.

4 CONVERSATION

A 07-10 **Listen or watch. Circle the correct answers.**

1. Jim forgot ___ name because he was so nervous.
   a. his　b. his boss's　c. his co-worker's
2. Jim and Su-min say their co-workers are ___.
   a. confident　b. supportive　c. experienced
3. Su-min is learning how to ___.
   a. be more confident　b. write marketing plans　c. plan a meeting

B 07-11 **Listen or watch. Complete the conversation.**

Jim: How's your internship going?

Su-min: It's going great. Better than I expected.

Jim: Oh, yeah?

Su-min: Yeah. I was a little nervous at first.

Jim: Well, that's understandable. But I'll bet you weren't ______________ I was when I started here!

Su-min: I'm not so sure about that! I was actually a little scared of *everyone*. But people here aren't __________ intimidating __________ I thought.

C 07-12 **Listen and repeat. Then practice with a partner.**

D PAIRS **Make new conversations. Use the words in 1A or your own ideas.**

5 TRY IT YOURSELF

A MAKE IT PERSONAL **Think about your classes, job, a sport, or hobby. How do they compare with what you expected? Make notes. Use the vocabulary in 1A.**

B PAIRS **Student A, talk about your expectations. Student B, ask follow-up questions.**

A: Learning English isn't as intimidating as I expected.
B: What do you mean?

☐ I CAN TALK ABOUT EXPECTATIONS.

LESSON 3 GIVE INSTRUCTIONS

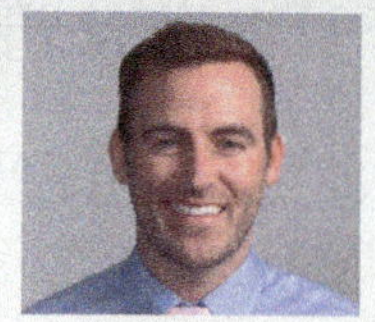

JIM STEVENS
@JimS
Looking forward to getting out of the city this weekend.

1 VOCABULARY Phrasal verbs

A 07-13 Listen. Then listen and repeat.

check in with: to talk with someone to make sure that everything is okay
run out of: to use all of something so that there is none left
get on: to connect to an online network to use a cell phone or computer
go over: to review something
go through: to look at or read something carefully
back up: to make a copy of information on a computer
put together: to prepare or produce something by collecting information, ideas, etc.
figure out: to understand someone or something after thinking about him, her, or it

B Write the phrasal verbs from 1A next to the correct word or phrase. More than one answer may be possible.

1. ________________ your computer
2. ________________ a problem
3. ________________ your files
4. ________________ your family
5. ________________ the information
6. ________________ paper

C PAIRS Compare your answers in 1B. Make sentences about how often you do these activities.

I almost never back up my files.
I often check in with my parents.

2 GRAMMAR Phrasal verbs with objects

Phrasal verbs are made up of a verb + particle. Particles look like prepositions (*with*, *of*, *on*), but together with the verb they have a different meaning.

Separable phrasal verbs

Subject	Verb	Particle	Object		Subject	Verb	Object	Particle
I	**put**	**together**	a plan.	or	I	**put**	a plan	**together**.
Arun	**backs**	**up**	the files.		Arun	**backs**	them	**up**.

Inseparable phrasal verbs

Subject	Verb	Particle	Object
Mira	**is getting**	**on**	the Internet.
We	**went**	**over**	the notes.

Notes

- With separable phrasal verbs, the object can come before or after the particle.
- When the object is a pronoun, it ***must*** come after the verb and before the particle.
  Compare these examples:
  *I put **a plan** together.* *I put **it** together.*
  *I put together **a plan**.* NOT ~~*I put together it.*~~
- With **inseparable** phrasal verbs, the object always comes after the particle.
  *We went over **the notes**.* *We went over **them**.*

>> FOR PRACTICE, GO TO PAGE 145

3 PRONUNCIATION

COACH

A 07-15 Listen. Notice the stressed words. Then listen and repeat.

Turn the TV on. I turned it on. Check in with me.

B 07-16 Underline the two stressed words in each phrasal verb + object. Then listen and check your answers.

1. A: Don't forget to back your files up.
   B: I already backed them up.
2. A: Do you know how to set this up?
   B: I think I can figure it out.
3. A: Turn the lights off when you leave, OK?
   B: I'm not sure how to turn them off.
4. A: Let's go over these notes.
   B: OK. Let's go over them after lunch.

C PAIRS Practice the conversations in 3B.

Stress in phrasal verbs

In most phrasal verbs, both the verb and the particle are stressed. If a phrasal verb has a noun object, stress sometimes shifts from the particle to the noun. Pronoun objects are not usually stressed.

4 LISTENING

A 07-17 Listen to the series of voicemail messages between Jim and his co-worker Peter. Put the pictures in the order that they happen.

LISTENING SKILL

Listen for instructions

When someone gives you instructions, listen for the imperative form of the verb. When you hear it, make a note of what the instruction is.

A

B

C

D
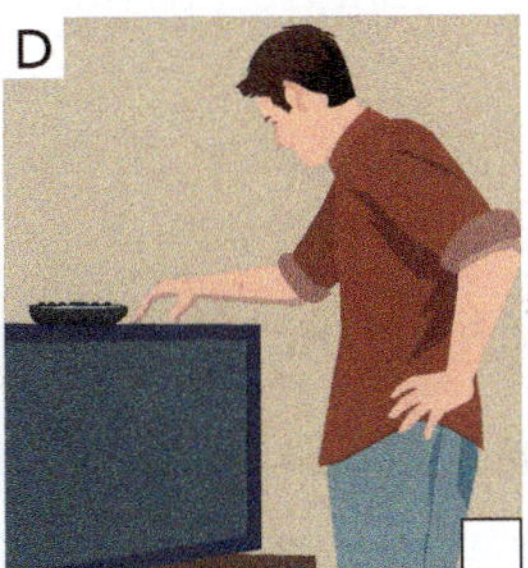

E

B 07-17 Read the Listening Skill. Listen again. Complete the sentences with *Jim* or *Peter*.

1. ______________ called to find out if ______________ backed up the North Pole files.
2. ______________ put together information and emailed it to ______________.
3. ______________ thought ______________ didn't have any cat food in the house.
4. ______________ couldn't figure out how to turn on the TV.
5. ______________ sent the email to ______________ again.
6. ______________ wrote about the wifi in his email, but ______________ didn't read it.

C PAIRS Look at the pictures in 4A. Give Peter instructions about what to do.

Picture A Look in the cabinet...

5 TRY IT YOURSELF

ROLE PLAY Imagine you are going away for the weekend and your classmate is housesitting for you. Make a list of 5-8 things you need to tell your classmate. Then give instructions about what to do and what not to do. When you finish, switch roles.

To get on the internet, choose the network "home sweet home." Then type in the password "homealone."

☐ I CAN GIVE INSTRUCTIONS.

LESSON 4 READ ABOUT GOOD WORK HABITS

JIM STEVENS
@JimS
Great tips in this article about how to be more productive without getting exhausted.

1 BEFORE YOU READ

A PAIRS How do you get everything done when you are at work?

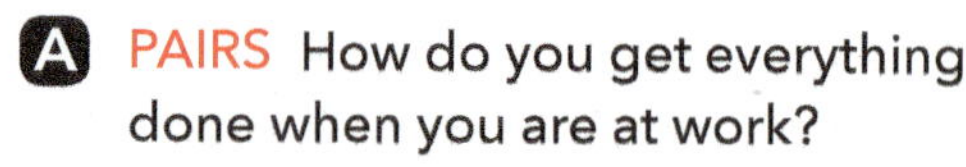

I close my door so no one bothers me.

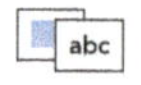

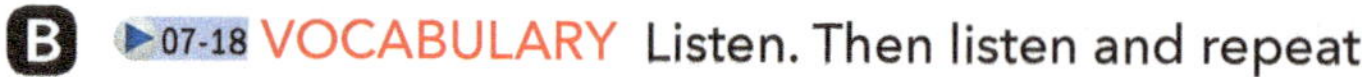

B 07-18 VOCABULARY Listen. Then listen and repeat.

a deadline: a date or time by which you must finish something
productive: achieving a lot
pile up: to increase (only if the things that are increasing are bad)
catch up: to do something you did not have time for earlier
dread: to worry about something that is going to happen
focus: to give a lot of attention to something or someone
a notification: a message about activity on your social media
distracted: confused or not paying attention because you are thinking of something else

>> FOR PRACTICE, GO TO PAGE 157

2 READ

A PREVIEW Read the title. What good work habits do you think the text will include?

B 07-19 Listen. Read the blog post.

Blog | About | Contact Logout

Good work habits

Last year was a disaster at work. I missed a lot of deadlines and I got a bad performance report. It's a new year and I need to be more productive. So, I asked a lot of successful people about their work habits. I got some good advice and some advice that's—well—a little unusual! Here is what they said:

Tarek, owner of multiple successful restaurants:

- I plan my day in 15-minute blocks, so I don't waste any time.
- I set goals and make a list of steps to meet each of them.
- I keep my meetings short by having "standing" meetings—that's right—no chairs!

Siguri, online store manager:

- It's hard, but I try to stay on top of my email. If I let it pile up, I never catch up.
- I have different music playlists for different purposes—electronic music for meeting deadlines; classical music for increasing creativity.

Kim, a writer and editor:

- I get the most unpleasant jobs out of the way as soon as I get to work. If I don't, I spend all day dreading them and I can't focus.
- I turn off my social media notifications, but I check them every few hours. That way, I don't get distracted with constant messages, but I still stay connected while I'm in the office.
- Every couple of hours, I stop working and do something silly, like watching cat videos. I can get back to work with a smile on my face and plenty of energy.

Vinod, a money manager:

- My job is very stressful. Plants make me feel calm and happy so I keep lots of them in my office. They also increase the amount of oxygen in the room, which helps me focus.
- I also keep fish in my office. They help me relax so I can be more creative. My best ideas come after watching my fish.

I've started following some of this advice. It's only been a few weeks, but I think it's already working. Yesterday, my boss told me how pleased she was with my work. She also asked about the goldfish in my office ☺ !

3 CHECK YOUR UNDERSTANDING

A **What is the main idea of the post? Circle the correct answer.**

a. No one really knows how we can increase productivity.
b. There are many different strategies for increasing productivity.
c. The author is confused about how to improve her performance.

B **Who probably said it? Write *T* (Tarek), *S* (Siguri), (K) Kim, or (V) Vinod in the blanks.**

___ 1. "Your deadline is when? Oh no! Put on some good music and let's get it done!
___ 2. "I'm going back to my office so I can think in peace and quiet."
___ 3. "I'm glad I finished that. Now I can start on the more interesting stuff."
___ 4. "This meeting won't take long."
___ 5. "I finished eight of the ten things on my list today."
___ 6. "Check out this video. It's so cute!"

C FOCUS ON LANGUAGE **Reread lines 16–25 in the blog post. Think about the phrases *on top of* and *out of the way*. Circle the correct answers.**

1. The expression *on top of* means ___.
   a. above   b. in control of   c. not knowing about
2. The expression *out of the way* means ___.
   a. finished   b. hidden   c. done by somebody else

D **Read the Reading Skill. Which of these ideas do the people discuss? Circle three answers.**

a. ways to use time efficiently
b. ways to become more confident
c. ways to increase focus
d. ways to keep a work-life balance
e. ways to be more creative

READING SKILL
Synthesize information

When you synthesize information, you read details from different sources and group similar ideas together. Look for parts of the text that say the same thing in different ways and try to figure out what all of these ideas have in common.

E PAIRS **For each of the ideas in 3D, what advice did the blog post provide?**

The post offers advice about…

Look online for more ideas about how to increase productivity in the workplace. Which ones do you think would be the most successful? Why?

4 MAKE IT PERSONAL

A **Think about how you work or study. Do you think any of the suggestions in the post would work for you? Take some notes in the chart.**

What would help me	Why
What would not help me	**Why**

B PAIRS **Discuss your answers in 4A.**

The idea about plants is very interesting. It would help me because I always feel relaxed in a garden.

☐ I CAN READ ABOUT GOOD WORK HABITS.

LESSON 5 WRITE ABOUT HOW PEOPLE LEARN

JIM STEVENS

@JimS

My friend can learn things just by watching a video! I wish I could. Here's my new post on learning.

1 BEFORE YOU WRITE

A What are some things that help you learn a new skill?

B Read Jim's post. What ways of learning does he talk about?

THE WAYS WE LEARN

Jim Stevens
Copywriter,
TSW Media

People learn in many different ways. Some of us are really good at reading written instructions; others prefer to look at pictures. Some people learn by watching other people do something first, while others learn by doing things themselves.

In my case, I need time to read and concentrate before I learn something new. Then I like to teach it to someone else right away. In this way, I gain a deeper understanding of the new skill. For example, I recently learned how to use a new computer program. Then I taught a co-worker how to use the program. After I taught my co-worker, I felt like I really understood the program. I no longer needed to check the written instructions.

In contrast, I have a friend who *never* reads written instructions. Instead, she prefers to watch videos online. Once, she watched a video about how to fix her laptop computer, and then she changed all the hardware in her laptop—all without reading anything! She is really good at figuring things out on her own, and she will always try to find solutions before she asks for help. That's one thing we have in common.

How do *you* learn? I'd love to hear your stories.

C Read the post again. Complete the chart.

Jim	Both	Jim's friend
• learns by ____________ instructions • also learns by ____________	• try to ____________ before ____________	• does not ____________ • learns by ____________

2 FOCUS ON WRITING

Read the Writing Skill. Then reread Jim's post. Underline the words or phrases that signal comparison or contrast.

> **WRITING SKILL Show comparison and contrast**
>
> Use **compare and contrast** signal words to show how two things are alike and how they are different.
>
> Compare: *alike, similarly, in common*
>
> Contrast: *in contrast, unlike, as opposed to, instead, some...others*

3 PLAN YOUR WRITING

A How do you learn? Complete the chart with your information.

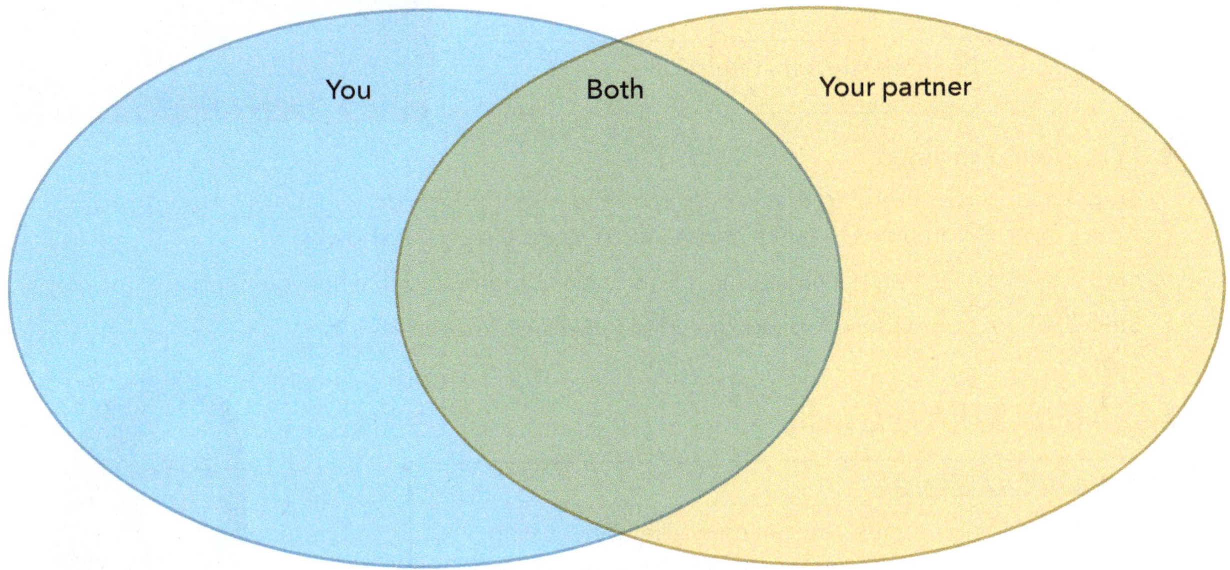

B PAIRS Interview your partner. Complete the chart in 3A with your partner's information.

4 WRITE

Write a post about how people learn using your and your partner's information from 3A and B. Remember to use signal words to show comparison and contrast. Use the post in 1B as a model.

5 REVISE YOUR WRITING

A PAIRS Exchange and read each other's posts.

1. Underline the signal words that show comparison and contrast.
2. Did your partner's use of signal words show you the different ways your partner and the other person learn? Why or why not?

B PAIRS Can your classmate improve his or her post? Make suggestions.

6 PROOFREAD

Read your post again. Can you improve your writing?

> Check your
> - spelling
> - punctuation
> - capitalization

☐ I CAN WRITE ABOUT HOW PEOPLE LEARN.

PUT IT TOGETHER

1 MEDIA PROJECT

A ▶07-20 **Listen or watch. What does Li Wei teach us?**

B ▶07-20 **Listen or watch again. Answer the questions.**

1. What does Li Wei need for his lesson?

   ____

2. Which parts of the guitar does he talk about?

   ____

3. What are the three steps that he shows?

   ____

C **Make your own video.**

Step 1 Choose something that is easy to teach. What things do you need? Are there any words you need to teach? What steps do you need to show?

Step 2 Make a 30-second video. Show how to do something. Say what you need and the steps.

Step 3 Share your video. Answer questions and get feedback.

2 LEARNING STRATEGY

Joe is as tall as Ron.

GRAMMAR CHALLENGE

To remember things better, you can create sentences with different grammar and vocabulary that you've learned. Review the grammar and try to put two or more grammar points together in one sentence. Add vocabulary from the unit.

grammar: phrasal verbs, embedded questions, as…as

They wanted to know when we backed up our files.

Review the grammar from the unit. Write five sentences using two or more grammar points. Try to combine different grammar points. Add at least one vocabulary word to each sentence.

3 REFLECT AND PLAN

A **Look back through the unit. Check (✓) the things you learned. Highlight the things you need to learn.**

Speaking objectives
- ☐ Ask about how to do something
- ☐ Talk about expectations
- ☐ Give instructions

Vocabulary
- ☐ Technology verbs
- ☐ Describe work and co-workers
- ☐ Phrasal verbs

Pronunciation
- ☐ Stress and linking in comparisons with *as…as*
- ☐ Stress in phrasal verbs

Grammar
- ☐ Embedded *wh-* questions
- ☐ Comparisons with *as…as*
- ☐ Phrasal verbs with objects

Reading
- ☐ Synthesize information

Writing
- ☐ Show comparison and contrast

B **What will you do to learn the things you highlighted? For example, use your app, review your Student Book, or do other practice. Make a plan.**

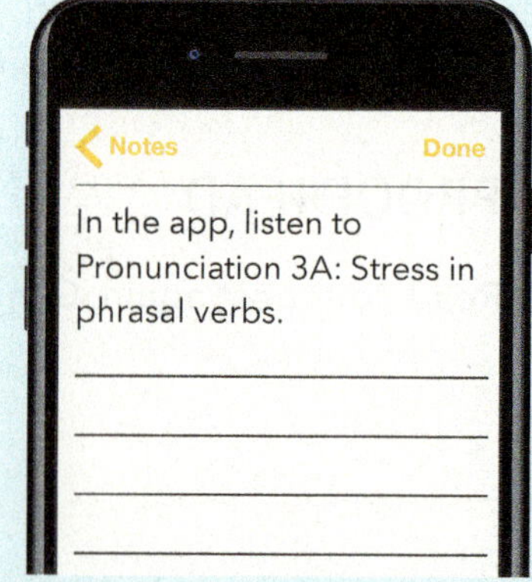

8 HOW ARE YOU FEELING?

LEARNING GOALS

In this unit, you

- talk about feeling sick
- talk about the flu
- discuss what happens when you get sick
- read about keeping cool
- write about being sick

GET STARTED

A Read the unit title and learning goals.

B Look at the photo of a health clinic. What do you see?

C Now read Diana's message. What does she remind people about?

DIANA OLVERA

@DianaO

Just a reminder that it's flu season again. Let's all stay healthy this year!

LESSON 1 TALK ABOUT FEELING SICK

DIANA OLVERA

@DianaO

Not feeling well this morning —please don't tell me I'm coming down with the flu!

 1 VOCABULARY Common health problems

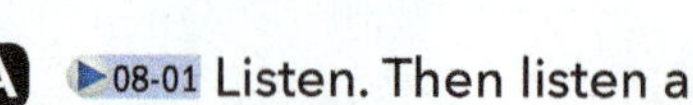

A 08-01 Listen. Then listen and repeat.

B 08-02 Listen. Write the health problem from 1A that each speaker talks about.

1. ______________ 3. ______________ 5. ______________

2. ______________ 4. ______________ 6. ______________

C PAIRS Compare your answers in 1B.

 COACH 2 GRAMMAR *May / might / could* with the continuous to show possibility

Use *may / might / could* + continuous form to express the possibility that something is happening at the time of speaking.

Affirmative				
Subject	**Modal**	***Be***	**Verb + *-ing***	
I	**may**		**getting**	sick.
He	**might**	**be**	**catching**	a cold.
They	**could**		**meeting**	now.
Negative				
He	**may not**	**be**	**feeling**	better.
We	**might not**		**going**	home.
Questions				
Modal	**Subject**	***Be***	**Verb + *-ing***	
Could	he	**be**	**sleeping**?	

Notes

- Do not use *could not* (*couldn't*) to express possibility. *Couldn't* means you are very certain.
  He couldn't be sick. = I am almost 100% certain he is not sick.
- Do not use *may* or *might* to form questions.
- Do not confuse *may be* (verb phrase) and *maybe* (adverb).
  *Tim **may be** talking to the doctor.*
  ***Maybe** Tim is talking to the doctor.*

>> FOR PRACTICE, GO TO PAGE 146

3 PRONUNCIATION

COACH

Silent letters

Some words have consonant letters that are silent, or not pronounced. For example, *know* begins with the letter *k*, but we don't pronounce that letter. The letter *k* is silent.

A ▶08-04 **Listen. Notice the silent letters. Then listen and repeat.**

know wrong listen

B ▶08-05 **Circle the one word in each line that does *not* have silent letters. Then listen and check your answers.**

1. might thought caught cough
2. could cold half talk
3. sign foreign migraine design
4. write why answer whole

C PAIRS **Create three sentences. Each sentence should include 2-3 words with silent letters.**

4 CONVERSATION

A ▶08-06 **Listen or watch. Circle the correct answers.**

1. What is wrong with Diana?
   a. She's allergic to seafood.
   b. She's coming down with the flu.
   c. She doesn't feel well.
2. What does Mehmet suggest that she do?
   a. leave work early
   b. go to the doctor
   c. take some medicine
3. What happens at the end of the scene?
   a. Diana decides to go home.
   b. Diana starts to feel better.
   c. Mehmet starts to feel sick.

B ▶08-07 **Listen or watch. Complete the conversation.**

Mehmet: Do you have a stomachache?
Diana: No, but I think I might have a fever.
Mehmet: Do you have a cough? You ____________ down with the flu.
Diana: Oh no, not again!
Mehmet: What are you looking for?
Diana: I'm looking for my tea. I take it when I think I ____________ sick.

CONVERSATION SKILL
Show concern

To show concern and to offer help, say:
Are you okay?
What's wrong?
Do you need anything?
Listen to or watch the conversation in 4A again. Underline the questions that you hear above.

C ▶08-08 **Listen and repeat. Then practice with a partner.**

D PAIRS **Make new conversations. Use these words or your own ideas.**

indigestion a stuffy nose a cold

5 TRY IT YOURSELF

A ROLE PLAY **Student A, imagine you are not feeling well. Talk about your symptoms. Student B, show concern. Guess what is wrong with Student A and give advice.**

A: I have a terrible headache. B: You might be getting a migraine. You should lie down.

B WALK AROUND **Take turns talking to four other classmates about different symptoms.**

☐ I CAN TALK ABOUT FEELING SICK.

TALK ABOUT THE FLU

DIANA OLVERA
@DianaO
Found a really informative podcast that helps you get through the flu season.

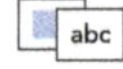

1 VOCABULARY The flu

A ▶08-09 Listen. Then listen and repeat.

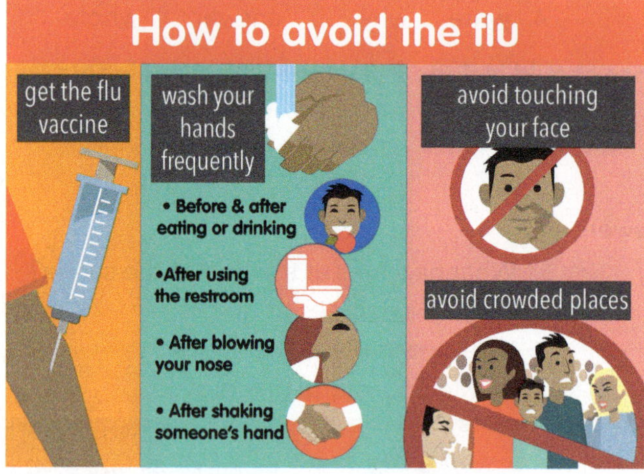

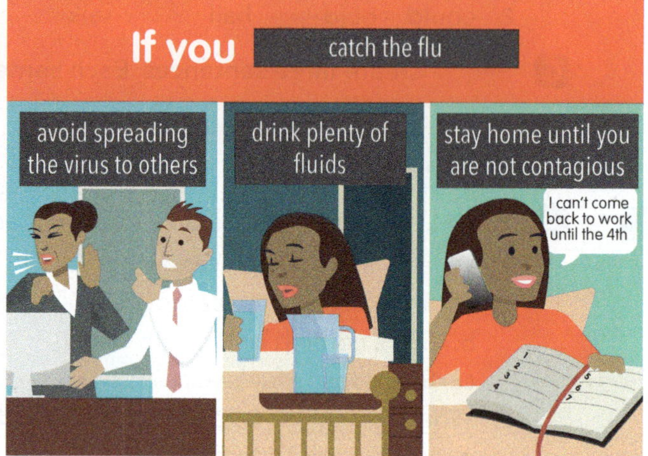

B If you have the flu, what should you do to make sure others don't catch it? Check (✓) all the correct answers.

- ☐ drink plenty of fluids
- ☐ get the flu vaccine
- ☐ avoid crowded places
- ☐ avoid touching your face
- ☐ wash your hands frequently
- ☐ stay home until you are not contagious

C PAIRS Compare your answers in 1B.

COACH

2 GRAMMAR Subordinating conjunctions in time clauses

A time clause tells when something happens. It begins with a subordinating conjunction.

Conjunction	Meaning	Example sentences with time clauses
after	at a later time	*Wash your hands **after** you touch anything in public.*
as soon as	happening shortly after an event	*He will call the doctor **as soon as** he finishes work.*
before	at an earlier time	*People should get the flu vaccine **before** flu season starts.*
once	from the moment something happens	***Once** you feel better, you can return to your normal activities.*
till / until	up to that time, and then no longer	*Don't go back to work **till / until** you feel better.*
when	at that time	***When** spring comes, she gets terrible allergies.*
whenever	every time	***Whenever** you can, avoid crowded places.*
while	at the same time	*They waited **while** he was taking a photo.*

Note: Time clauses are dependent clauses. This means they are **not** complete ideas.
In formal speech and writing, they must be used with **independent clauses.**
***When** I see the doctor, I'll ask her about a flu shot.*
(dependent clause) (independent clause)

>> FOR PRACTICE, GO TO PAGE 147

3 PRONUNCIATION

COACH

A ▶08-11 **Listen. Notice the pronunciations of *can* and *can't*. Then listen and repeat.**

/kən/	/kæn(t)/
What can we do?	I can't always stay home.
Maybe I can help you.	Whenever you can, avoid crowds.

B ▶08-12 **Listen. Circle the word that the *second* person says.**

1. can / can't 2. can / can't 3. can / can't 4. can / can't

Can* and *can't

Negative contractions like *can't* usually do not have a clear /t/ sound at the end. Stress and the sound of the vowel help us hear the difference between *can't* and *can*. *Can't* is stressed and has the clear vowel sound /æ/. *Can* is usually unstressed and has the weak vowel /ə/, though it is stressed before a pause.

4 LISTENING

A ▶08-13 **Listen to the podcast. Check (✓) all the true statements about the flu.**

1. ☐ It is very easy to pass on to others.
2. ☐ It can kill you.
3. ☐ Everyone should get the flu vaccine.
4. ☐ You can go back to work or school as soon as you feel better.

B ▶08-13 **Read the Listening Skill. Listen again. Use the words in the box to help you complete the chart. Then check your answers.**

avoid touching your face	avoid all public places
wait a couple of days	stay home and rest
get the flu vaccine	wash your hands
stay away from other people	drink plenty of fluids

Here are two easy things you can do to protect yourself.
First: ____________________
Second: • ____________________
• ____________________
Now here's my third piece of advice. If you catch the flu…
• ____________________
• ____________________
• ____________________
• ____________________
Finally, once you feel better…
____

LISTENING SKILL
Listen for signal words

Speakers sometimes use signal words to let us know what they are going to talk about, for example:
*Here are **two** easy things you can do. **First**, most healthy people should…*
When you hear signal words, use them to help you follow the speaker's important ideas.

C TAKE A POLL **How many of your classmates have had the flu in the past two years?**

5 TRY IT YOURSELF

A MAKE IT PERSONAL **Think about what you do during flu season to stay healthy. Use information from the podcast and your own ideas. Take notes.**

As soon as flu season starts, I get the flu vaccine.

B PAIRS **Discuss. What do you do during the flu season to stay healthy? Do you both do the same things?**

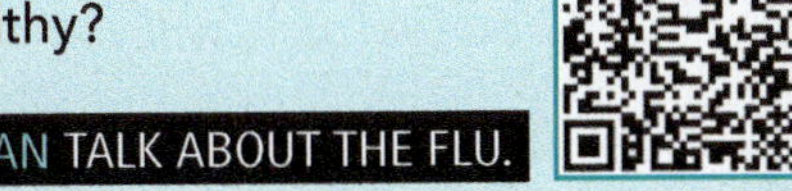

LESSON 3 DISCUSS WHAT HAPPENS WHEN YOU GET SICK

DIANA OLVERA
@DianaO
You can never be too careful during the flu season.

1 VOCABULARY When you are sick

A ▶08-14 Listen. Then listen and repeat.

go to the doctor: to see a doctor when you are sick
miss work: to not go to work, usually because you are sick
make others sick: to spread a virus or bacteria to other people
get worse: to become sicker
call in sick: to inform people that you are sick and won't go to work or school
stay in: to not go outside of your house
get over (something): to become well again after a difficult time, for example after being sick
get better: to feel better, usually after an injury or illness

B Complete the sentences with the words in 1A.

1. Stay home when you are sick so that you don't spread your illness and ______________.
2. Go to the doctor before you ______________.
3. If you take medicine, you will ______________ your cold faster.
4. You should ______________ and get some rest today.
5. If you rest, you will ______________ faster.

C PAIRS Make five new sentences with the expressions from 1A.

2 GRAMMAR Future real conditional

COACH

Use the future real conditional to talk about what will likely happen under certain conditions. The *if*-clause gives the condition.

Statements

***If*-clause**				**Result clause**			
If	**Subject**	**Simple present**		**Subject**	***Will / Won't***	**Base form of verb**	
If	I you people	**feel** **don't take** **get**	sick, this medicine, sick,	I you they	**will** **won't** **will**	**stay** **get** **miss**	home. better. work.

Questions

***If*-clause**				**Result clause**				
If	**Subject**	**Simple present**		***Wh-* word**	***Will / Won't***	**Subject**	**Base form of verb**	
If	you he	**feel** **gets**	sick, better,	who –	**will** **will**	you he	**call**? **come**	to work?

Note: The *if*-clause can come at the beginning or end of a sentence. Use a comma when the *if*-clause comes at the beginning of a sentence.

***If** you come to work**,** you'll make others sick.* *You'll make other sick **if** you come to work.*
***If** you feel sick**,** will you come to work?* *Will you come to work **if** you feel sick?*

>> FOR PRACTICE, GO TO PAGE 148

3 CONVERSATION

A 08-16 Listen or watch. Circle the correct answers.

1. Why is Diana worried?
   a. She could make others sick.
   b. She could catch the flu.
   c. They could lose business.
2. What does Diana give Mehmet?
   a. a mask
   b. a message from his sister
   c. meeting notes
3. What does Mehmet say about getting sick?
   a. He doesn't get sick.
   b. He hates being sick.
   c. He should protect himself.
4. What does Mehmet do at the end of the scene?
   a. He wears a mask.
   b. He sneezes.
   c. He goes to the doctor.

B 08-17 Listen or watch. Complete the conversation.

Mehmet: Diana? What's wrong? Why are you wearing a mask?
Diana: Oh, this. I'm just being careful. It's the flu season.
Mehmet: You've had the flu shot, right?
Diana: Yes, of course. But you never know. ____________ sick, ____________ work, and we ____________ our deadline.

C 08-18 Listen and repeat. Then practice with a partner.

D PAIRS Make new conversations. Use the words in 1A or your own ideas.

4 TRY IT YOURSELF

A ROLE PLAY What will happen if you get sick? Student A, start a sentence about getting or being sick. Student B, finish the sentence and start a new one. Continue the story. Keep the story going as long as you can.

A: I'm sick. If I don't get better soon, I'll go to the doctor.
B: But if you go to the doctor, you...

B WALK AROUND Change partners and role-play a different story.

☐ I CAN DISCUSS WHAT HAPPENS WHEN I GET SICK.

LESSON 4 READ ABOUT KEEPING COOL

DIANA OLVERA
@DianaO
This is the most interesting way to stay cool. Has anyone else heard of this?

1 BEFORE YOU READ

A PAIRS How hot does it get where you live? What do you do to stay cool?

On hot, summer days, I spend time in cool, indoor places like the café near my house.

B ▶08-19 VOCABULARY Listen. Then listen and repeat.

tropical: in or from the hottest, wettest parts of the world
evidence: information or something you see that helps you decide if something is true
a surface: the outside or top part of something
sweat (noun): the liquid that comes out of your skin when you are hot, nervous, or have a fever
sweat (verb): when you sweat, liquid comes out of your skin because you are hot
evaporate: when liquid evaporates, it changes into a gas
a signal: a sound or action that tells someone or something to act
leave out: to not include

>> FOR PRACTICE, GO TO PAGE 158

2 READ

A PREVIEW Read the title and look at the photos. How could these foods help you keep cool?

B ▶08-20 Listen. Read the article.

KEEPING COOL

spicy salsa–Mexico

hot chai tea–India

It's hot, really hot. There's no swimming pool or air conditioning. You should reach for an ice-cold glass of water or maybe a dish of ice cream, right? Wrong, at least according to people who live in hot, tropical climates. How about a cup of hot tea or a spicy dish full of chilies instead? Just listen to people in India, where hot tea is the most popular drink. Or ask people in Mexico, where archeologists have found evidence that ancient people were cooking up hot, spicy drinks more than 2,400 years ago!

So why are hot drinks and spicy foods so popular in hot climates? At first glance, this doesn't make a lot of sense. But if you look a little closer—at the science behind body temperature—it makes perfect sense because hot drinks and chilies can actually cool you down. Here's how it works: Your body temperature stays within about one degree of the normal body temperature. If your temperature goes higher, your blood begins to move toward the surface of your body. This causes your body to sweat. As a result of the sweat evaporating, you start to feel cooler and your body temperature goes back down.

How do the hot drinks and chilies fit into this picture? You have temperature sensors in your mouth, along your tongue, and all the way down into your stomach. When hot drinks, like tea or coffee, hit those sensors, they send a signal to your brain. Some foods, like ginger and black pepper, but most of all, chili peppers, cause those sensors to respond in the same way. Then the brain sends out a message: Start sweating! You may not like sweating, but it is extremely important, especially in hot climates, because the body cools down when sweat evaporates.

So, what about that ice-cold glass of water? Will it cool you off? It can actually have the opposite effect. The sensors in your mouth will tell your brain, "Ah, nice and cool." As a result, the brain sends out the message, "Time to stop sweating"—exactly what you don't want. However, keep in mind that when you sweat, your body loses water, so drinking water on hot days is still very important. You just might want to leave out the ice cubes.

3 CHECK YOUR UNDERSTANDING

A **What is the main thing readers can learn from this article? Circle the correct answer.**

a. Hot drinks and spicy foods can keep you cool.
b. Your body sometimes has trouble keeping you cool.
c. Sweating is a signal that you are too hot.

B **Circle the correct answers.**

1. What causes body temperature to go down?
   a. body staying at normal temperature
   b. blood getting cooler
   c. sweat evaporating
2. What do hot drinks have in common with spicy food?
   a. They keep your body temperature within one degree of the normal temperature.
   b. They block temperature sensors from sending signals to the brain.
   c. They cause your body to sweat.
3. Why is important to drink a lot of water when it is hot?
   a. It replaces the water we lose in sweat.
   b. It keeps your blood moving quickly.
   c. It makes your sweat evaporate more quickly.

C FOCUS ON LANGUAGE **Reread lines 8–15 in the blog post. Think about the phrases *make sense* and *fit into the picture*. Circle the correct answers.**

1. The expression *make sense* means ___.
   a. have a meaning you can understand b. be useful c. feel right
2. The expression *fit into the picture* means ___.
   a. be related
   b. explain something difficult
   c. show how something looks

D **Read the Reading Skill.**

1. Reread the article. Underline words and phrases that signal cause or effect.
2. Write *C* (cause) and *E* (effect) next to the correct event in each pair.
   a. ___ you sweat
      ___ your blood moves to the skin's surface
   b. ___ you drink something hot or eat something spicy
      ___ sensors in your mouth send a signal to your brain
   c. ___ you feel cooler
      ___ sweat evaporates

> READING SKILL
> **Identify cause and effect**
>
> Writers use signals like *because*, *so*, *as a result*, *cause*, *result in*, *lead to*, *consequently*, and *therefore* to show a cause-and-effect relationship. Sometimes the order in which the writer reports the events or actions can also help you see the cause-and-effect relationship.

E PAIRS **What did you learn from the article? Retell the most important ideas in your own words.**

I learned about foods that can...

> Look online to find other foods that can help you keep cool. Was any of the information you found surprising?

4 MAKE IT PERSONAL

A **Have you ever eaten spicy food or hot drinks to stay cool? What was your experience? What else do you do to stay cool?**

B PAIRS **Discuss your answers in 4A.**

I always drink hot tea in the summer.

☐ I CAN READ ABOUT KEEPING COOL.

LESSON 5 WRITE ABOUT BEING SICK

1 BEFORE YOU WRITE

A When you are sick, who do you have to tell about it? How do you tell them?

B Read Diana's emails. What is wrong with her?

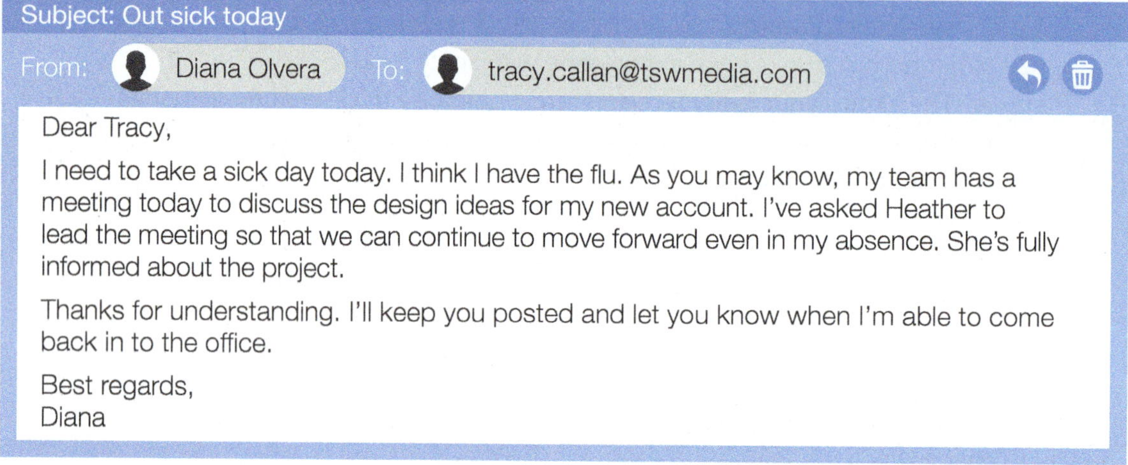

Subject: Out sick today

From: Diana Olvera To: tracy.callan@tswmedia.com

Dear Tracy,

I need to take a sick day today. I think I have the flu. As you may know, my team has a meeting today to discuss the design ideas for my new account. I've asked Heather to lead the meeting so that we can continue to move forward even in my absence. She's fully informed about the project.

Thanks for understanding. I'll keep you posted and let you know when I'm able to come back in to the office.

Best regards,
Diana

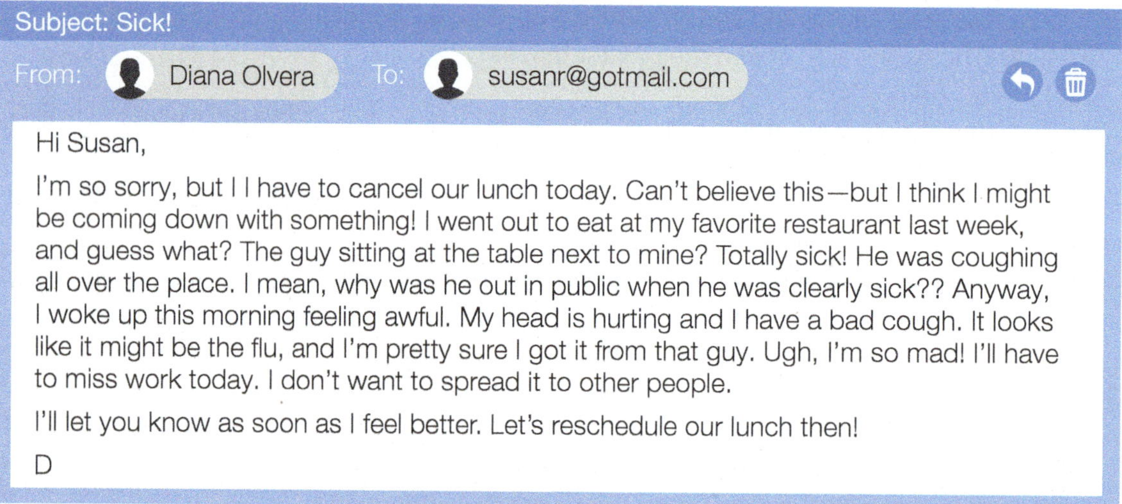

Subject: Sick!

From: Diana Olvera To: susanr@gotmail.com

Hi Susan,

I'm so sorry, but I I have to cancel our lunch today. Can't believe this—but I think I might be coming down with something! I went out to eat at my favorite restaurant last week, and guess what? The guy sitting at the table next to mine? Totally sick! He was coughing all over the place. I mean, why was he out in public when he was clearly sick?? Anyway, I woke up this morning feeling awful. My head is hurting and I have a bad cough. It looks like it might be the flu, and I'm pretty sure I got it from that guy. Ugh, I'm so mad! I'll have to miss work today. I don't want to spread it to other people.

I'll let you know as soon as I feel better. Let's reschedule our lunch then!

D

C Read the emails again. Complete the chart.

	Who will read this?	*What* are the important details?
Email 1	Diana's manager, Tracy	She needs to take ______________________. She has ______________________. Her team has ______________________ today. Heather will ______________________. She will let Tracy know ______________________.
Email 2	Diana's ______________, Susan	She has to cancel ______________________. She has ______________________. She caught it from ______________________. She will let Susan know ______________________.

2 FOCUS ON WRITING

A Read the Writing Skill. Then reread Diana's emails. Which email is formal? Which email is informal?

B In the informal email, underline the extra details. Double underline the incomplete sentences. Circle the exclamations and other emotional language.

WRITING SKILL Use formal and informal writing

Choose to write in a **formal or informal** style depending on who will read your writing. Formal writing should have complete sentences, only important details, no exclamations points or emotional language. Informal writing can have incomplete sentences, extra details, and emotional language.

3 PLAN YOUR WRITING

A Imagine you need to take a sick day. Who will you email and what will you tell them? Complete the chart with your information.

	Who will read this?	*What* are the important details?
Email 1	your manager,	
Email 2	your friend,	

B PAIRS Talk about who you will email and what you will tell each person.

First, I'll email my manager, John. I'll tell him that my colleague Sara can help with...

4 WRITE

Write a formal email to a manager and an informal email to a friend to tell them you are sick. Use your information from 3A. Remember to add extra details and emotional language to the informal email. Remember to use complete sentences in the formal email. Use the emails in 1B as models.

5 REVISE YOUR WRITING

A PAIRS Exchange and read each other's emails.

1. Underline examples of informal writing (extra details, emotional language, incomplete sentences).
2. Did your partner use an informal style for the email to the friend and a formal style for the email to the manager? In what ways?

B PAIRS Can your classmate improve his or her email? Make suggestions.

6 PROOFREAD

Read your emails again. Can you improve your writing?

Check your
- spelling
- punctuation
- capitalization

☐ I CAN WRITE ABOUT BEING SICK.

PUT IT TOGETHER

1 MEDIA PROJECT

A ▶08-21 **Listen or watch. Why does Hae-young show the items?**

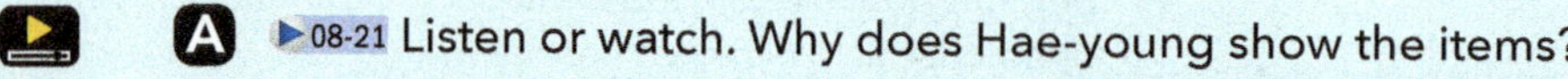

B ▶08-21 **Listen or watch again. Answer the questions.**

1. What items does Hae-young show?
____
2. How does she get enough vitamin C?
____
3. What makes her throat feel better?
____

C **Make your own video.**

Step 1 Think of 3–5 tips for staying healthy. How do these tips help you stay well or feel better?

Step 2 Make a 30-second video. Tell why each tip is helpful.

Step 3 Share your video. Answer questions and get feedback.

2 LEARNING STRATEGY

CONNECT VOCABULARY TO PERSONAL EXPERIENCE

When you learn a new word, think about how it relates to your life. What does it remind you of? For example, if you are studying words about being sick, which words help you talk about a time when you were sick?

Review the vocabulary from the unit. What words do you need to practice? Choose five words or phrases that you want to learn. Write a sentence for each that connects to you personally.

3 REFLECT AND PLAN

A **Look back through the unit. Check (✓) the things you learned. Highlight the things you need to learn.**

Speaking objectives
- ☐ Talk about feeling sick
- ☐ Talk about the flu
- ☐ Discuss what happens when I get sick

Vocabulary
- ☐ Common health problems
- ☐ The flu
- ☐ When you are sick

Pronunciation
- ☐ Silent letters
- ☐ *Can* and *can't*

Grammar
- ☐ *May / might / could* with the continuous to show possibility
- ☐ Subordinating conjunctions in time clauses
- ☐ Future real conditional

Reading
- ☐ Identify cause and effect

Writing
- ☐ Use formal and informal writing

B **What will you do to learn the things you highlighted? For example, use your app, review your Student Book, or do other practice. Make a plan.**

Notes Done

Review the grammar chart in lesson 3, page 94.

9 CAN YOU TELL ME A STORY?

LEARNING GOALS

In this unit, you

- tell a personal story
- retell a story
- explain how you learned to do something
- read about the power of stories
- write about a funny experience

GET STARTED

A Read the unit title and learning goals.

B Look at the photo of a group of friends. What do you see?

C Now read Flavio's message. Why is he happy to work with Jim?

FLAVIO VEGA

@FlavioV

Nice to be working with Jim again. He's a great guy—always interesting to talk to.

LESSON 1 TELL A PERSONAL STORY

FLAVIO VEGA

@FlavioV

I had a relaxing weekend. How was *your* weekend?

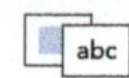

1 VOCABULARY Adjectives to describe emotions

A ▶09-01 Listen. Then listen and repeat.

proud of: happy about something good you did
mad at: angry or disappointed about something
surprised at: shocked by something you did
disappointed in: sad about something you did
satisfied with: happy because something happened the way you wanted
unhappy with: not happy because you don't like what is happening

B Put the phrases from 1A in the correct category. One expression can be in both.

Positive	Negative

C PAIRS Think of a time when you felt one of the emotions in 1A. What happened to make you feel that way? Talk about the experience.

I remember I was really proud of my sister when she learned to drive.

COACH

2 GRAMMAR Reflexive pronouns

Subject	Verb	Adjective	Reflexive pronoun	
I You He She We You They	feel feels	proud of	**myself** **yourself** **himself** **herself** **ourselves** **yourselves** **themselves**	for passing the test.

Notes

- Adjectives commonly used with reflexive pronouns: *proud of, mad at, surprised at, disappointed in, satisfied with, unhappy with, ashamed of, hard on*
- Verbs commonly used with reflexive pronouns: *promise, blame, enjoy, help, teach, introduce, hurt*

  I ***promised myself*** that I'd fix the problem one day.

  He ***blames himself*** for having a fear of heights.
- *By* + a reflexive pronoun means "alone" or "without help."

  *The students did this **by themselves**.*

>> FOR PRACTICE, GO TO PAGE 149

COACH

3 PRONUNCIATION

A ▶09-03 **Listen. Notice the number of sounds in each consonant group. Then listen and repeat.**

/sk/ /kl/	/ks/ /ksp/	/md/ /lvz/
a skydiving class	an exciting experience	ashamed of ourselves

Consonant groups

Many words have groups of two or three consonant sounds next to each other. We say the consonants in a group together, and we do not add a vowel sound between them.

B ▶09-04 **Underline the consonant groups in these words. Then listen and check your answers.**

1. flying on a plane
2. speaking to a group
3. crowded streets
4. small spaces
5. driving on bridges
6. spiders or snakes

C PAIRS **Talk about the things in 3B. Are you or is someone you know afraid of any of them?**

4 CONVERSATION

A ▶09-05 **Listen or watch. Circle the correct answers.**

1. Jim has been afraid of heights since ___.
   a. he fell from a tall building b. he was a teenager c. he flew in an airplane
2. Jim lost his fear by ___.
   a. taking a class b. going to a doctor c. taking pictures from a plane
3. Jim wants to ___.
   a. go skydiving again
   b. never go skydiving again
   c. take skydiving lessons

B ▶09-06 **Listen or watch. Complete the conversation.**

Jim: I went skydiving last weekend!

Flavio: Skydiving? But wait–you're afraid of heights!

Jim: Not anymore! I promised __________ that this year I was finally going to deal with my fear.

Flavio: Incredible. You must be proud of __________.

C ▶09-07 **Listen and repeat. Then practice with a partner.**

D PAIRS **Make new conversations. Use the words in 1A or your own ideas.**

5 TRY IT YOURSELF

A MAKE IT PERSONAL **Choose one of the expressions from 1A, and think of a story about a time when you felt that way. Take notes.**

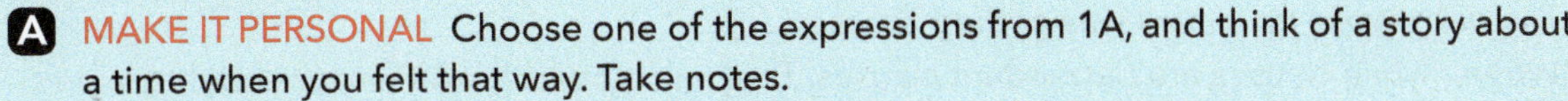

I was surprised at myself when I figured out how to...

B PAIRS **Student A, talk about how you felt about yourself. Student B, ask follow-up questions.**

LESSON 2 RETELL A STORY

FLAVIO VEGA
@FlavioV
Every day is an adventure as a new dad.

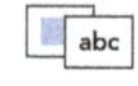 1 VOCABULARY Morning routines

A ▶09-08 Listen. Then listen and repeat.

grab a cup of coffee: to get a cup of coffee quickly, on your way somewhere
oversleep: to sleep later than you planned to
run late: to be late on your way somewhere
rush out the door: to leave a place quickly
catch the bus: to get on the bus before it leaves
make it on time: to arrive somewhere on time

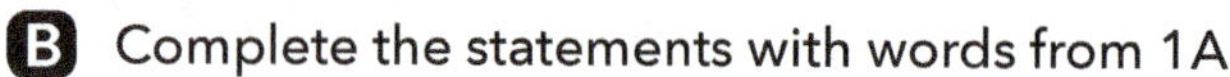

B Complete the statements with words from 1A.

1. If a meeting is important, you need to ________________________.
2. If your alarm clock doesn't work, you could ________________________.
3. If you are in a hurry, you ________________________.
4. If you don't have time to eat, you should at least ________________________.
5. If you car doesn't work, you need to ________________________.
6. If you miss the bus, you will ________________________.

C PAIRS Compare your answers in 1B.

 2 GRAMMAR Past continuous with *while* and *when*

Use the past continuous with *while* and *when* to show that one action was in progress when a second action occurred.

While / When	Subject 1	*Was / Were*	Verb + *-ing*	Subject 2	Simple past verb	
While / When	I she we	**was** **was** **were**	**waiting** for the bus, **shopping**, **working**,	it she the power	**started** **saw** **went out**.	to rain. David.

Notes

- The action in the *while / when* clause happened first.
  *While I **was waiting** for the bus, people **gave** me strange looks*
  (happened first) (happened second)
- The *when / while clause* may appear at the beginning or end of a sentence.
  *While I **was getting** dressed, the baby **woke up**.*
  *The baby **woke up** while I **was getting** dressed.*
- *When / while* clauses are dependent clauses. They must be used with independent clauses:
  *When I **was getting** on the elevator, I **got** some more looks.*
  (dependent clause) (independent clause)

>> FOR PRACTICE, GO TO PAGE 150

3 PRONUNCIATION

COACH

A ▶09-10 **Listen. Notice the intonation. Then listen and repeat.**

I didn't want to **wake** them.

I didn't want to **wake** them, so I didn't turn the **light** on.

Intonation to end or continue a thought

At the end of a statement, the intonation usually goes down. This shows that the thought, or sentence, is finished. If the intonation falls and then rises a little, it shows that we have more to say. We often use this intonation in the first part of a longer sentence.

B ▶09-11 **Listen and notice the intonation. Add a period (.) if the sentence sounds finished. Add a comma (,) if the speaker has more to say.**

1. I tried to call you
2. He was telling me a funny story
3. I was watching a movie with a friend
4. She was walking her dog in the park

4 CONVERSATION

A ▶09-12 **Listen or watch. Circle the correct answers.**

1. Flavio ___.
   a. was running late
   b. missed the bus
   c. didn't make it to work on time
2. People gave Flavio strange looks because he ___.
   a. was rushing out the door
   b. was late to a meeting
   c. shaved only half his face

B ▶09-13 **Listen or watch. Complete the conversation.**

Flavio: You'll never believe what happened last week.
Jim: Yeah? What?
Flavio: Well, I got dressed for work in the dark because I didn't want to wake up Carmen and the baby.
Jim: Makes sense.
Flavio: ________________ for the bus, a couple of people ________________ me strange looks.
Jim: Oh no!

CONVERSATION SKILL
Show interest

To show that you are interested in someone's story, use short expressions. Here are some examples:

Makes sense. Right. No way!
Oh no! You've got to be kidding!

Listen to or watch the conversation in 4A again. Raise your hand when you hear the phrases above.

C ▶09-14 **Listen and repeat. Then practice with a partner.**

5 TRY IT YOURSELF

A MAKE IT PERSONAL **Think about something funny or unusual that happened while you were doing something else. Complete the chart.**

What I was doing...	What happened...

B PAIRS **Student A, tell your story using notes from 5A. Student B, respond with expressions to show interest or ask questions.**

☐ I CAN RETELL A STORY.

LESSON 3 EXPLAIN HOW YOU LEARNED TO DO SOMETHING

FLAVIO VEGA

@FlavioV

It's so cool how people learn new things.

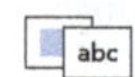

1 VOCABULARY Verbs for thinking and understanding

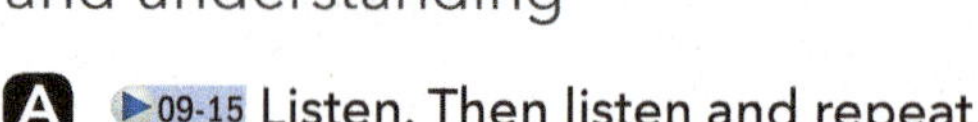

A ▶09-15 Listen. Then listen and repeat.

discover: to find out something that you did not know before
grasp: to understand something, especially something difficult
master: to learn something so well that you understand it completely and have no difficulty with it
memorize: to learn something so that you will remember it perfectly
get it: to understand something
catch on: to begin to understand
work on: to spend time improving something
get good at: to learn how to do something well

B Circle the correct words to complete the sentences. There may be more than one answer.

1. When learning to play an instrument, you should ***work on* / *discover* / *grasp*** it every day.
2. I ***memorized* / *discovered* / *caught on*** that I liked to do things with my hands.
3. Keep trying, and you'll ***work on* / *catch on* / *get it*** eventually.
4. It isn't necessary to ***memorize* / *master* / *grasp*** every word when you're learning a new language.
5. We want to ***get good at* / *get it* / *master*** tennis, so we're taking lessons.

C PAIRS Talk about a time you learned something new, using at least four of the verbs in 1A.

2 GRAMMAR Infinitives of purpose

Use the infinitive (*to* + base form of the verb) to explain the purpose–the reason for doing something.

Subject	Verb	Infinitive	
I	watch videos	**to learn**	new things.
He	called the show	**to share**	his story.
They	went to Mexico	**to practice**	their Spanish.

Notes

- Infinitives of purpose answer the question: *Why?*
  *A: **Why** do you watch online videos?*
  *B: I watch them **to learn** how to do things.*
- In informal speech, you can answer this question with just the infinitive phrase.
  A: Why do you watch online videos?
  *B: **To learn** how to do things.*

>> FOR PRACTICE, GO TO PAGE 151

3 LISTENING

A ▶09-17 **Listen to the podcast. What is it about? Circle the correct answer.**

a. Experts' opinions about people's different learning styles
b. How different people learn new skills
c. Ways people can learn how to do something without a teacher
d. apps and videos that are useful for learning

B ▶09-17 **Read the Listening Skill. Listen again. Check (✓) all the details that apply.**

1. Steve learned how to play the piano by...
   - [ ] a. using an app called *8-Keys*.
   - [ ] b. reading all the reviews.
   - [ ] c. playing games that taught him to read music.
   - [ ] d. working on correct finger positions.
   - [ ] e. practicing simple musical chords on his piano.
   - [ ] f. buying a real piano.

2. Mary learned how to change the oil in her car by...
   - [ ] a. watching her mechanic.
   - [ ] b. watching many videos.
   - [ ] c. watching one video.
   - [ ] d. memorizing each step on a video.
   - [ ] e. practicing doing each step on real cars.
   - [ ] f. imagining each step in her head under a real car.

C PAIRS **Student A, talk about how Steve learned to play the piano. Student B, talk about how Mary learned how to change the oil in her car. Are you more like Steve or Mary? Discuss.**

LISTENING SKILL
Listen for details

When you listen for details, you don't need to understand every word. Pay attention to the specific kind of information you need—how someone learned how to do something—and try to listen for words related to those details.

4 TRY IT YOURSELF

A MAKE IT PERSONAL **Think about how you learned to do something. You can use one of the ideas in the chart or your own idea. Think about what you did first and what you did next to learn it. Make notes.**

drive a car	speak a foreign language	do a hobby or sport	your own idea

I took lessons to learn how to drive. But first I had to save enough money to pay for the lessons.

B WALK AROUND **Find someone who learned the same thing as you. Talk about the similarities and differences in how you learned.**

☐ I CAN EXPLAIN HOW I LEARNED TO DO SOMETHING.

LESSON 4 READ ABOUT THE POWER OF STORIES

FLAVIO VEGA
@FlavioV
I just read this article about stories. Really interesting! Now I understand why I love them so much.

1 BEFORE YOU READ

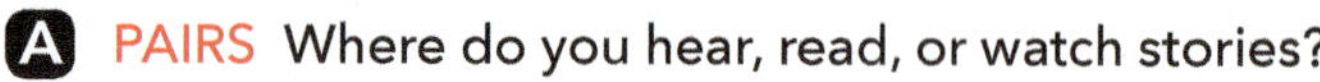

A PAIRS Where do you hear, read, or watch stories?

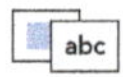

B ▶09-18 VOCABULARY Listen. Then listen and repeat.

a psychologist: a person who studies the human mind and behavior
a discovery: finding something out for the first time
invent: to make, design, or think of something that is new and different
respond: to do something because of something that has happened
survive: to continue to live after an accident, illness, or dangerous experience
an advantage: something that helps you be successful

>> FOR PRACTICE, GO TO PAGE 158

2 READ

A PREVIEW Read the title of the article and look at the image. What kind of power do you think stories have?

B ▶09-19 Listen. Read the article.

THE HUMAN BRAIN AND THE POWER OF STORIES

In a famous experiment, psychologists Fritz Heider and Marianne Simmel made a surprising discovery about the human mind. They created a short film in which simple shapes moved around the screen. Then they asked 34 people to describe what they'd seen. Only one person described the movements of the shapes. All the others invented stories. One person said, "The triangles were in love with the circle." Another said, "The circle was running away from the angry triangles." Since then, other researchers have repeated the experiment with similar results. Why did so many people choose to give the shapes human actions and feelings? Many psychologists believe it's because our brains are wired to look for and respond to stories.

Why are stories so important to us? One answer may be that stories helped early humans survive in a dangerous world. Thousands of years ago, people learned how to stay alive by passing along stories. For example, stories taught them what was safe to eat: "Do you see those berries over there? Don't eat them! My cousin ate some and got very sick." Stories prepare us for real situations and let us solve problems before we experience them.

By sharing stories, early humans also learned important information about the people around them. They learned where others were from, how they lived, and if they were friendly. They learned how they thought and felt and then compared these to their own emotions and experiences. In creating these connections, stories helped humans build relationships and work together—giving humans a big advantage over other animals.

In fact, stories are so important that our brains are programmed to remember them over other kinds of information. In another experiment, psychologists Gordon Bower and Michael Clark tested people's ability to remember information. They gave a group of people a list of ten words and asked them to memorize the list. They gave another group the same list, but asked them to make up stories with the ten words. The group that made up stories with the words were able to remember six to seven times as many words as the other group. Think about the article you are reading now. In six months will you remember the facts, the numbers, and the other details? Or will you remember the story of the circle and the angry triangles?

3 CHECK YOUR UNDERSTANDING

A **Which statement best describes the main idea? Circle the correct answer.**

a. Our brain's ability to remember stories helped early humans to survive.
b. Early humans learned information about other people through stories.
c. Our brains use stories to share and remember information.

B **Circle the correct answers.**

1. After watching the simple shapes video, most people ___ the shapes.
   a. described the movements of b. made up stories about c. couldn't remember
2. Stories helped early humans ___.
   a. find new places b. find food c. build relationships
3. Bower and Clark learned that people remember things best when information is ___.
   a. written down b. in a list c. told as a story

C FOCUS ON LANGUAGE **Reread lines 8–10 in the article. Think about the phrase *wired*. Circle the correct answers.**

The expressions *wired* means ___.
a. not prepared to do something
b. ready to become emotional
c. designed to work a certain way

READING SKILL **Find supporting evidence**

Writers use supporting evidence to show the reader that their opinions and ideas are true. Evidence can be in the form of a quotation (something someone said), an example, or a fact.

D **Read the Reading Skill. Find evidence that the writer uses to support each idea. Complete the chart.**

Idea	Supporting evidence
In the shapes experiment, people invented stories to make sense of what they saw.	(quotations) a. b.
Stories helped early humans survive in a dangerous world.	(example)
Stories help us remember important information.	(fact)

E PAIRS **What was the article about? Retell the most important ideas in the article. Use your own words.**

The article is about the importance of...

Find the Heider-Simmel video. Describe what you see.

4 MAKE IT PERSONAL

A **Think of some examples of powerful stories in your life. Take notes.**

- a story that helped you solve a problem
- a story that helped you in your job
- a story you tell people that helps explain who you are
- a story that helped you remember something you learned in school
- ______________ (*your own idea*)

B PAIRS **Tell each other your story.**

I CAN READ ABOUT THE POWER OF STORIES.

LESSON 5 WRITE ABOUT A FUNNY EXPERIENCE

FLAVIO VEGA

@FlavioV

Remember the headphones, Carmen? That was a good one! I just had to share it!

1 BEFORE YOU WRITE

A Think about your own birthday. What do you usually do to celebrate?

B Read Flavio's story. What was surprising about his experience?

Blog | About | Contact Search

About
RSS Feed
Social Media
Recent Posts
Archives
Email

Birthdays...

My wife, Carmen, and I have the same birthday, and I always try to find the perfect birthday present for her.

Two weeks before our birthday a few years ago, we went out for lunch together. Afterwards, we went shopping because I needed a jacket and she wanted to look at shoes. As we passed by the electronics department, we saw a pair of wireless headphones. Carmen wanted to buy it, but she didn't because she thought it was too expensive. Then, while I was shopping for the jacket, Carmen went to look at the shoes. I thought, "I'm going to buy those headphones for her!" I went back to the store the next day and bought them.

On our birthday, Carmen and I met for dinner, and we exchanged gifts. We both had similar sized boxes! We opened the gifts at the same time and—surprise!—it was the headphones! We had bought each other the same gift. "No way!! How—?" I started to ask. "While you were looking at jackets, I bought it for you!" she explained. We both laughed. And we love our presents!

Leave a Reply

Enter your comment here...

C PAIRS Did you expect the surprise in this story? Have you ever been surprised on your birthday? Or have you ever surprised someone else?

2 FOCUS ON WRITING

WRITING SKILL Show sequence

Use time expressions such as *then*, *while*, *next*, *afterwards*, *the next day* or *before* to show the order in which the events happened.

A Read the Writing Skill. Then reread Flavio's story. Underline all the time expressions that show sequence in the story. Then write them in the chart.

Earlier	Same time	Later
Before		

B PAIRS Add your own time expressions to the chart in 2A.

C Read the story again. What happened? Complete the notes in the chart.

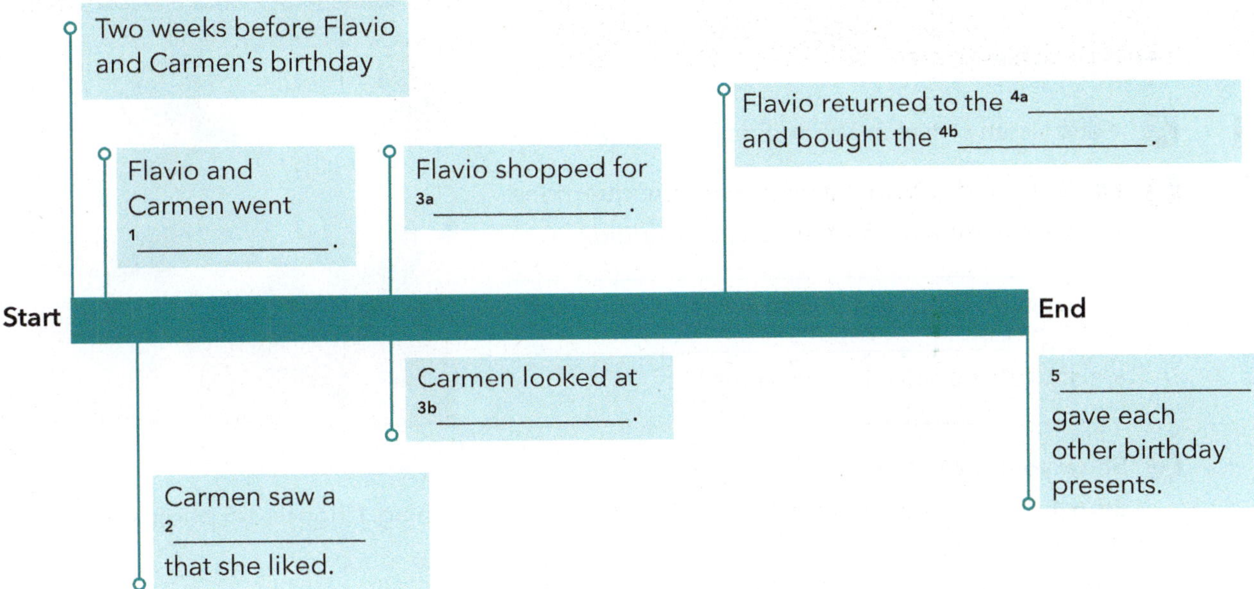

3 PLAN YOUR WRITING

A Think about a funny or surprising experience you had. How did it begin? What happened next? How did it end? Write the events in a timeline like the one in 2C.

B PAIRS Tell your stories. Use your timelines to help you.

On the first day of my job, I...

4 WRITE

Write about the story you planned in 3A. Remember to use time expressions. Use the story in 1B as a model.

5 REVISE YOUR WRITING

A PAIRS Exchange and read each other's stories.

1. Did your partner clearly explain the sequence of events?
2. Underline all the time expressions.
3. Did your partner add something funny or surprising to the story?

B PAIRS Can your classmate improve his or her story? Make suggestions.

6 PROOFREAD

Read your story again. Can you improve your writing?

Check your
- spelling
- punctuation
- capitalization

☐ I CAN WRITE ABOUT A FUNNY EXPERIENCE.

PUT IT TOGETHER

1 MEDIA PROJECT

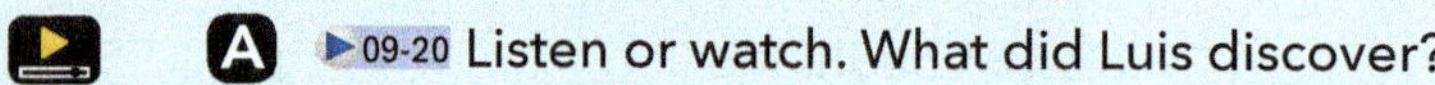

A ▶09-20 **Listen or watch. What did Luis discover?**

B ▶09-20 **Listen or watch again. Answer the questions.**

1. What was the hardest thing Luis ever did?
____
2. What problems did Luis have?
____
3. How did he solve his problems?
____

C **Show your own photos.**

Step 1 Think about when you worked hard to learn something. Choose 3-5 photos to show it.

Step 2 Show the photos to the class. Talk about what happened.

Step 3 Answer questions and get feedback.

2 LEARNING STRATEGY

WATCH TV OR A MOVIE IN ENGLISH

Practice listening to authentic English pronunciation by watching TV or movies in English. Try to imitate the pronunciation you hear. For example, English speakers may say "wanna" instead of "want to." Copying their pronunciation can help you sound more natural when you speak.

Find an English speaking TV show or movie to watch. Try to practice your pronunciation by copying what you hear. Practice at least once a week.

3 REFLECT AND PLAN

A **Look back through the unit. Check (✓) the things you learned. Highlight the things you need to learn.**

Speaking objectives
- ☐ Tell a personal story
- ☐ Retell a story
- ☐ Explain how I learned to do something

Grammar
- ☐ Reflexive pronouns
- ☐ Past continuous with *while* and *when*
- ☐ Infinitives of purpose

Vocabulary
- ☐ Adjectives to describe emotions
- ☐ Morning routines
- ☐ Verbs for thinking and understanding

Reading
- ☐ Find supporting evidence

Writing
- ☐ Show sequence

Pronunciation
- ☐ Consonant groups
- ☐ Intonation to end or continue a thought

B **What will you do to learn the things you highlighted? For example, use your app, review your Student Book, or do other practice. Make a plan.**

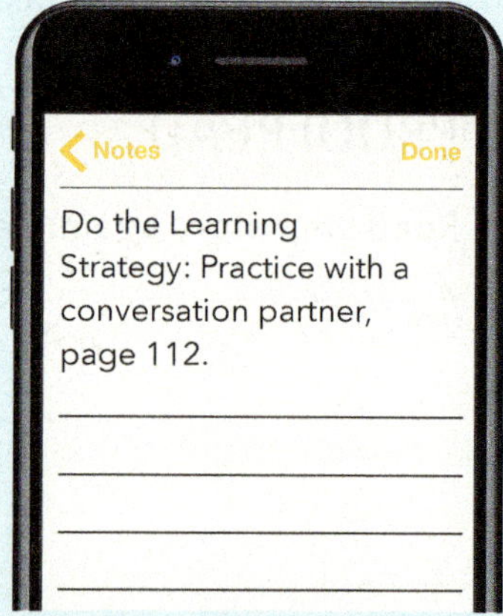

10 WHAT WILL THE FUTURE BRING?

LEARNING GOALS

In this unit, you

- discuss hopes and dreams
- talk about *what if* situations
- tell someone's success story
- read about reducing waste
- write about good advice

GET STARTED

A Read the unit title and learning goals.

B Look at the photo. What do you see?

C Now read Liz's message. Why is change not easy?

LIZ FLORES

@LizF

Change can be good, but it's never easy!

LESSON 1 DISCUSS HOPES AND DREAMS

LIZ FLORES

@LizF

Working with Su-min on our first project together today. Looking forward to it!

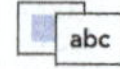 1 VOCABULARY Dreams and ambitions

A  10-01 Listen. Then listen and repeat.

go to law school

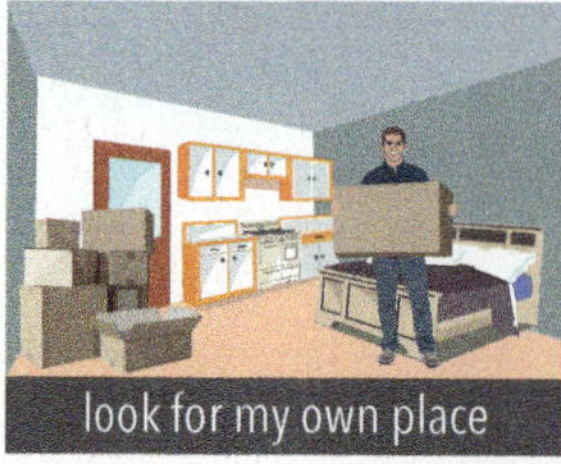
look for my own place

start a business

get a promotion

open a restaurant

start a family

take care of my parents

B Put the phrases from 1A in the correct category.

Personal goals	Career goals

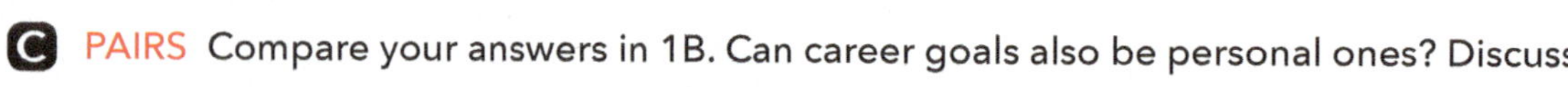

C PAIRS Compare your answers in 1B. Can career goals also be personal ones? Discuss.

 2 GRAMMAR Noun clauses with *that*

COACH

Noun clauses are a group of words that includes a subject and a verb and functions as a noun.

			Noun clause as object		
Subject 1	**Verb 1**	***(That)***	**Subject 2**	**Verb 2**	
I They	can't believe hope	**(that)**	I **someone**	**didn't bring** **will find**	my phone. them.

				Noun clause as adjective complement		
Subject 1	***Be***	**Adjective**	***(That)***	**Subject 2**	**Verb**	
I It	am is	glad awesome	**(that)**	I **you**	**met** **are running**	you. a marathon.

Notes

- Use the word *that* to introduce noun clauses in sentences. When *that* introduces a noun clause, it can be omitted.
- An *object* of a sentence is the person or thing that receives the action of the verb.
- An *adjective complement* is a clause or phrase that modifies an adjective. It is often a noun clause.

>> FOR PRACTICE, GO TO PAGE 152

3 CONVERSATION

A 10-03 **Listen or watch. Circle the correct answers.**

1. What do Su-min and Liz usually talk about?
   a. the marathon
   b. work
   c. charities
2. Why is Liz moving to New York?
   a. She got a promotion.
   b. She wants to live on her own.
   c. She wants to leave Lima.
3. What does Liz say about Mehmet?
   a. He wants to open a restaurant.
   b. He's taking cooking classes.
   c. He wants to join his family business.
4. What does Su-min say about Diana?
   a. Diana wants to become an artist.
   b. Diana owns an art gallery.
   c. Diana wants to start her own business.

B  **Listen or watch. Complete the conversation.**

Liz:	It's awesome ______________________ a marathon! So why are you doing it?
Su-min:	I like to challenge myself. Also, I'm raising money for charity.
Liz:	Wow. Good for you! How's the training going?
Su-min:	It's going well! I found some trainers to work with at the gym here. They're very helpful.
Liz:	______________ you'll do great!
Su-min:	What about you? What's going on in your life?

CONVERSATION SKILL
Respond with encouragement

When you want to show someone encouragement, you can say:
I'm sure (*you will do great.*)
I hope (*you can do it!*)
I think / know (*you're a great runner.*)
I'm glad (*you decided to go for it.*)
Listen to or watch the conversation in 3A again. Underline the phrases that you hear above.

C 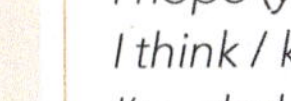 10-05 **Listen and repeat. Then practice with a partner.**

D PAIRS **Make new conversations. Use the words in 1A or your own ideas.**

4 TRY IT YOURSELF

A MAKE IT PERSONAL **Think about your dreams for the future. Use the ideas in 1A or your own ideas.**

B PAIRS **Student A, talk about your dreams. Student B, ask follow-up questions. Give Student A encouragement.**

A: I want to open a restaurant someday.
B: Really? What kind of restaurant?
A: A Turkish restaurant. I think people will like traditional Turkish food.
B: Sounds like a great idea. I hope you can do it!

☐ I CAN DISCUSS HOPES AND DREAMS.

LESSON 2 TALK ABOUT *WHAT IF* SITUATIONS

LIZ FLORES
@LizF
How can we all make the world a better place?

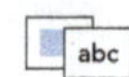

1 VOCABULARY Helping others

A 10-06 Listen. Then listen and repeat.

world hunger: the problem of not having enough food for people in many places around the world
a homeless shelter: a place for people who don't have a place to live
medical research: the activity of finding information about different health problems
animal welfare: health, comfort, and happiness of animals
human suffering: the pain people feel due to physical, mental, or emotional problems
a local school: a school that is close to you such as in your city or neighborhood

B Write two words from 1A under each box to complete the phrase.

bring an end to...	volunteer at...	raise money for...

C PAIRS Compare your answers in 1B. Which of the activities are the easiest ways to do good? Which are more difficult?

2 GRAMMAR Present unreal conditional

Use present unreal conditionals to talk about untrue or imagined situations and their results.

Statements

If-clause				Result clause			
If	**Subject**	**Simple past**		**Subject**	***Would / Wouldn't***	**Base form of verb**	
If	I	**were**	rich,	I	**would**	**donate**	more money.
	she	**had**	more time,	she	**would**	**volunteer**	every day.
	people	**didn't care**,	-	they	**wouldn't**	**help**.	

Questions

If-clause				Result clause				
If	**Subject**	**Simple past**		***Wh-* word**	***Would / Wouldn't***	**Subject**	**Base form of verb**	
If	you	**had**	more money,	what	**would**	you	**do**?	
	they	**had**	the time,	-	**would**	they	**help**	us?

Note

- The *if-clause* uses the simple past, but this is not a past statement. It's about the present.
- For the *be* verb, use *were* for all subjects: *If he* **were** *president... If they* **were** *free...*
- The *if-clause* can come at the beginning or end of a sentence. Use a comma when the *if-clause* comes at the beginning of a sentence.

>> FOR PRACTICE, GO TO PAGE 153

3 PRONUNCIATION

A ▶10-08 **Listen. Notice the blended pronunciations of *would you* and *did you*. Then listen and repeat.**

/wʊʤə/ /dɪʤə/

What would you do to help? Did you know he could cook?

B ▶10-09 **Listen. Circle the words you hear.**

1. What **would you / did you** study in college?
2. **Would you / Did you** go to medical school?
3. **Would you / Did you** volunteer at a homeless shelter?

Blended pronunciations of *would you* ("wouldja") and *did you* ("didja")

When we link words together, sounds that are next to each other sometimes blend together and change. When we ask questions with *would you* and *did you*, we often blend *would* and *you* together as "wouldja" /wʊʤə/, and *did* and *you* together as "didja" /dɪʤə/.

C PAIRS **Ask each other and answer the questions in 3B, choosing *would you* or *did you*.**

4 CONVERSATION

A ▶10-10 **Listen or watch. Circle the correct answers.**

1. Where does Su-min volunteer?
   a. at a hospital
   b. at a school
   c. at a children's center
2. What happens at the end of the scene?
   a. Liz and Su-min decide to volunteer together.
   b. Liz and Su-min continue talking about what-if situations.
   c. They receive a message that the elevator will be moving soon.

B ▶10-11 **Listen or watch. Complete the conversation.**

Su-min: ____________ you didn't have to work, what ____________ you do?
Liz: That's a good question. I'd like to help children get a better education.
Su-min: How would you do that?
Liz: ____________ with local schools to start reading programs. What about you? What ____________?

C ▶10-12 **Listen and repeat. Then practice with a partner.**

D PAIRS **Make new conversations. Use the words in 1A or your own ideas.**

5 TRY IT YOURSELF

A MAKE IT PERSONAL **Think about a world problem you want to help improve. Use ideas from 1A or your own.**

B PAIRS **Student A, talk about your ideas. Student B, ask follow up questions.**

A: If I had more time, I'd try to raise money for animal welfare.
B: How would you do that?

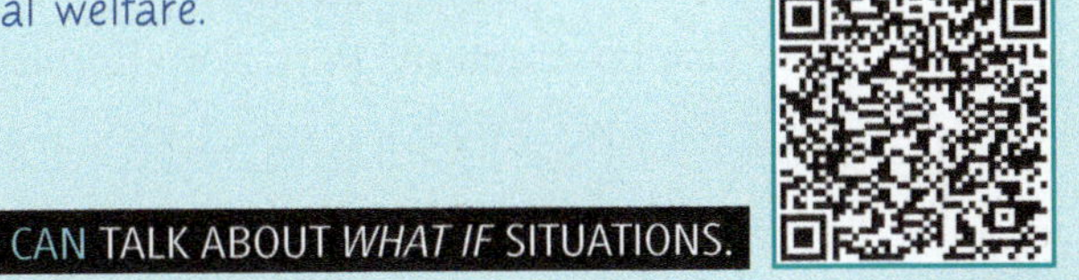

LESSON 3 TELL SOMEONE'S SUCCESS STORY

LIZ FLORES

@LizF

Inspiring story about a woman who was adopted, who is using her experience to help other families.

1 VOCABULARY Making decisions

A ▶10-13 Listen. Then listen and repeat.

realize: to start to understand something that you had not thought about before
make a choice: to decide what you want from two or more options or possibilities
fall into: to gradually get into a particular condition, especially a bad condition
come to a crossroads: to need to make an important decision
change your mind: to make a new decision about something
have a change of heart: to change your opinion about something
happen by chance: to happen without planning
end up: to finally be in a particular place or situation

B Answer the questions with the words and phrases from 1A.

1. What expression is related to understanding? ________________
2. What are four expressions related to making decisions?
   ________________ ________________
   ________________ ________________
3. What are three expressions related to how something happens?
   ________________ ________________
   ____

C PAIRS Compare your answers in 1B.

2 GRAMMAR Past perfect

COACH

Use the past perfect to show that one event happened before another event in the past.

Statement			
Subject	***Had* (not)**	**Past participle**	
I	**had not**	**tried**	Korean food until I moved to Korea.
My sister	**had**	**lived**	in five different homes by the time she was ten.
They	**had**	**been**	homeless when they moved into the apartment.

Question				
***Wh*-word**	***Had* (not)**	**Subject**	**Past participle**	
What	**had**	you	**done**	by 8:30?
-	**Had**	you	**seen**	him before?

Notes

- The past perfect is often used with the simple past. The past perfect shows the event that happened first / earliest.
  *He **had lived** in a shelter for years when he **moved** into a real home.*
  (happened first) (happened later)
- Use contractions in spoken English and informal writing: *I'd, he'd, they'd, hadn't.*

>> FOR PRACTICE, GO TO PAGE 154

3 PRONUNCIATION

A ▶10-15 **Listen. Notice how we break the sentences into thought groups. Then listen and repeat.**

She always **knew** / that she was **adopted**.
She lived in **shelters** / for five **years** / before she was **adopted**.
She made a **choice** / that **no** mother / should have to **make**.

Thought groups

To make long sentences easier to say and easier to understand, we break them into thought groups. Each thought group has a main stress. We often pause a little between each group.

B ▶10-16 **Draw lines (/) to break each sentence into three thought groups. Listen and check your answers. Then listen and repeat.**

1. I moved into a new apartment two weeks ago.
2. She wanted to do something to make the world a better place.
3. They've built houses in five states so far.
4. I didn't know where my brother was until a year ago.
5. I can't believe that I left my phone in my car!

C PAIRS **Practice saying the sentences in 3B. Then write a sentence about your own life that includes three thought groups.**

4 LISTENING

A ▶10-17 **Listen to the podcast. Check (✓) the true statements about Janine's story.**

☐ 1. Janine found out she had brothers and sisters when she was 16.
☐ 2. She started a charity to help homeless families.
☐ 3. She never found her mother again.
☐ 4. Her sister donates money to the charity.

B ▶10-17 **Read the Listening Skill. Put the important events from Janine's life in order.**

Her father died before she was born. ___
Her mother gave the children up for adoption. ___
Her mother moved into one of her homes. ___
She started a charity for homeless families. ___
She was adopted. ___

LISTENING SKILL Listen for key words in questions and answers

When you listen to two people talking as in an interview, listen carefully to the questions, then listen for key words that are repeated in the answers.

C PAIRS **Talk about the interview with Janine. Which part made the strongest impression on you? Give reasons.**

5 TRY IT YOURSELF

A MAKE IT PERSONAL **Think about when you were younger. What had you learned, done, or decided by that time? Fill in the chart with specific ages. Make notes.**

___ years old ___ years old ___ years old ___ years old

B PAIRS **Student A, talk about your ideas from 5A. Student B, ask follow-up questions. Were you surprised about anything you learned about your partner?**

A: By the time I was 10, I had decided I wanted to be a physical therapist.
B: What made you decide that?

☐ I CAN TELL SOMEONE'S SUCCESS STORY.

LESSON 4 READ ABOUT REDUCING WASTE

LIZ FLORES
@LizF
Lots of inspiration this week! Here's something to think about the next time you eat.

1 BEFORE YOU READ

A PAIRS In what ways do people waste food?

People buy more food than they need.

B ▶10-18 VOCABULARY Listen. Then listen and repeat.

peel: to remove the skin from fruit or vegetables
a scrap: a small piece of something
sustainability: the ability of something to continue without damaging the environment
a landfill: a place where waste is put under the ground
compost: a mixture of rotten vegetables, fruit, and plant parts used to make soil better
transport: to move things in a vehicle
a profit: money that you gain by selling things or doing business
a perspective: a way of thinking about something

>> FOR PRACTICE, GO TO PAGE 158

2 READ

A PREVIEW Read the title and look at the image. How big a problem is food waste?

B ▶10-19 Listen. Read the article.

Do you peel potatoes, carrots, and peaches before you eat them? A lot of people do. But those scraps are food—food that goes to waste. A third of food produced for human use is wasted every year. The United Nations says if we could reduce waste by just 25 percent, world hunger would disappear. The biggest losses are in fresh food, especially fruits and vegetables. One company in New York wants to change this.

Thomas McQuillan is a director at Baldor Foods, a company that cuts up and packages fruits and vegetables to sell to stores and restaurants. One of his responsibilities is sustainability. He saw lots of food scraps going into landfills, and he decided the company needed to reduce waste. His first idea was to take the scraps to farms, to be used as compost. But transporting the scraps was expensive. One day, an obvious idea came to him: All these scraps were not waste; they were food. Maybe there was a way to recycle them as food. And that's when Baldor's journey to a zero-waste company began.

First, McQuillan decided to give the scraps a creative name and sell them as food. He named it SparCs. That's "scraps" spelled backwards, with a capital C. Restaurants and juice companies buy SparCs to make soups, sauces, and fresh juices. Today, Baldor sells about 30,000 pounds or 13,600 kg of SparCs every week. The company also sells healthy powders they make with dried scraps. The powder can be added to soups, drinks, and other foods. Finally, scraps that can't be turned into human food are sold as food for farm animals. Nothing is wasted; no food goes to landfills. It's good for the planet, but it's good for the company, too. Instead of throwing food scraps away, the company is selling them at a profit.

McQuillan says it's all about changing your perspective. In his case, he stopped seeing scraps as waste and started seeing them as food. He hopes that other businesses involved in food service, such as hotels and restaurants, will start paying more attention to the food they waste. Think about this: Not too long ago, most restaurants threw away their potato skins. Today, baked potato skins filled with cheese are a popular appetizer. Who knows what tasty scrap might be next on the menu?

3 CHECK YOUR UNDERSTANDING

A **What does McQuillan want readers to understand? Circle the correct answer.**

a. Peeling fruit and vegetables creates a lot of waste.
b. It's sometimes hard to change your perspective.
c. All food should be treated as food, not waste.

B **What are Baldor's strategies for turning food waste into profit? Check (✓) all the correct answers.**

☐ 1. Use food scraps to feed hungry people.
☐ 2. Send food scraps to landfills.
☐ 3. Use food scraps as compost.
☐ 4. Package food scraps with a new name to be used as food.
☐ 5. Make a healthy powder from food scraps.
☐ 6. Use scraps to feed animals.

C FOCUS ON LANGUAGE **Reread lines 1-3 in the article. Think about the phrase *goes to waste*. Circle the correct answer.**

The expression *goes to waste* means ___.
a. it is not used and therefore thrown away
b. it is unnecessary and therefore thrown away
c. it is damaged and therefore thrown away

> READING SKILL **Make inferences**
>
> Sometimes writers don't directly say what they mean. In this case, you can make an inference by looking at the text and using your own general knowledge to figure out what is not directly said.

D **Read the Reading Skill. Then read the sentences below. Circle the correct answers.**

"One of McQuillan's responsibilities is sustainability."
1. What do you think is important to McQuillan?
   a. protecting the environment b. ending world hunger c. making food healthy

"First, McQuillan decided to give the scraps a creative name and sell them as food."
2. Why do you think McQuillan decided to give scraps a creative name?
   a. to make people want to buy it b. to show his creativity c. to describe what it is

"Not too long ago, most restaurants threw away their potato skins. Today, baked potato skins filled with cheese are a popular appetizer."
3. Why does McQuillan talk about baked potato skins?
   a. He believes sale of SparCs will increase.
   b. He wants more people to eat baked potato skins.
   c. He believes it's possible to find new uses for food that was once thrown away.

E PAIRS **How has Baldor become a zero-waste company? Retell the most important ideas. Use your own words.**

Baldor created a new product...

Look online for other ways to reduce food waste. Describe a step that is easy—one that anyone could take. 

4 MAKE IT PERSONAL

A **What else can businesses do to reduce food waste? Take some notes.**

B PAIRS **Discuss your answers in 4A.**

Restaurants or grocery stores can donate food to food banks.

☐ I CAN READ ABOUT REDUCING WASTE.

WRITE ABOUT GOOD ADVICE

LIZ FLORES
@LizF
I've received a lot of advice in my life, and I've given a lot, too. My post today is about the best advice I've ever received.

1 BEFORE YOU WRITE

A Who are some people in your life that give you advice? Do you listen to them?

B Read Liz's post. What skill did she learn as a result of following the advice from her teacher?

I once had a teacher who shared with me this quote from Albert Einstein: "A person who never made a mistake never tried anything new." I was only 12 years old when she told me this, but I've never forgotten it. It's definitely the best advice I've ever received.

Before my teacher gave me that advice, I was sometimes afraid to try new things. I was smart, curious, and creative. However, I worried that I would make a mistake, or that the results wouldn't be very good. But this quote really made me think. Einstein was a brilliant man, so if *he* wasn't afraid to make mistakes, why should *I* be afraid?

I loved computer games and apps. So I started playing around with my computer and trying different things. And, yes, I made a lot of mistakes. Most of my ideas didn't work. But from each mistake, I learned something new. Eventually, I figured out how to create my own apps. It felt so amazing. I realized that it's really worth it to keep trying, to keep pushing, and not to give up just because of a few mistakes.

I truly believe that Einstein's quote made it possible for me to have more success in my life.

C Complete the chart with information from Liz's post.

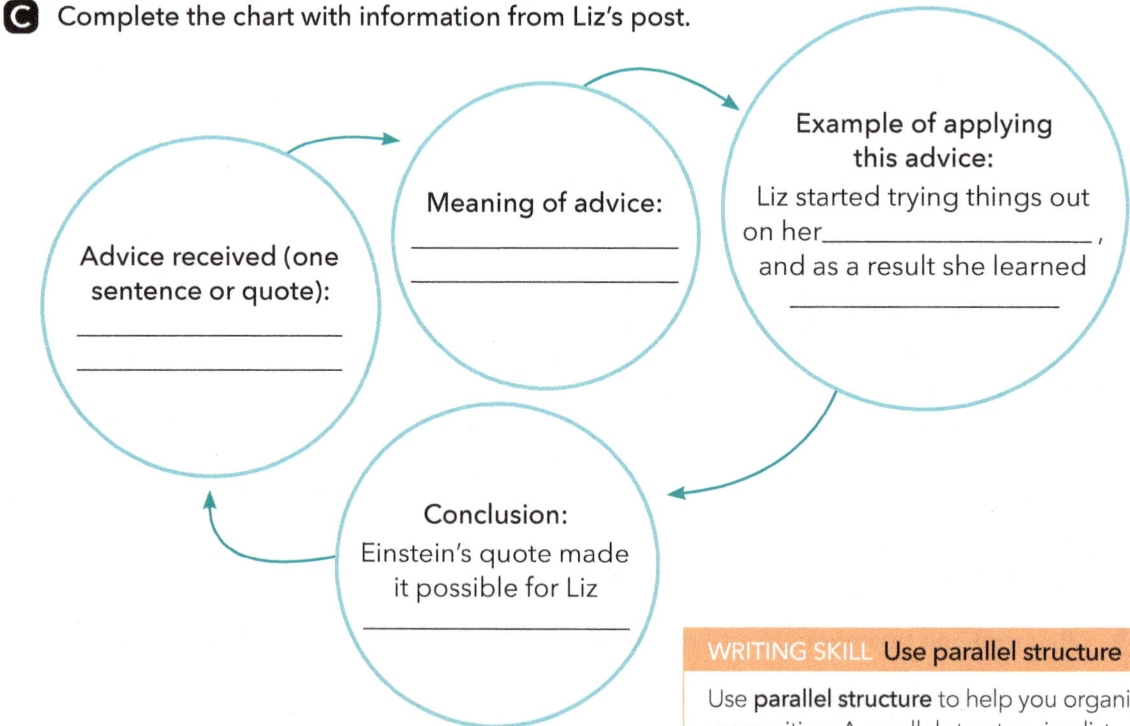

WRITING SKILL Use parallel structure

Use **parallel structure** to help you organize your writing. A parallel structure is a list of words, phrases, or clauses in a sentence that follow the same grammar pattern: *Mary is happy, kind, and thoughtful.* (three adjectives)

2 FOCUS ON WRITING

Read the Writing Skill. Then reread Liz's post. Underline all the examples of parallel structure.

3 PLAN YOUR WRITING

A What is the best advice you've ever received? Complete the chart with your information.

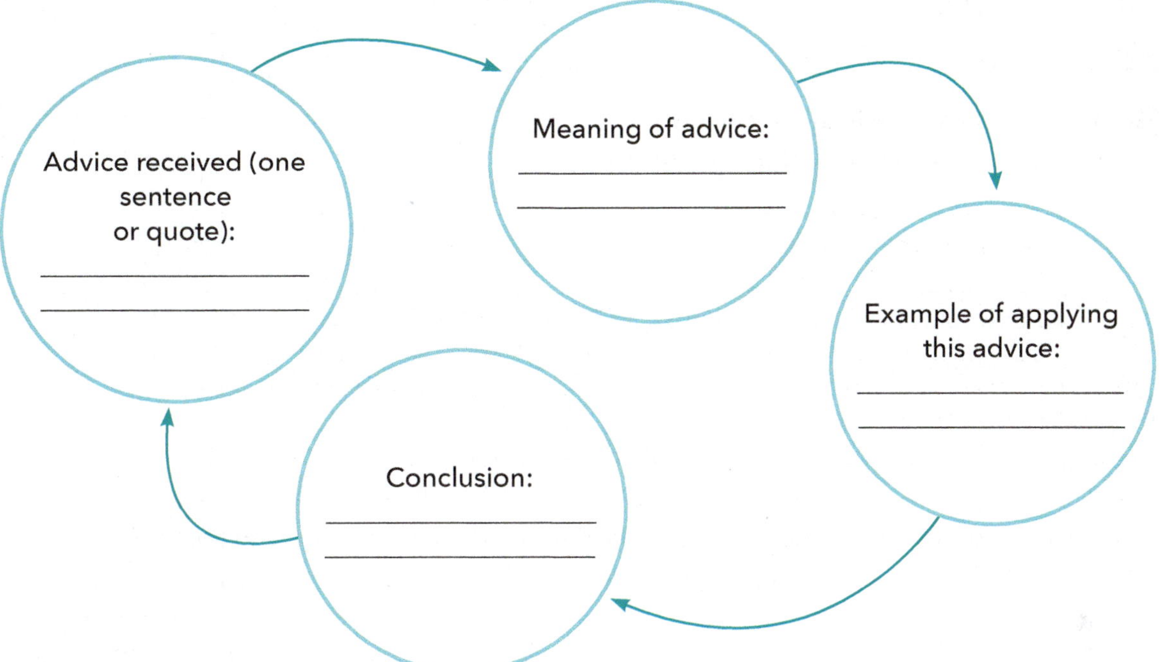

B PAIRS Use your chart to talk about the best advice you've ever received.

My mother told me to do everything one step at a time...

4 WRITE

Write a post using your information from 3A. Remember to use parallel structure. Use the post in 1B as a model.

5 REVISE YOUR WRITING

A PAIRS Exchange and read each other's posts.

1. Underline examples of parallel structure.
2. Did your partner's use of parallel structure help to make the writing clear? Why or why not?
3. Did your partner provide a good example of how the advice given has helped him or her?

B PAIRS Can your classmate improve his or her post? Make suggestions.

6 PROOFREAD

Read your post again. Can you improve your writing?

Check your
- spelling
- punctuation
- capitalization

☐ I CAN WRITE ABOUT GOOD ADVICE.

PUT IT TOGETHER

1 MEDIA PROJECT

A  **10-20 Listen or watch. What is Daniela's future dream?**

B  **10-20 Listen or watch again. Answer the questions.**

1. Why did Daniela become interested in Bali?

   ____

2. What types of art do people in Bali do?

   ____

3. What would she study if she could go Bali?

   ____

C Show your own photos.

Step 1 Think of a future hope or dream of yours that is not related to work or school. Choose 3–5 photos to show what you would do if you could.

Step 2 Show the photos to the class. Describe what you want to do and tell why.

Step 3 Answer questions and get feedback.

2 LEARNING STRATEGY

STUDY THE SOUNDS OF NEW WORDS

When you learn a new word, find a way to hear it pronounced by a native speaker, for example, by using your StartUp app or an online dictionary. Practice the pronunciation.

Review the vocabulary from the unit. What words are difficult for you to pronounce? Listen to the correct pronunciation of the words and practice the pronunciation of those words daily.

3 REFLECT AND PLAN

A Look back through the unit. Check (✓) the things you learned. Highlight the things you need to learn.

Speaking objectives
- ☐ Discuss hopes and dreams
- ☐ Talk about *what if* situations
- ☐ Tell someone's success story

Vocabulary
- ☐ Dreams and ambitions
- ☐ Helping others
- ☐ Making decisions

Pronunciation
- ☐ Blended pronunciations of *would you* ("wouldja") and *did you* ("didja")
- ☐ Thought groups

Grammar
- ☐ Noun clauses with *that*
- ☐ Present unreal conditional
- ☐ Past perfect

Reading
- ☐ Make inferences

Writing
- ☐ Use parallel structure

B What will you do to learn the things you highlighted? For example, use your app, review your Student Book, or do other practice. Make a plan.

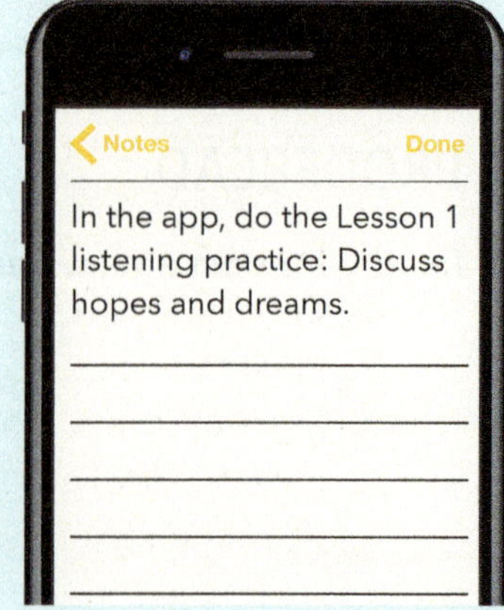

UNIT 1, LESSON 1 NO ARTICLE

A ▶01-02 Listen. Check (✓) the article you hear (*a*, *an*, or *the*). If you don't hear an article, check "no article."

	a	an	the	no article
1.	☐	☐	☐	☑
2.	☐	☐	☐	☐
3.	☐	☐	☐	☐
4.	☐	☐	☐	☐
5.	☐	☐	☐	☐
6.	☐	☐	☐	☐
7.	☐	☐	☐	☐
8.	☐	☐	☐	☐
9.	☐	☐	☐	☐

B Anna and Jun are new students. They are talking after their English class. Complete the sentences. Write *a*, *an*, *the*, or Ø (no article).

Anna: Hey Jun! How do you like ___the___ (1) class?

Jun: Oh, it's great! Everyone is so nice. But learning ___________ (2) English is difficult!

Anna: I agree! I took ___________ (3) English class in my home country, but it seemed a lot easier then! So, some of us are getting together to watch ___________ (4) soccer game tonight at Joe's Pizza. Would you like to join us?

Jun: Yes! I love ___________ (5) soccer! What time is ___________ (6) game?

Anna: It starts at 7:00, but we're meeting at 6:00 in ___________ (7) school parking lot.

Jun: I have ___________ (8) math test at 5:00, so I might be a little late.

Anna: You can meet us at ___________ (9) restaurant, then.

Jun: Perfect! I'll see you there!

C Complete the sentences with *a*, *an*, *the*, or Ø (no article).

1. All children should get an equal ___Ø___ education.
2. The dove is a symbol of ___________ peace.
3. Did you meet ___________ new English teacher?
4. I visited ___________ art gallery last weekend.
5. Did you see ___________ baseball game last night?
6. I learned ___________ Japanese when I lived in Japan.
7. My friends are really into ___________ table tennis.
8. I want to find ___________ book about French cooking.
9. She teaches ___________ history to college students.

RESTRICTIVE RELATIVE CLAUSES

A **Complete the sentences with *who, that, when,* or *where.* If a relative pronoun can be deleted, write *X* in the space. More than one answer may be possible.**

1. I found the same ring ___that / X___ you bought.
2. The friend ________________ knitted my scarf is an artist.
3. She told the police about the ring ________________ had been stolen.
4. Do you remember the day ________________ you bought that dress?
5. Did you ever find the watch ________________ you lost?
6. The store ________________ I bought the tie didn't accept returns.
7. The diamond necklace ________________ the movie star wore cost $10,000.
8. He helped the man ________________ was buying earrings for his wife.
9. We visited a market ________________ they sold handmade items.

B **Combine the sentences using *who, that, when,* or *where*. Then read each sentence again and cross out the relative pronoun if it can be deleted.**

1. I love the necklace. You are wearing it.
   I love the necklace ~~that~~ you are wearing.
2. This is the silver bracelet. I bought it in New Mexico.
   ____
3. A man is wearing a red tie. The man is my brother.
   ____
4. He's the celebrity. He always wears expensive jewelry.
   ____
5. Can you tell me the name of a store? I can buy some cool sunglasses there.
   ____
6. I'll always remember the day. My mother gave me this ring on that day.
   ____
7. Can you show me the silver watch? It is behind the gold one.
   ____
8. The coffee shop is around the corner. I ate delicious cake there.
   ____
9. Do you see the girl? She looks like a famous singer.
   ____

C ▶01-09 **Listen. Complete the sentences with the restrictive relative clause you hear.**

1. He bought it at the store ___where my sister works___.
2. Those are the shoes ________________________________.
3. This is the watch ________________________________.
4. I got these at a store ________________________________.
5. I can take you any weekend ________________________________.
6. Do you know the designer ________________________________?
7. The artist ________________________________ is a good friend.
8. Do you know a shop ________________________________?

UNIT 1, LESSON 3 SEQUENCE OF ADJECTIVES

A ▶01-16 Listen. Write the adjectives in the blanks.

1. She still has an ___old___ ___black-and-white___ TV.
2. There was a ________ ________ scarf in the drawer.
3. I'd love to get a ________ ________ sofa for my living room.
4. The ________, ________, ________ boots need repairing.
5. She kept a ________, ________, ________ dish on the table.
6. I've had this ________ ________ table for years.
7. Unfortunately, this ________ ________ watch no longer works.
8. He wore a ________, ________, ________ tie.
9. There was a ________ ________ mirror in the hall.

B Complete the sentences. Put the adjectives in parentheses in the correct order.

My friends Robert and Yoko love to shop at the flea market. They always find the most ___interesting old___ (1 (old / interesting)) items. They usually drive their ________ (2 (red / big)) truck so they can carry a lot of stuff. Their living room is full of things that they have found, such as a ________ (3 (wooden / tall)) clock, some ________ (4 (glass / pretty)) vases, ________ (5 (antique / beautiful)) furniture, and a ________ (6 (Turkish / wool)) rug. Last week, I joined them on a shopping trip when they bought a ________ (7 (rectangular / large)) picnic table for their backyard. I saw a ________ (8 (colorful / cotton)) tablecloth. It was Yoko's birthday so I bought the tablecloth as a gift for her. When we went home, she put it right on the table, took out two ________ (9 (shiny / porcelain)) cups and invited me for a cup of coffee.

C Complete the sentences. Use the adjectives in parentheses in the correct order. Add commas where necessary.

1. The ___blue cotton___ (cotton / blue) blanket belonged to my grandmother.
2. He cleaned the ________ (shiny / metal) spoon.
3. The ________ (leather / new / Italian) boots were expensive.
4. Be careful with that ________ (glass / fancy) vase!
5. We bought a(n) ________ (wooden / antique) desk.
6. The waiter put a(n) ________ (white / plain) tablecloth on the table.
7. I found a ________ (rectangular / black) box in the basement.
8. You have the most ________ (long / brown / beautiful) hair.

UNIT 2, LESSON 1 *MUST / MAY / MIGHT / COULD* FOR CONCLUSIONS

A **Circle the correct modal.**

1. It's been raining all day. The picnic ***must*** / ***couldn't*** be cancelled.
2. It's clearing up. The storm ***might*** / ***must not*** be over.
3. The ground is covered in ice. The road ***could*** / ***may not*** be closed.
4. Temperatures are dropping. You ***must not*** / ***may*** need your coat.
5. Tree branches are falling down. It ***couldn't*** / ***must*** be a strong storm.
6. He is soaking wet. He ***might not*** / ***must not*** have an umbrella.
7. Did you watch the weather forecast? It ***might*** / ***must*** clear up in a few hours.
8. It's bright and sunny outside. It ***couldn't*** / ***must*** be raining.
9. The storm damaged the station. The train ***must*** / ***couldn't*** be running.

B **Complete the sentences with words in the box.**

couldn't be	could lose	~~may need~~	must be
might not need	must not have	could be	might like

1. It's snowing outside. You ____may need____ your snow boots.
2. We ________________ our electricity because of the storm.
3. John is out of town for the weekend. That ________________ him.
4. Sara doesn't mind being out in the cold. She ________________ to go outside and play.
5. It's supposed to clear up later. You ________________ your umbrella.
6. His clothes are all wet. He ________________ a raincoat.
7. You should check the bus schedule before you leave. They ________________ running late.
8. You've been outside in this cold without a coat? You ________________ freezing!

C ▶02-03 **Listen to each conclusion. Circle the answer that is likely to be true based on the sentence you hear.**

1. a. It has almost stopped raining. b. It has just started raining.
2. a. Trees aren't moving. b. Trees have fallen over.
3. a. The sky is turning dark gray. b. The sky is clearing up.
4. a. The roads are wet. b. The roads aren't wet.
5. a. It's snowing very hard. b. It has stopped snowing.
6. a. I can't find my sun hat. b. I know where my sun hat is.
7. a. She is very nervous during thunderstorms. b. She isn't very nervous during thunderstorms.
8. a. I can see the road in the rain. b. I can't see the road in the rain.

UNIT 2, LESSON 2 PRESENT PERFECT AND PRESENT PERFECT CONTINUOUS

A Complete the sentences with the present perfect or present perfect continuous form of the verb.

1. It has been snowing (snow) since 6:00 A.M.
2. Heavy rains ______ (cause) landslides and closed down the roads.
3. I ______ (watch) the news programs all morning.
4. Several tornadoes ______ (come) through the area this year.
5. It ______ (snow) only once this month.
6. Firefighters ______ (fight) strong winds for hours.
7. Local news channels ______ (report) the storm since yesterday.
8. We ______ (drive) in the heavy rain for two hours.
9. The hurricane ______ (damage) hundreds of homes.

B Complete the sentences with the present perfect or present perfect continuous form of the verb.

The weather service has issued (1 issue) severe weather warnings for the eastern region of the Texas Coast. A hurricane ______ (2 form) in the Gulf of Mexico since Tuesday. People in the area ______ (3 prepare) for the hurricane's arrival for days. Many stores ______ (4 sell out) of water and other necessities. This is the fourth hurricane in the area this season. Two hurricanes ______ (5 hit) the western coast of Florida already. There ______ (6 not be) a hurricane this large in the Gulf of Mexico area in many years. A lot of people ______ (7 leave) their homes and moved to safer areas. Local governments ______ (8 ask) people to be careful while traveling. Flooding is possible, and strong winds ______ (9 cause) major damage already.

C ▶02-10 Listen. Check (✓) the correct box.

1. ☑ completed action ☐ continuing action
2. ☐ completed action ☐ continuing action
3. ☐ completed action ☐ continuing action
4. ☐ completed action ☐ continuing action
5. ☐ completed action ☐ continuing action
6. ☐ completed action ☐ continuing action
7. ☐ completed action ☐ continuing action
8. ☐ completed action ☐ continuing action
9. ☐ completed action ☐ continuing action

UNIT 2, LESSON 3 EXPRESSING CAUSE AND EFFECT WITH *SO / SUCH...THAT*

A ▶02-15 **Listen. Complete the sentences.**

1. They were scared because ___the lightening was so close___.
2. We couldn't take much with us because ______________________.
3. There was a lot of damage because ______________________.
4. Our yard is flooding because ______________________.
5. Jim and Sara helped us during the storm because ______________________.
6. The roof blew off the house because ______________________.

B **Complete the sentences. Use *so* or *such*.**

1. The hurricane was ___so___ strong that stores were closed for weeks.
2. The building is damaged __________ badly that it will take years to repair.
3. It snowed __________ much that we couldn't leave the house.
4. It was __________ a large fire that thousands of trees were destroyed.
5. The thunder was __________ loud that it made me jump.
6. It's raining __________ heavily that I can't see the road.
7. We had __________ a strong blizzard that all flights were canceled.
8. The firefighters worked __________ quickly that everyone was rescued.
9. The storm caused __________ terrible traffic that it took two hours to get to work.

C **Combine the sentences to make one sentence. Use *so* or *such* + *that*.**

1. The rain was bad. We lost power for days.
   ___The rain was so bad that we lost power for days.___
2. The roads are icy. Cars are sliding everywhere.
   ____
3. It was a powerful earthquake. Large cracks appeared in the ground.
   ____
4. The tornado was weak. No damage was done.
   ____
5. The wildfire burned slowly. People had time to evacuate.
   ____
6. The landslide caused terrible damage. Many homes were destroyed.
   ____
7. The trees were burnt badly. Their trunks were black.
   ____
8. They are having a severe drought. Lakes are drying up.
   ____
9. The water on the streets is deep. People are using boats instead of cars.
   ____

UNIT 3, LESSON 1 OBJECT COMPLEMENTS

A Combine the sentences into one sentence that has an object complement.

1. We saw him. He was working late.
   We saw him working late.
2. They elected Mr. Jones. Mr. Jones became president.
   ______
3. I found the email. It was sitting in my inbox.
   ______
4. They will be painting my office. It will be light blue.
   ______
5. We heard the copy machine. It was making strange noises.
   ______
6. She considered the award. It was an honor.
   ______
7. I saw the new manager. She was walking into her office.
   ______

B Read each conversation. Complete the reply with a direct object and object complement, using the words in parentheses. Change verbs as needed.

1. A: Traffic is terrible here!
   B: I hate it, too. It makes me frustrated. **(make / frustrated)**
2. A: Did the boss like your presentation yesterday?
   B: Yes, she ______. **(find / interesting)**
3. A: Are you the new manager?
   B: Yes, I'm Robert, but please ______. **(call / Rob)**
4. A: The coffee is not very good this morning.
   B: I know. Someone ______. **(make / too strong)**
5. A: Gaby, your office is always so clean!
   B: Thanks. I like to ______. **(keep / neat)**
6. A: I'm glad they're painting these dull white walls.
   B: Me too. They're going to ______. **(paint / yellow)**
7. A: I heard Amir is getting a promotion.
   B: Yes, they are ______. **(make / a senior designer)**
8. A: Our new project is going to be huge!
   B: That's for sure. It will ______. **(keep / busy)**
9. A: How do you like working with the people at that new company?
   B: Unfortunately, I am ______. **(find / difficult to work with)**

C ▶03-03 Listen. Complete the sentences.

1. The presentation was boring.
2. Everyone is getting ______.
3. I think Simon is ______.
4. Elena said John was ______.
5. Ana was ______.
6. Lucas thinks May is ______.
7. Lan is ______.
8. The room will be ______.

UNIT 3, LESSON 2 MAKING SUGGESTIONS

A **Complete the sentences. Use the words in parentheses to make a suggestion.**

1. A: What time should I set up the meeting for?
   B: You ___could set up___ the meeting for 9:00. **(could / set up)**
2. A: It's late. I don't think we can finish tonight.
   B: ______________________ tomorrow? **(What if / finish)**
3. A: What kind of food should Lisa order for the client meeting?
   B: She ______________________ some sandwiches. **(could / order)**
4. A: I'm so frustrated! I can't think of any good ideas!
   B: ______________________ together? **(How about / brainstorm)**
5. A: How should we give them feedback?
   B: ______________________ an email. **(suggest / send)**
6. A: When can we meet to work on this?
   B: ______________________ on Wednesday? **(Why don't / meet)**

B **Rewrite the suggestions.**

1. What if we give them some feedback?
   I suggest ___that we give them some feedback___.
2. Let's talk to the designers about it.
   Why don't ______________________?
3. How about setting up a daily meeting?
   What if ______________________?
4. How about we give them another chance?
   Let's ______________________.
5. Why don't we set some goals for the project?
   How about we ______________________?
6. I suggest that we brainstorm some ideas together.
   What if ______________________?
7. What if we meet this morning?
   I suggest ______________________.
8. Let's offer some suggestions.
   Why don't ______________________?

C ▶03-10 **Listen to the sentences. Write the words you hear.**

1. How about ___we meet___ tomorrow morning?
2. I suggest that ______________________ a different company next time.
3. Why don't ______________________ some goals for the project?
4. I suggest that ______________________ on Thursday and Friday so we can stay on schedule.
5. ______________________ a meeting to give them feedback.
6. ______________________ some ideas with the design team?
7. ______________________ that company another chance?
8. ______________________ a daily team meeting?

UNIT 3, LESSON 3 IMPERATIVES IN REPORTED SPEECH

A **Read the email. Complete the sentences about the email.**

From: Design Manager To: Design Department

Team,

Tomorrow morning, we will have visitors from Rainbow Printing. There will be a design department meeting at 10:00 A.M. Then Rainbow will tour our department. I have a few requests:

1. Please set up the room ahead of time.
2. Clean up all workspaces in advance.
3. Please arrive by 9:30 and greet the visitors.
4. Don't be late.
5. Don't bring laptops to the meeting.
6. Be available for questions after the meeting.

Thank you everyone for your help! See you at the meeting.

1. She told us ___to set up the room ahead of time___.
2. She asked us ______.
3. She said ______.
4. She told us ______.
5. She said ______.
6. She asked us ______.

B **Read the sentences. Then write a sentence using reported speech using the same verb.**

1. Sara said, "Please arrive by 9:00 A.M."
   Sara ___said to arrive by 9:00 A.M.___.
2. The office manager told us, "Reserve the meeting rooms online."
   The manager ______.
3. We told him, "Please get coffee for the meeting."
   We ______.
4. Carmen said, "Review the brochure."
   She ______.
5. My boss told me, "Please pick up the client at the hotel."
   My boss ______.
6. The president told us, "Don't be late for the company meeting."
   The president ______.
7. They said, "Don't come in tomorrow."
   They ______.

C ▶03-15 **Listen to the conversation. What did Mary tell Ana and Jim to do? Circle the correct instructions.**

1. (bring) / don't bring laptops
2. take / don't take notes
3. arrive / don't arrive late
4. fix / don't fix mistakes in the brochure
5. print / don't print the brochure
6. finalize / don't finalize the design
7. book / don't book a room
8. order / don't order coffee

A Complete the sentences. Use *used to*, *would*, or the simple present and the verbs in parentheses. Write *used to / would* if both are possible.

1. People ___didn't use to have___ (not have) smart phones. Now everyone ___has___ (have) one.
2. In the past, friends ___________ (write) letters. Now they ___________ (send) texts.
3. Everyone ___________ (have) cell phones these days. But remember when people ___________ (have) a phone on the wall?
4. My mother ___________ (shop) in stores. She ___________ (buy) everything online now.
5. My father ___________ (own) a typewriter. Now he ___________ (use) a computer.
6. My grandmother ___________ (not get on) social media. But she ___________ (use) it every day now!

B Read each conversation. Complete the sentences with *used to* or *would* and the verbs in parentheses.

1. A: ___Did___ you ___use to work___ (work) at CaB Design?
   B: Yes, I did. I worked there for three years.
2. A: Remember when people ___________ (go) to the bank in person?
   B: I know! Now it's so easy to bank online.
3. A: How did you ___________ (stay in touch) with your friends in school?
   B: We ___________ (call) each other. Now we only text.
4. A: Do you use social media?
   B: I ___________ (post) on social media a lot, but I stopped.
5. A: Do you talk to your family in India?
   B: We video chat a lot. But when I was young, we ___________ (not talk) so often.
6. A: I didn't know your sister was a writer!
   B: Yes. In college, she ___________ (write) for magazines. Today she writes a blog.

C ▶ 04-02 Listen to the conversation. Check (✓) what people did in the past and what they do in the present.

		Past	Present
1.	a. have a desktop	✓	☐
	b. have a laptop	☐	☐
2.	a. send cards in the mail	☐	☐
	b. post birthday messages	☐	☐
3.	a. visit grandparents	☐	☐
	b. video chat with grandparents	☐	☐
4.	a. post stories on his website	☐	☐
	b. write for an online magazine	☐	☐

A Read the lists. Complete the conversations with the correct response.

Hideo
- designs websites
- speaks Japanese, English, and Spanish
- plays the guitar
- loves rock music
- doesn't like jazz
- doesn't like scary movies

Teresa
- designs websites
- speaks Spanish, English, and French
- plays the piano
- loves rock music
- doesn't like jazz
- doesn't like scary movies

1. A: Hideo designs websites.
   B: ___So does___ Teresa.
2. A: Teresa doesn't like jazz.
   B: Hideo __________.
3. A: Hideo plays a musical instrument.
   B: Teresa __________.
4. A: Hideo doesn't like scary movies.
   B: __________ Teresa.
5. A: Hideo speaks three languages.
   B: __________ Teresa.
6. A: Teresa doesn't speak Russian.
   B: Hideo __________.

B Read each conversation. Write the correct response using the word in parentheses. There is more than one correct response.

1. A: I love science fiction stories.
   B: ___I do, too___ (I). They're my favorite.
2. A: We don't really like this band.
   B: __________ (we). The other band is much better.
3. A: I enjoy watching action/adventure movies.
   B: __________ (I). They're so exciting.
4. A: It's raining. I don't feel like going out.
   B: __________ (I). Let's watch a movie.
5. A: We want to go to the new photography show.
   B: __________ (we). Do you want to go together?
6. A: I hope Dave Bodie's new album is good.
   B: __________ (I). The last one was awful.

C ▶04-09 Listen to the conversation. Check (✓) the facts that are true for Jack and Nina.

	Jack	Nina
1. loves jazz music	✓	✓
2. likes The Cool Cats		
3. loves rock music		
4. loves The Corr's new album		
5. saw The Corr's concert		
6. doesn't like the band Fires		
7. plays the piano		
8. plays the guitar		

UNIT 4, LESSON 3 SIMPLE PRESENT AND PAST PASSIVE

A Read the sentences. Write each one in the passive.

1. Someone made the movie in 1994.
   The movie was made in 1994.
2. Jazz musician Toni Brown wrote the soundtrack.
   ____
3. Many critics did not like the movie.
   ____
4. Frida French plays the character Arlene in a new musical, *The Watchers*.
   ____
5. They did not complete the movie on time.
   ____
6. People know Warren Oakes for his action films.
   ____
7. Beth Atwood creates the most amazing theater costumes.
   ____

B Read the movie review. Complete the text with the correct passive form of the verbs in parentheses.

TRENDING BINGE GUIDE **REVIEWS** WHAT'S HOT COMPETITIONS Search

The pilot makes a big landing

The movie *The Pilot* tells the story of airline pilot Marvin Jones, who lands a plane on Lake Michigan in the middle of winter. The movie was adapted **1 (adapt)** from the book *The Big Landing*. *The Big Landing* ______ **2 (write)** by Jennifer Strong in 2001. *The Pilot* is set in Michigan in the winter. The role of Marvin Jones ______ **3 (play)** by actor Fred Murphy.

Murphy ______ **4 (not know)** for his roles in action movies. But he does a great job as the calm and confident pilot. Soon after the plane takes off, an engine problem ______ **5 (discover)**. Jones must land the plane. Helping Jones through the emergency is his co-pilot, Emily Street. Actress Sylvia Garcia puts in a fantastic performance as Street. Many scenes ______ **6 (shot)** outdoors in terrible weather, but the result was worth the effort.

Earlier this year, director John Chung ______ **7 (give)** a Best Director award for the film.

C ▶04-16 Listen to the passive sentences. Complete each active sentence with the correct verb form.

1. They made the movie in 2008.
2. Henry Houston ______ the movie.
3. Jason Ito ______ the role of the fire chief.
4. They ______ Ann Castro to play the role of the city mayor.
5. They ______ the movie on location.
6. They ______ the actors awards for their performances.

UNIT 5, LESSON 1 TAG QUESTIONS

A Read each question. Write the correct tag.

1. You like seafood, ___don't you___?
2. You haven't eaten here before, ____________?
3. You like chocolate, ____________?
4. You don't like fast food, ____________?
5. The service wasn't very efficient, ____________?
6. Small restaurants have the best atmosphere, ____________?
7. Tomato ice cream sounds strange, ____________?
8. It's nice to eat outside, ____________?
9. The desserts are homemade, ____________?

B ▶05-02 Listen to the tag questions. Is the speaker expecting information or expecting agreement? Check (✓) the right answer.

1. ☐ information ☑ agreement
2. ☐ information ☐ agreement
3. ☐ information ☐ agreement
4. ☐ information ☐ agreement
5. ☐ information ☐ agreement
6. ☐ information ☐ agreement
7. ☐ information ☐ agreement
8. ☐ information ☐ agreement
9. ☐ information ☐ agreement

C ▶05-03 Listen to parts of a conversation. Check (✓) *True* or *False* for each statement.

		True	False
1.	a. The man doesn't like the restaurant.	☐	☑
	b. The woman doesn't like the restaurant.	☐	☐
	c. The man and woman agree about the atmosphere.	☐	☐
2.	a. The man likes the pasta dish.	☐	☐
	b. The woman agrees with the man about the pasta.	☐	☐
3.	a. The woman likes spinach.	☐	☐
	b. The man likes spinach.	☐	☐
4.	a. The woman thinks the service is bad.	☐	☐
	b. The man agrees with the woman about the service.	☐	☐

UNIT 5, LESSON 2 EXPRESSING PREFERENCE WITH *WOULD RATHER* AND *WOULD PREFER*

A Read each conversation. Complete the sentence with *would prefer* (*not*) or *would rather* (*not*).

1. A: We have some delicious cakes tonight.
   B: No, thanks. I ___prefer not___ to have dessert.
2. A: Did the team decide on sandwiches or tacos for the meeting?
   B: They ____________ to have tacos.
3. A: Do you feel like eating Mexican food tonight?
   B: I ____________ eat Chinese food.
4. A: What do you think about trying the shrimp?
   B: I ____________ try the beef.
5. A: ____________ you ____________ to take a cab to the restaurant?
   B: It's a nice night. Why don't we walk?
6. A: Why don't we stay home and cook tonight?
   B: I ____________ to cook. Let's go out.
7. A: What about sitting at this table?
   B: We ____________ sit here. It's too close to the kitchen.
8. A: ____________ you ____________ have soup or a salad with your meal?
   B: I'll have a salad, please.
9. A: Why don't we go to Peppers restaurant for dinner?
   B: I ____________ go to Peppers. Their food is too spicy.

B Complete the conversations with the words in parentheses.

1. A: Do you want hamburgers tonight?
   B: ___No, I'd rather eat pizza___.
   (rather / eat / pizza)
2. A: ____________?
   (prefer / have / soup or salad)
   B: Salad, please.
3. A: Would you like ice cream for dessert?
   B: No, thank you. I ____________.
   (rather / have / cake)
4. A: When should we go out, Friday or Saturday?
   B: We ____________.
   (prefer not / go out / on Saturday)
5. A: Should we just go and see if there is a table?
   B: No, I ____________.
   (rather / call ahead / for a table)
6. A: Should we meet at the restaurant at 6:00?
   B: That's a little early. I ____________.
   (prefer / meet / at 7:00)
7. A: What kind of dressing would you like?
   B: I ____________.
   (rather not / have / any dressing)
8. A: Would you like to try the steak?
   B: No, thanks. I ____________.
   (prefer not / eat / red meat)
9. A: ____________?
   (rather / sit / by the window)
   B: Yes, that sounds nice.

C ▶05-10 Listen to the conversation. What would each person rather do? Check (✓) the boxes.

	Man	Woman
1. have the chicken salad	☐	✓
2. have the grilled shrimp	☐	☐
3. have the side salad	☐	☐
4. sit outside	☐	☐
5. order second	☐	☐
6. have water	☐	☐

QUANTIFIERS

A **Read each conversation. Circle the correct answer.**

1. A: Do we have three eggs to make the cake?
   B: No, we only have two. We don't have ***a little*** / ***enough*** eggs.
2. A: How ***much*** / ***many*** money do you need for a snack?
   B: I just need ***a few*** / ***a little*** dollars.
3. A: Do we have ***enough*** / ***a little*** paper plates for the party?
   B: No, we have ***few*** / ***little*** plates. We need a lot more.
4. A: This cookbook is in Spanish. Can you help me read it?
   B: Sure. I can speak ***a little*** / ***a few*** Spanish.
5. A: Oh, no! There isn't ***many*** / ***much*** coffee left.
   B: I'll go and get ***some*** / ***any*** coffee now.
6. A: There are ***a lot of*** / ***much*** new restaurants in town.
   B: I know! Five years ago, there were only ***a few*** / ***a little***.
7. A: I'm taking ***some*** / ***any*** classes at a cooking school.
   B: That's interesting. Do you have ***a lot of*** / ***some*** homework?
8. A: We have ***a lot of*** / ***much*** things to get. Let's make a shopping list.
   B: OK. I need ***a piece of*** / ***a few*** paper.

B **Look at the picture. Complete the conversations with the words in the box.**

a few	a jar of	a little	any	enough	much	a bottle of

1. A: Is there any cheese for cheese and crackers?
   B: There is only ___a little___ cheese. Let's get more.
2. A: Do we have any carrots to go with the hummus?
   B: We only have ________ carrots. We need some more.
3. A: How ________ soda do we have?
   B: We have ________ soda. Is that enough?
4. A: Do we have any salsa?
   B: Yes, we have ________ salsa. Do we need more?
5. A: How many eggs do we have?
   B: We have ________ eggs. We don't need more.
6. A: How much milk do we have?
   B: We don't have ________ milk at all. Let's get some.

C ▶05-17 **Listen. Complete the sentences with the quantifier and noun you hear.**

1. Here are ___a few dollars___ for the tip.
2. We don't have ________ to make dinner.
3. I've made ________ at cooking school.
4. That coffee shop only has ________.
5. Do you have ________ for dessert?
6. Cooking and shopping for a party is ________.
7. There is not ________ in this kitchen.
8. ________ were in the restaurant that night.

UNIT 6, LESSON 1 GERUNDS AS SUBJECTS AND OBJECTS

A Read the information. Correct seven errors, changing verbs to gerunds as necessary.

DO YOU HATE ~~GO~~ going TO THE GYM? DO YOU ENJOY DO THINGS OUTSIDE?

Then join the Outdoor Fitness Club!

We are a group of people that love be active outdoors.

- We enjoy rock climb at Big Rock State Park.
- Run is our most popular activity. Run with us on Saturday mornings.
- We love hike in nearby parks and forests.
- We offer beginning and advanced groups for cycle. Join a monthly ride.

The Outdoor Fitness Club has something for everyone. Come join us today!

B Put the words in the correct order to make sentences.

1. sports / on / is / watching / exciting
   Watching sports on TV is exciting.
2. enjoy / exercise / videos / I / watching
   ____
3. talking / are / about / we / on Saturday / meeting
   ____
4. is / tiring / marathon / a / running
   ____
5. fast food / will help / not eating / lose weight / you
   ____
6. likes / being / outdoors / Arun / active
   ____
7. his doctor / eating / less sugar / suggested
   ____
8. not running / your foot / will help / heal
   ____

C ▶06-02 Listen. Write the gerunds you hear.

When I was younger, I didn't use to exercise. Now, I enjoy ___exercising___ (1). It took a while to decide what kind of exercise I liked. I tried ______________ (2) at first. I liked it. I loved ______________ (3) active outdoors, so I started ______________ (4) some short races. It was exciting! But then I tried to run a marathon. I did not enjoy that. I still run, but I don't do any long races.

This year, a new gym opened nearby. I am not a gym person. I don't like ______________ (5) with a lot of people. But my friend suggested that I try it. So I went to a class. I tried ______________ (6). It was fantastic! I also did some ______________ (7) with a coach, and I already feel a lot stronger. Maybe ______________ (8) to the gym isn't so bad after all.

UNIT 6, LESSON 2 PAST FORM OF *BE* + *GOING TO* FOR PAST INTENTIONS

A **Complete the conversations with a form of *be* (*not*) + *going to* + the base form of the verb.**

1. A: How was your run this morning?
   B: Well, I ___was going to run___ **(run)** before work, but I woke up late.
2. A: It's 9:00 P.M.! You should go home!
   B: Well, I ______ **(work)** late, but I wanted to finish tonight.
3. A: When are you going on vacation?
   B: I ______ **(go)** in April, but I'll probably wait until May.
4. A: When is your family coming to visit?
   B: They ______ **(come)** this weekend, but they had to cancel.
5. A: Did you see the doctor about your sore foot?
   B: I ______ **(make)** an appointment today, but I've been so busy.
6. A: Why are you still here?
   B: We ______ **(take)** a break, but we decided to keep working.
7. A: You're not working on your vacation, are you?
   B: No, I'm not. I ______ **(take)** my laptop, but I need some time offline.

B **Complete the sentences with a form of *be* (*not*) + *going to* + a verb in the box.**

~~answer~~	check	cycle	exercise	finish	run	text	visit	work

1. I ___wasn't going to answer___ the phone, but it was my boss calling.
2. I ______ after work, but I forgot my gym shoes.
3. We ______ the designs tonight, but everyone needed to go home.
4. Anna ______ in the marathon, but she hurt her foot.
5. ______ you ______ me before you left?
6. We ______ late, but we had too much to do.
7. Rob ______ his inbox after work, but he did.
8. Yoko ______ her family in Japan, but the tickets were too expensive.
9. ______ Dan ______ with his friends before his bike broke?

C ▶06-09 **Listen to the conversations. Circle *T* for *True* and *F* for *False*. If the answer is false, write the reason why.**

		Reason
1. He went to the party.	T / F	His car broke down.
2. He woke up early.	T / F	
3. They visited Mexico.	T / F	
4. She talked to her boss this morning.	T / F	
5. She stayed until 9:00.	T / F	
6. He finished the designs.	T / F	
7. They'll take the train to the city.	T / F	
8. She's going to China.	T / F	
9. He's working out this evening.	T / F	

UNIT 6, LESSON 3 PREPOSITIONS OF TIME

A Read Marta's schedule. Circle the correct answers.

1. Marta got up ***in*** / ***at*** 6:00 this morning.
2. Marta finished her report ***during*** / ***until*** breakfast.
3. She ate lunch ***between*** / ***from*** 12:00 and 1:00.
4. She had a call with a client ***for*** / ***since*** one hour.
5. She worked ***by*** / ***until*** 5:30 P.M.
6. She went to the gym ***at*** / ***in*** 6:00 P.M.
7. She had to arrive for dinner ***by*** / ***on*** 7:00 P.M.
8. She has been awake ***for*** / ***since*** 6:00 this morning.

10:01

< menu Schedule add ⊕

Monday, May 5

6:00	get up
7:00	finish report/breakfast
8:00	
9:00	team meeting
10:00	project meeting
11:00	
12:00	lunch (12:15? 12:30?)
1:00	meeting with manager
2:00	call with client
3:00	
4:00	
5:00	leave office—5:30
6:00	gym
7:00	dinner with Nina—Don't be late!

B Complete the conversations with the correct word in the box.

after	~~before~~	by	during
for	on	since	until

1. A: You should stretch ___before___ you run.
   B: Thanks for the tip!
2. A: How long have you been a member at this gym?
   B: I have been a member ______________ 2015.
3. A: Can you meet ______________ 3:00? We need to start at 3:15.
   B: Sure, no problem. I won't be late.
4. A: How long did you run?
   B: I ran ______________ 5:00 P.M. I had to get home by 5:15.
5. A: When would you like to start with a personal trainer?
   B: How about starting ______________ Monday?
6. A: Do you always work out early in the morning?
   B: Yes, I don't like working out ______________ the day. It's too hot.
7. A: I'm getting tired! How long do we have left?
   B: Try to keep going ______________ one more minute.
8. A: What will you want to do ______________ the marathon?
   B: I'll want to rest!

C ▶06-16 Listen to two parts of a conversation. Match the words and phrases to finish the sentences.

Part 1: Yesterday, Yoko...

1. got up early	after	her run.
2. ran	in	the morning.
3. had coffee and breakfast	for	7:30.
4. went to the store	until	about an hour.

Part 2: Yesterday, Ben...

5. went rock climbing	after	the afternoon.
6. didn't put away his phone	before	the climb.
7. couldn't answer his phone	during	dinner.
8. called his father back	in	rock-climbing.

UNIT 7, LESSON 1 EMBEDDED *WH-* QUESTIONS

A **Rewrite each question as an embedded question.**

1. Where is the copier?
   Do you know where ___the copier is___?
2. When does Ava need this?
   Can you tell me when ______________________?
3. Why are my files missing?
   I don't understand why ______________________.
4. Where is Mona?
   Do you know where ______________________?
5. How do we install the program?
   Can you explain how ______________________?
6. What should I do about this problem?
   I'm not sure what ______________________.
7. Where can I find some pens?
   Do you know where ______________________?
8. When are we meeting?
   Can you tell me when ______________________?
9. Who should I email about this?
   I don't know who ______________________.

B **Read the email. Rewrite each question as an embedded question.**

1. Do you know ___where the meeting is___?
2. I don't know ______________________.
3. I'm not sure ______________________.
4. Do you know ______________________?
5. Can you tell me ______________________?
6. Can you explain ______________________?
7. I don't know ______________________.
8. Can you tell me ______________________?

Subject: Project meeting

From: May Chen To: Paula

Hi Paula,

I'm new to the design department. (Today is my first day!) My manager, Carlos, asked me to come to the project meeting tomorrow. He said to email you for more information about the meeting. I have a few questions.

Where is the meeting?
What time does it start?
What is the purpose of the meeting?
Who is attending?
What topics are we discussing?
How can I access the project documents?
What do I need to bring?
How do I add my name to the meeting list?

Thanks so much for your help!
May

C ▶07-02 **Listen to each embedded question. What does the speaker want to know? Add the missing word.**

1. ___Where___ are the presentation files?
2. ___________ can I download these files?
3. ___________ is the client meeting?
4. ___________ does Nina need these files today?
5. ___________ should I send this email to?
6. ___________ is May?
7. ___________ can I call about this problem?
8. ___________ is his name?

A **Complete the email. Make comparisons with *as...as* and the words in parentheses.**

From: Ying Lee To: Lan

Hi, Lan.

Greetings from Houston! Moving overseas and starting a new job has been a little scary. But it's not nearly as scary as (1 not nearly / scary) I thought it would be! Everyone has been so kind and helpful. My new coworkers are ______ (2 supportive) my old co-workers. And the atmosphere at the office is ______ (3 not / intimidating) I had imagined. The work is ______ (4 challenging) I had expected, but I know it will get easier. And I love the city. Houston is ______ (5 just/hot) Shanghai. The traffic is also bad, but it's ______ (6 not nearly / bad) the traffic back home. My new co-worker from the office is ______ (7 just / enthusiastic) I am about live music. So we are going to see some bands this weekend.

I can't wait! I hope everything is going well with you. Send an email or text me when you can.

Ying

B **Rewrite the sentences. Make comparisons with *as...as* and the words in parentheses.**

1. Dan is not very busy. Marc is very, very busy.
   Dan is not nearly as busy as (not nearly / busy) Marc.
2. Kelly has two years of experience. Yuko has two and a half years of experience.
   Kelly is ______ (almost / experienced) Yuko.
3. I think learning English is challenging. But learning Chinese is a lot more challenging.
   Learning English ______ (not nearly / challenging) learning Chinese.
4. Marco was confident in the review. Lucas wasn't so confident.
   Lucas was ______ (not / confident) Marco.
5. Alba is very talented. Diego is also very talented.
   Alba is ______ (just / talented) Diego.
6. This project is easy. The last project was really intense.
   This project ______ (not nearly / difficult) the last one.
7. My old manager was laid-back. My new manager is not laid-back at all.
   My new manager is ______ (not nearly / laid-back) my old one.

C 07-07 **Listen to the conversations. Circle the correct answer.**

1. The presentation was ***more useful*** / ***less useful*** than he had hoped.
2. Her new job is ***more exciting than*** / ***as exciting as*** her old job.
3. The new project is ***much more challenging*** / ***much less challenging*** than the last one.
4. He would like his boss to be ***more supportive*** / ***less supportive***.
5. Yesterday, she was ***a lot more*** / ***a lot less*** tired.
6. He hoped the designs would be ***better*** / ***worse***.
7. She thought she would be ***more nervous*** / ***less nervous*** about the interview.
8. His new office is ***a little bigger*** / ***a little smaller*** than his old office.
9. Both of them are ***excited*** / ***not excited*** about our trip to New York.

UNIT 7, LESSON 3 PHRASAL VERBS WITH OBJECTS

A Put the words in the correct order to make sentences. If the phrasal verbs are separable, write the sentence in two ways.

1. with / will/ my manager / I / check / in I will check in with my manager.
2. run / have / paper / of / we / out ______
3. I / can / up / set / the projector ______
4. the feedback / go / let's / tomorrow / over ______
5. get / need to / the internet / on / I ______
6. out / hasn't / it / Pedro / figured / yet ______
7. a plan / put / Fatima / for the party / together ______
8. the process / Dana / went / carefully / through ______

B Read each conversation. Complete the sentences using the phrasal verb and a pronoun as the object.

1. A: Did you back up your hard drive?
   B: Yes I backed it up an hour ago
2. A: Are you going to check in with Sara?
   B: Yes, I will ______ this afternoon.
3. A: Did we run out of printer ink?
   B: Yes, we ______ yesterday.
4. A: Do you want to go over the notes together?
   B: Sure, but let's ______ later.
5. A: Have you figured out the problem?
   B: No, I haven't ______ yet.
6. A: Did you put together the agenda for the meeting?
   B: Yes, I ______ this morning.
7. A: Would you mind setting up the tables and chairs for the presentation?
   B: Sure. I'll ______ now.
8. A: Should we go through the client feedback now?
   B: Sure. Let's ______ in my office.
9. A: Did he remember to turn on the computer?
   B: Yes, he ______ already.

C ▶07-14 Listen. Complete the sentences with the phrasal verbs you hear.

1. It's too dark in here. Can you turn on the lights?
2. Let's ______ the new designs in the meeting.
3. We have a problem. Can you help us ______?
4. Please ______ your files every day.
5. Will you help me ______ the room for the meeting?
6. Why don't you ______ with Tom?
7. Can we ______ before tomorrow?
8. Yuko ______ the process step-by-step.

UNIT 8, LESSON 1 *MAY / MIGHT / COULD* WITH THE CONTINUOUS FOR POSSIBILITY

A **Rewrite the sentences with the modal in parentheses.**

1. Dana might be getting sick. (may)
   Dana may be getting sick.
2. Ahmet may be coming down with the flu. (might)
   ______
3. They might be talking to the doctor now. (may)
   ______
4. Ari may be resting. (could)
   ______
5. Sara may not be working today. (might)
   ______
6. I may be getting a migraine. (could)
   ______

B **Complete the conversations with the words in parentheses. Use the continuous or simple form of the verb.**

1. A: What's wrong?
   B: I think I ___might be getting___ **(might / get)** the flu.
2. A: I think I ______ **(might / come down with)** a cold.
   B: Why don't you go home for the afternoon?
3. A: Is Pedro here? He was sick yesterday.
   B: I haven't seen him. He ______ **(might not / feel)** better.
4. A: Where is Ava? ______ she ______ **(could / sleep)**?
   B: Probably. She said she was tired.
5. A: I ______ **(might / get)** a rash. My arm is itching a lot.
   B: Let me look at it.
6. A: Who is Lisa talking to?
   B: She ______ **(could / make)** an appointment with the doctor.

C ▶08-03 **Listen to each conversation. What do Marco, Trina, and Ed think is possible? Check (✓) all the correct answers.**

1. It's possible that Marco…
   a. ☐ has a rash
   b. ☑ is getting the flu
2. It's possible that Trina…
   a. ☐ is getting sick
   b. ☐ has allergies
   c. ☐ has the flu
   d. ☐ needs to see the doctor
3. It's possible that Ed…
   a. ☐ is getting a migraine
   b. ☐ needs to take some medicine
   c. ☐ wants to lie down
   d. ☐ needs to go to the store

UNIT 8, LESSON 2 SUBORDINATING CONJUNCTIONS IN TIME CLAUSES

A Read the web page. Circle the correct answers.

HEALTH A-Z LIVING HEALTHY **SELF HELP** NEWS & EXPERTS SYMPTOM CHECKER Search

How to Treat a Cold

There is no cure for a cold, but here are some tips to feel better faster.

1. ***As soon as*** / ***Until*** you feel sick, start drinking fluids like water or juice.
2. Don't drink coffee or sodas ***before*** / ***while*** you are sick.
3. Get lots of rest ***after*** / ***when*** you have a cold.
4. Talk to you doctor ***before*** / ***as long as*** you give cold medicine to a child.
5. Stay home from work or school ***once*** / ***until*** you are better.
6. ***After*** / ***While*** you blow your nose, wash your hands.
7. Boil a pot of water and breathe in the steam ***as long as*** / ***before*** you can.
8. Eat chicken soup ***until*** / ***whenever*** you are sick.

B Put the words in parentheses in the correct order to complete the sentences.

1. Take this medicine before you go to bed. **(go / before / you / to bed)**
2. You should avoid crowded places ________________. **(while / are contagious / you)**
3. Read the information on the package ________________. **(you / before / any medicine / take)**
4. ________________, I always get sick, too! **(my family / whenever / gets sick)**
5. I stayed home ________________. **(my cold / until / was gone)**
6. ________________, you shouldn't come to work. **(have / as long as / the flu / you)**
7. ________________, I felt so much better. **(took / I / after / the cold medicine)**
8. ________________, you can pass the virus to others. **(you / are contagious / when)**
9. You can return to work ________________. **(you / feel better / as soon as)**

C ▶08-10 Listen to the conversation. Match the parts to make sentences based on the doctor's advice.

e 1. Dan should get the flu vaccine ___ he can.
___ 2. He should take his medicine ___ he eats a meal.
___ 3. He should try to stay away from people ___ he is contagious.
___ 4. He should drink plenty of water ___ he is sick.
___ 5. He should have a hot drink ___ he goes to bed.
___ 6. He should wash his hands ___ he coughs.
___ 7. He should stay home and rest ___ his cold is gone.
___ 8. He should make another appointment ___ he feels better.

a. as long as
b. until
c. while
d. once
e. as soon as
f. before
g. when
h. after

UNIT 8, LESSON 3 FUTURE REAL CONDITIONAL

A Complete each future real conditional sentence using the words in parentheses.

1. If I ___get___ (get) sick, I ___will miss___ (miss) the meeting.
2. If you ________ (not rest), you ________ (not get) better.
3. Her throat ________ (feel) better if she ________ (drink) this tea.
4. If I ________ (be) still contagious, I ________ (not come) to work.
5. ________ you ________ (call) the doctor if you ________ (feel) worse?
6. If you ________ (get) worse, you ________ (end up) in the hospital.
7. If he ________ (take) this medicine, his headache ________ (go away).
8. What ________ you ________ (do) if you ________ (get) sick?
9. If you ________ (not treat) that rash, it ________ (spread).

B Complete each future real conditional sentence using the words in parentheses. Add a comma when needed.

1. ___If I get the flu,___ (get the flu) it will be terrible.
2. If I don't feel better in the morning ________ (call the doctor).
3. ________ (feel bad) he will go home early.
4. ________ (be contagious) you will make everyone else sick.
5. ________ (take this medicine) you will get healthy soon.
6. ________ (not come to the party) if I feel worse.
7. ________ (have time) will you make me some hot tea?
8. ________ (not recover) if you don't rest.

C ▶08-15 Listen to each conversation. Circle the correct ending for each sentence.

1. If she gets better,
   a. they will have dinner tonight.
   (b.) they will do something on the weekend.
2. If he listens to the doctor,
   a. he will be able to go to work.
   b. he will get over the flu.
3. If she goes out,
   a. she will make other people sick.
   b. she will be bored.
4. If he doesn't feel well tomorrow,
   a. his friend will take the day off.
   b. his friend will take him to the doctor.
5. If he gets sick,
   a. he will rest.
   b. he will miss the party.
6. If she drinks the tea,
   a. her throat will hurt.
   b. her throat will feel better.
7. If he doesn't rest,
   a. he will get worse.
   b. he will get tired.
8. If she doesn't take the medicine,
   a. she won't get better.
   b. she won't like it.
9. If he doesn't wear a mask,
   a. he will look strange.
   b. he will spread the virus.

UNIT 9, LESSON 1 REFLEXIVE PRONOUNS

A **Complete the sentences with a reflexive pronoun.**

1. She was mad at ___herself___ for losing her keys.
2. Carlos will be disappointed in ________________ if he doesn't finish the race.
3. We didn't enjoy ________________ at the company party.
4. The people helped ________________ to the free cookies.
5. I was surprised at ________________ for going rock climbing.
6. You shouldn't blame ________________ for what happened.
7. Did Ana draw these designs by ________________?
8. The boy looked proud of ________________ for spelling his own name.
9. Why don't we introduce ________________ before we start the meeting?

B **Complete the sentences using the word in parentheses and a reflexive pronoun. Use correct prepositions with the adjectives, if necessary.**

1. I was ___disappointed in myself___ **(disappointed)** for not passing the exam.
2. She should be ________________ **(ashamed)** for being so rude.
3. Don't ________________ **(blame)**. The accident wasn't your fault.
4. We really ________________ **(enjoyed)** on our trip to Vietnam.
5. I never took piano lessons. I ________________ **(taught)** how to play.
6. There's plenty of food for all of you. Please ________________ **(help)** to whatever you want.
7. I was ________________ **(surprised)** for trying skydiving.
8. That was a terrible kick! He looks really ________________ **(mad)** for missing the goal.
9. I ________________ **(told)** I would quit smoking this year.

C ▶09-02 **Listen to the conversations. Complete the sentences using the words in the word box and a reflexive pronoun.**

blames	disappointed in	helped	mad at	promised	~~proud~~ of

1. She was ___proud of herself___ for winning the race.
2. They were ________________ for losing an important game.
3. She was ________________ for breaking the vase.
4. He ________________ that he would exercise more.
5. They ________________ to the sandwiches.
6. He ________________ for what happened.

UNIT 9, LESSON 2 PAST CONTINUOUS WITH *WHILE* AND *WHEN*

A Complete the sentences with the correct form of the verbs in parentheses.

1. While I ___was walking___ (walk) down the street, I ___saw___ (see) an accident.
2. While Kay ______ (drive) to work, her car ______ (run out) of gas.
3. When I ______ (get) dressed, I accidently ______ (put on) two different socks!
4. Jon's boss ______ (walk) in while he ______ (play) a game on his phone.
5. When they ______ (surf), they ______ (see) a shark!
6. We were so tired! We ______ (not hear) a thing when we ______ (sleep).
7. While they ______ (sing) on stage, the microphones ______ (stop) working.
8. The soccer player ______ (hurt) himself when he ______ (kick) the ball.

B Read the timeline of Mei's life. Write sentences with the verbs in parentheses. Use correct tense.

1985 born in China
1991 starts learning English
2003 gets scholarship; starts college in California
2005 gets a part-time job; meets Adam
2007 starts graduate school
2008 starts work at TCI Group
2010 finishes graduate school
2011 gets married; gets promoted
2013 starts own business
2014 has a baby daughter
2016 expands business

1. While she was living in China, she started learning English.
(live in China / start learning English)
2. ______
(live in China / get a college scholarship)
3. ______
(get a part-time job / attend college)
4. ______
(go to college / meet Adam)
5. ______
(start work at TCI Group / go to graduate school)
6. ______
(work at TCI Group / gets married)
7. ______
(run her own business / have her daughter)
8. ______
(raise her daughter / expand her business)

C ▶09-09 Listen to the conversation. Write the numbers 1 or 2 to show the order of the actions.

1. _2_ starts graduate school
   _1_ lives in New York
2. ___ meets wife
   ___ goes to graduate school
3. ___ works at Brown Engineering
   ___ gets married
4. ___ company goes out of business
   ___ looks for a larger apartment
5. ___ hears about a job in Houston
   ___ talks to college roommate in Houston

UNIT 9, LESSON 3 INFINITIVE OF PURPOSE

A Complete the sentences using the words in parentheses in the correct form and infinitives of purpose.

1. She drinks coffee to stay awake.
   (drink coffee / stay awake)
2. He ______________________.
   (read / relax)
3. She ______________________.
   (practice a lot / get better)
4. He ______________________.
   (sat down / rest)
5. They ______________________.
   (went to the cafeteria / eat)
6. He ______________________.
   (work out / stay fit)
7. I ______________________.
   (used my phone / take a selfie)
8. We ______________________.
   (had a party / surprise our parents)
9. Are you ______________________?
   (going to Egypt / see the pyramids)

B Rewrite the two sentences as one sentence with an infinitive of purpose.

1. I went to China. I wanted to study Chinese. I went to China to study Chinese.
2. My parents called. They wanted to wish me a happy birthday.
   ____
3. Rasha got up early. She had to take the kids to school.
   ____
4. I watch American movies. I want to improve my English.
   ____
5. Matt went outside. He needed to get some fresh air.
   ____
6. I will get a part-time job. I need to earn some extra money.
   ____
7. We are going on vacation. We need to relax.
   ____
8. Gina always shops online. She wants to save time.
   ____
9. I went to the doctor. I needed to get a flu shot.
   ____

C ▶09-16 Listen to each conversation. Circle the correct answer.

1. She wants to stop at the store ***to get ice cream*** / ***to get dinner***.
2. She left her car at the shop ***to fix her brakes*** / ***to get new brakes***.
3. He is going to France ***to meet a friend*** / ***to learn French***.
4. She runs ***to relax*** / ***to exercise***.
5. They're stopping at the gas station ***to get coffee*** / ***to get gas***.
6. She's going to Florida ***to visit the Kennedy Space Center*** / ***to visit her son***.
7. He got up at 4:00 A.M. ***to catch his plane to India*** / ***to pick up his family***.
8. She has to go to the store ***to buy rice*** / ***to buy bread***.

UNIT 10, LESSON 1 NOUN CLAUSES WITH *THAT*

A **Put the words in the correct order to make sentences.**

1. Youri / that / she / hopes / graduates / law school
   Youri hopes that she graduates law school.
2. think / is / Marco / a good boss / I
   ____
3. to visit / dreamed / her parents / were coming / Luisa
   ____
4. Tara / found / scientists / read / a cure for allergies
   ____
5. next term / hope / we / will be better / our grades
   ____
6. will start / Rose / her own business / I / heard
   ____
7. to set / we / need / I / agree / some goals right away
   ____

B **Read the sentences. Answer the question using a noun clause.**

1. Alan can't afford a new car right now. Why is Alan worried?
   Alan is worried (that) he can't afford a new car right now.
2. Jack didn't get a promotion. Why is Jack disappointed?
   ____
3. Ana and Lucas have to move. Why are Ana and Lucas sad?
   ____
4. Dan is moving back to China. Why is Dan's family happy?
   ____
5. The team got an award. Why was the team excited?
   ____
6. Murat's friends forgot his birthday. Why is Murat surprised?
   ____

C ▶10-02 **Listen. Write the missing words.**

1. I hope that ______ my roommate gets ______ accepted into law school.
2. James is excited that ______________________ a promotion.
3. Ever since we got married, we've dreamed ______________________ South Africa.
4. I heard that ______________________ this week.
5. Tranh hopes ______________________ his parents this year.
6. I guess that ______________________ with his parents when he goes back to Peru.
7. Jill forgot that ______________________ away on vacation and has to miss Eric's wedding.
8. They're not sure ______________________ the new designs.

UNIT 10, LESSON 2 PRESENT UNREAL CONDITIONAL

A Complete each present unreal conditional sentence.

1. If I __didn't work__ (not work) so much, I __would volunteer__ (volunteer) more.
2. If you ________ (not be) a scientist, ________ you ________ (what / do)?
3. If everyone ________ (drive) electric cars, we ________ (help) the environment.
4. I ________ (travel) the world if I ________ (have) enough time.
5. If Kelly ________ (not be) so busy, she ________ (exercise) more.
6. If she ________ (ask) me for help, I ________ (help) her.
7. What ________ you ________ (do) if you ________ (have) more time?
8. If we all ________ (work) together, we ________ (achieve) great things.

B Complete each present unreal conditional sentence with the information in parentheses.

1. __If I weren't so busy__ (not so busy), I would travel more often.
2. If I had enough money, ________ (get my own apartment).
3. ________ (start a business) if I saved more money.
4. ________ (not be happy) if she weren't helping animals.
5. ________ (what / do) if you were a world leader?
6. We would move if ________ (find new jobs).
7. ________ (they need help), I would help them immediately.
8. ________ (get a promotion) if he worked harder.

C ▶10-07 Listen. Write the words you hear.

1. __If I were rich__, __I'd build__ houses in poor communities.
2. ________, ________ at an animal shelter.
3. ________, ________ for world peace.
4. ________, ________ for Doctors Without Borders.
5. ________, ________ 10% of my profits to charity.
6. ________, ________ to end world hunger.
7. ________, ________ the elephant.
8. ________, ________ about injustice.

UNIT 10, LESSON 3 PAST PERFECT

A Look at Erika's daily schedule. Complete the sentences using the past perfect or past simple form of the verbs in parentheses.

10:01		
< menu	Schedule	add ⊕
7:00	gym	
9:00	meeting with team	
10:00	set daily goals	
12:00	lunch with client	
2:00	project meeting	
3:30	finish report for manager	
4:30	meet with manager	
5:30	leave office	
6:00	dinner with Carol	

1. Erika ___had gone___ (go) to the gym by 7:30 A.M.
2. She __________ (attend) the team meeting before she __________ (set) her daily goals.
3. By 11:30, she __________ (not eat) lunch yet.
4. By the time she __________ (have) lunch, she __________ (set) her goals.
5. After she __________ (be) to the project meeting, she __________ (write) her report.
6. She __________ (finish) her report by the time she __________ (meet) with her manager.
7. By 5:00, she __________ (not leave) the office yet.
8. She __________ (work) all day by the time she __________ (have) dinner with Carol.

B Read both actions. Complete the sentences. Use the past perfect.

1. After my car ___had broken down___, I took the bus.
   2:00 P.M. — car broke down; 2:45 P.M. — took the bus
2. Yuko __________ before she moved there for school.
   visited the United States — moved there for school
3. By the time Jake got a full-time job, he __________.
   did volunteer work — got a full-time job
4. Until I went to veterinary school, I __________.
   didn't realize I loved horses — went to veterinary school
5. After Maria __________, she ended up becoming a lawyer.
   got an engineering degree — ended up becoming a lawyer

C ▶10-14 Listen to each conversation. Write the numbers 1 or 2 to show the order of the actions.

1. _1_ left her job
   _2_ wrote a book
2. ___ was 25 years old
   ___ became president of the company
3. ___ worked in restaurants
   ___ opened own restaurant
4. ___ volunteered
   ___ got a job
5. ___ became famous
   ___ went to the moon
6. ___ visited a company's offices
   ___ didn't make a decision
7. ___ got an offer
   ___ stuck in a job
8. ___ raised money
   ___ ran the race

VOCABULARY PRACTICE

UNIT 1, LESSON 4

Complete the sentences with words from the box.

network	eat out	joy	significant	last	immediate	temporary	possession

1. Dana's sunglasses didn't ________________ long. They broke after two days.
2. Helping others is a ________________ part of Matteo's life. He reads to children at the library every Saturday.
3. His ________________ of friends helped Tom when he broke his leg. They brought him dinner every night for a month.
4. I hate to cook so I always ________________ on the weekends.
5. Pete's new job was only ________________. It was just for one month.
6. Kara felt better that day. She took the medicine and it brought her ________________ relief from pain.
7. The bracelet my mother gave me is my most important ________________.
8. Hana smiled with ________________ as everyone began to sing "Happy Birthday!"

UNIT 2, LESSON 4

Circle the correct answers.

1. When storms are *frequent* that means they happen ___.
   a. sometimes
   b. often
   c. every day
2. Everyone likes to work with Rosa. They say that she is *logical*. That means she is ___.
   a. clear thinking
   b. extreme
   c. unusual
3. A *creature* could be any type of ___.
   a. pond
   b. weather
   c. animal
4. The book *inspired* Lei Wi to get more exercise. It ___.
   a. gave him the idea
   b. was based on clear thinking
   c. was very unusual
5. Because of the *extreme* weather conditions, school was cancelled. That means that the weather conditions were ___.
   a. happening very often
   b. trying to hurt someone
   c. very bad and unusual
6. A *body of water* is ___.
   a. an animal, an insect, or a fish
   b. a lake, a pond, or an ocean
   c. very unusual or very bad
7. Don't come too close to the tigers. They can *attack* and ___ you.
   a. like
   b. hurt
   c. play with

UNIT 3, LESSON 4

Complete the sentences with words from the box.

obvious	assumptions	flexible	arrest	relevant	criminal

1. When we meet new people we sometimes make ________________ about them.
2. The police had to ________________ the man for stealing computers.
3. The lawyer said that any information about the car accident could be ________________.
4. The ________________ broke into the house and stole diamond jewelry and watches.
5. The mistakes Ken made were so ________________. He didn't pass the driving test.
6. At our office some people work from 9-5. I work from 12 to 8 P.M. We have ________________ working hours.

UNIT 4, LESSON 4

Complete the paragraph with words from the box.

scenes	industry	remote	authentic	bonus	shoot

The whole film ________________ (1) is waiting for the release of Harold Dean's new movie about Australia in the 1930s. The director decided to ________________ (2) most of the movie ________________ (3) in a ________________ (4) town in Australia. He wanted to make it look more ________________ (5). There's a DVD coming out shortly after the movie opens, with a special ________________ (6) soundtrack and interviews with the filmmakers.

UNIT 5, LESSON 4

Complete the sentences with words from the box.

intimate	tender	superb	skip	tough	options	to order

1. The service at the restaurant yesterday was perfect. It was ________________.
2. The meat in the dish was cooked very well. It was soft and ________________.
3. The menu at this restaurant is very flexible. Most of the meals can be made ________________.
4. There were so many different entrée ________________. I had trouble making a choice.
5. Tonight I prefer to ________________ the appetizers and order the main course right away.
6. The vegetables were so ________________ that they were too hard to cut. I didn't eat them.
7. We loved the new restaurant. The atmosphere was warm and ________________.

UNIT 6, LESSON 4

Circle the correct answers.

1. A word used to describe the type of food you usually eat is ___.
   a. an incentive
   b. a feature
   c. a diet
2. The grocery store clerk reads the ___ on the package of food that you buy.
   a. bar code
   b. diet
   c. feature
3. She won the race thanks to her hard work and a lot of ___ from her trainer.
   a. adjustment
   b. incentive
   c. encouragement
4. To give an opinion to a restaurant or movie is to ___ it.
   a. rate
   b. adjust
   c. keep track of
5. The new running app has many great ___.
   a. barcodes
   b. features
   c. incentives
6. The company is offering a special low price as ___ to buy their product.
   a. an incentive
   b. a feature
   c. an adjustment
7. I try to change and ___ my workout so that I don't get bored with it.
   a. rate
   b. encourage
   c. adjust
8. Mike's coach told him to ___ his daily workouts so he can see his improvement over time.
   a. adjust
   b. keep track of
   c. encourage

UNIT 7, LESSON 4

Complete the sentences with words from the box.

productive	distracted	dread	pile up
deadline	catch up	focus	notifications

1. Dan hates to check his email. He lets the messages ________________ so sometimes he misses an important one.
2. Ana never turns off her ________________. She always wants to know what's happening.
3. Gabby had to rush so that she didn't miss the last ________________.
4. I was on vacation for two weeks. Now I have to work this Saturday to ________________.
5. My son can get ________________ easily except when he's playing video games.
6. Sometimes Paul listens to music while he works. It helps him ________________.
7. I ________________ going to long meetings. They are so boring.
8. Rita was the best employee. She always got everything done. She was the most ________________.

UNIT 8, LESSON 4

Circle the correct answers.

1. The surface of an object is on the ***bottom / outside / inside.***
2. When liquid evaporates it ***changes to gas / turns into water / comes out of your skin.***
3. When you visit a tropical place it will be very ***dry and cool / cold and snowy / hot and wet.***
4. If someone is looking for evidence, they are searching for ***a sound / new information / a signal.***
5. When people sweat, liquid ***is turning to gas / disappears / comes out of their skin.***
6. When you leave out the ice cubes that means you ***add them / don't include them / increase the amount.***
7. Sweating could occur if someone is ***happy / nervous / cold.***
8. When you signal to get someone's attention, you can ***make a sound or action / decide if something is true / leave out important information.***

UNIT 9, LESSON 4

Match each word with the words that describe it. Write the letter on the line.

___	1. invent	a.	to react to something
___	2. survive	b.	the situation when someone finds something new
___	3. a discovery	c.	a doctor that studies human behavior
___	4. an advantage	d.	to create an new type of thing or solution
___	5. respond	e.	to continue to live after a dangerous event
___	6. a psychologist	f.	a better position to be in

UNIT 10, LESSON 4

Complete the sentences with words from the box.

transport	peel	perspective	sustainability
scrap	compost	profit	landfill

1. Using renewable resources like wind and solar power helps achieve the goal of ________________.
2. Lucia's co-workers say that she has an unusual ________________ because she always "thinks outside the box."
3. They were so hungry that there wasn't a ________________ of food left after they had finished dinner.
4. When Yoka Mia started her own business she didn't see a ________________ for a few months. It was a difficult time.
5. After the storm the employer provided ________________ for all of the workers to get home safely.
6. Members of the community garden collected old food and used it to make ________________.
7. The chef didn't ________________ the potatoes before baking them, he left the skins on.
8. Tons of waste go into the local ________________ every month.

UNIT 2, LESSON 1 *WILL, MAY,* AND *MIGHT* TO EXPRESS LIKELIHOOD

Use *will* to talk about something that is certain to be true in the future. Use *may* or *might* when you are unsure of something.

Subject	*Will / May / Might*	*Not*	Base form of verb
It	**will**	**not**	**solve** the problem.
You	**may**	**not**	**be** connected to the Internet.
The problem	**might**	**not**	**happen** again.

Notes

- Use *will (most / very) likely* or *will probably* to talk about something that is expected to be true.
  That ***will most likely*** *solve the problem.*
  That ***won't likely*** *solve the problem. That* ***likely won't*** *solve the problem.*
  That ***will probably*** *solve the problem. That* ***probably won't*** *solve the problem.*
- Use *will definitely* to talk about something that is going to happen for sure.
  We ***will definitely*** *be there tomorrow. We* ***definitely won't*** *be there tomorrow.*

UNIT 2, LESSON 2 PRESENT PERFECT FOR PAST EXPERIENCES

Use the present perfect to show that something has or hasn't happened at an indefinite time in the past. The present perfect is formed with *have* or *has* + past participle.

Questions			Statements			
Have / Has	**Subject**	**Past participle**	**Subject**	***Have / Has***	***Not***	**Past participle**
Have	you	**been** to the theater?	I	**have**		**been** to the theater.
Has	she	**seen** the play?	She	**has**		**seen** the play.
Have	they	**taken** a bus tour?	They	**have**	not	**taken** a bus tour.

Notes

- The adverbs *yet* and *already* are often used with the present perfect. Use *yet* in questions and negative statements. Use *already* in affirmative statements.
  Have you seen the play ***yet****? I haven't seen the play* ***yet****.*
  She has ***already*** *seen the play.* or *She has seen the play* ***already****.*
- It is possible to have more than one verb after *have* or *has*.
  It is not necessary to repeat *have* or *has*.
  I ***have traveled*** *to Paris and* ***have seen*** *the Eiffel Tower.*
  More common: *I* ***have traveled*** *to Paris and* ***seen*** *the Eiffel Tower.*
- Use the simple past when the specific time of the event is mentioned. *I* ***took*** *a tour* ***last week****.*

UNIT 2, LESSON 2 PRESENT CONTINUOUS: REVIEW

Affirmative statements

Subject	*Be*	Verb + *-ing*	Object
I	**am**		
She	**is**	**doing**	chores.
We	**are**		

Negative statements

Subject	*Be* + *not*	Verb + *-ing*	Object
I	**am not**		
She	**is not**	**having**	dinner.
We	**are not**		

Questions

Wh- word	*Be*	Subject	Verb + *-ing*
What	**are**	you	**doing?**
Where	**is**	he	**going?**
	Is	she	**working?**
	Are	you	

Answers

I'm doing the laundry.	
He's taking out the trash.	
Yes, she **is**.	No, she **isn't**.
Yes, we **are**.	No, we **aren't**.

Notes

- We almost always contract the subject pronoun + *be* in speaking and informal writing.
- Do not use contractions in short, affirmative answers. Yes, she is. NOT ~~Yes, she's~~.

Spelling rules for *-ing* verbs:

- For most verbs, add *-ing* to the base form of the verb. study → studying
- For verbs ending in a consonant + *-e*, drop the *e* and add *-ing* come → coming
- For most verbs ending in consonant / vowel / consonant, double the final consonant and add *-ing*. set → setting begin → beginning

UNIT 4, LESSON 3 SIMPLE PAST, REGULAR VERBS: REVIEW

Affirmative statements

Subject	Verb	
I She	**visited**	Miami.
	watched	the sunset.

Negative statements

Subject	*Did* + *not*	Verb	
I She We	**did not**	**like**	the beaches.

Notes

- We almost always use the contraction *didn't* in speech and informal writing.

Spelling rules for regular verbs

- For most verbs, add *-ed* to the base form. enjoy → enjoy**ed** walk → walk**ed**
- For verbs that end in *e*, add only *d*. like → like**d** love → love**d**
- For verbs that end in a consonant + *y*, change the *y* to *i* and add *-ed*.
  stud**y** → stud**ied** tr**y** → tr**ied**
- For most verbs that end in consonant + vowel + consonant, double the last consonant.
  sto**p** → sto**pped** pla**n** → pla**nned**

UNIT 4, LESSON 3 SIMPLE PAST, IRREGULAR VERBS: REVIEW

Affirmative statements

Subject	Verb	
I	**ate**	at a restaurant.
She	**swam**	at the beach.
We	**got**	a massage.

Negative statements

Subject	*Did + not*	Verb	
I		**eat**	at the hotel.
She	**did not**	**swim**	in the pool.
We		**get**	a double room.

Note: We almost always use the contraction *didn't* in speech and informal writing.

Common irregular verbs

Base form	Simple past	Base form	Simple past	Base form	Simple past
be	was, were	go	went	sit	sat
bring	bought	hang out	hung out	sleep	slept
buy	brought	have	had	spend	spent
come	came	make	made	take	took
cost	cost	say	said	wake	woke
drink	drank	see	saw	write	wrote

UNIT 5, LESSON 1 TAG QUESTIONS

A tag question is a question added to the end of a sentence. Use an auxiliary verb and the subject of the sentence in a tag question. Speakers sometimes use tag questions to confirm information. When the main verb of the sentence is affirmative, the tag question is negative.

Affirmative sentence	Negative tag
She's here for the interview,	**isn't she**?
I've given you a copy of my résumé,	**haven't I**?
They'll be here soon,	**won't they**?

I am becomes *aren't I* in a negative tag. ***I'm** a little late today, **aren't I**?*

When the main verb of the sentence is negative, the tag question is affirmative.

Negative sentence	Affirmative tag
You didn't have any trouble,	**did you**?
The interviews haven't started yet,	**have they**?
We can't park here,	**can we**?

Notes

- When the questioner's statement is correct, we use *yes* to agree with an affirmative sentence and *no* to agree with a negative sentence. The verb in the answer agrees with the main verb in the sentence.
- When the questioner's statement is ***not*** correct, we use *no* to disagree with an affirmative sentence and *yes* to disagree with a negative sentence. The verb in the answer contradicts the main verb in the sentence.

UNIT 5, LESSON 3 COUNT AND NON-COUNT NOUNS WITH *SOME, ANY,* AND *NO*

Count nouns		Non-count nouns	
Singular count nouns	**Plural count nouns**	tomato soup	ketchup
a tomato	two tomato**es**	fruit salad	salad dressing
an apple	some apple**s**		

Questions				Short answers	Answers with *some, any,* and *no*				
Are	there	any	burgers?	Yes. Yes, there are.	Yes,	there	are	**some**	burgers.
					No,	there	aren't	**any**	
						There	are	**no**	
Is			ketchup?	No. No, there isn't.	Yes,	there	is	**some**	ketchup.
					No,	there	isn't	**any**	
						There	is	**no**	

Notes

- Use *any* in questions and negative statements. Do not use *any* in affirmative statements.
- Do not use *no* with a negative verb.
- Many nouns have both a count and a non-count meaning.
  I love ***chocolate.*** (chocolate in general) *Do you want* ***a chocolate****?* (one piece of chocolate)

UNIT 5, LESSON 3 *MUCH / MANY / A LOT OF* AND *HOW MUCH / HOW MANY*

Use *much* with non-count nouns. Use *many* with plural count nouns. Use a *lot of* with both non-count nouns and plural count nouns.

Questions with *How much / How many*			Statements with *Much / Many / A lot of*		
How much / How many	**Noun**			***Much / Many / A lot of***	**Noun**
How much	water	do you drink?	I drink	**a lot of**	water.
	meat	did she eat?	She didn't eat	**much**	meat.
How many	vegetables	did they cook?	They didn't cook	**many**	vegetables.

Notes

- We usually use *much* in questions and negative statements. Do not use *much* in affirmative statements. *I usually drink* ***a lot of water****.* not *I usually drink* ~~much~~ **water***.*
- *Many* and *a lot of* are often used the same way.
  I like ***many*** *different* ***vegetables****. I like* ***a lot of*** *different* ***vegetables****.*
- Use *how many* with words like *cartons, bottles, bags, pounds, bowls,* and *cups.*
  How much water *do you drink?* ***How many bottles of water*** *do you drink?*

UNIT 5, LESSON 3 *ENOUGH* AND *TOO MUCH / TOO MANY* + NOUNS

Enough + noun				
	Not	***Enough***	**Noun**	
We have		**enough**	hamburgers.	We don't need any more.
There are	**not**	**enough**	hot dogs.	We need some more.

Note: *Enough* means the right amount. *Not enough* means less than you need.

Too much / Too many + noun			
	Too Much / Too Many	**Noun**	
We have	**too much**	food.	We can't finish everything.
There are	**too many**	hamburgers.	We can't finish all of them.

Note: *Too much* and *too many* have negative meanings. They describe a quantity that is more than you need. Use *too much* with non-count nouns and *too many* with count nouns.

UNIT 6, LESSON 1 VERBS + INFINITIVES AND GERUNDS

Some verbs take infinitives or gerunds. Some verbs take only infinitives or only gerunds.

Verb + gerund/infinitive, infinitive, or gerund			
Subject	**Verb**	**Infinitive or Gerund**	
I	love	to listen listening	to music.
		Infinitive only	
He	wants	to go	to a concert.
		Gerund only	
We	dislike	watching	TV.

Common verbs for ...	
Infinitive or gerund	
love like don't like hate	
Infinitive only	**Gerund only**
want	enjoy
plan	dislike
hope	avoid

UNIT 6, LESSON 1 GERUNDS AS OBJECTS OF PREPOSITIONS

A gerund is a verb + *ing*. It is used the same way as a noun. A gerund is often the object of a preposition.

	Preposition	Object	
I'm interested	**in**	**learning**	more about Mexico City.
She's responsible	**for**	**planning**	the trip.
We look forward	**to**	**hearing**	all about it.
They talked	**about**	**going**	to an unusual restaurant.
He's afraid	**of**	**flying**	too far.

UNIT 7, LESSON 1 INDIRECT QUESTIONS

Use indirect questions to be polite or if you're not sure the person will know the answer to the question.

Direct *wh-* questions				Indirect questions			
***Wh-* word**	**Auxiliary verb**	**Subject**	**Main verb**		***Wh-* word**	**Subject**	**Verb**
Where	**is**	he?		I wonder	where	he	**is**.
Why	**isn't**	she	**answering**?	I don't know	why	she	**isn't answering**.
When	**did**	you	**plan** to leave?	Can you tell me	when	you	**planned** to leave?

In *yes / no* questions, use *if* or *whether* before the subject.

Direct *yes / no* questions			Indirect questions			
Auxiliary verb	**Subject**	**Main verb**		***If / Whether***	**Subject**	**Verb**
Is	he	**here** yet?	Do you know	**if**	he	**is here** yet?
Were	they	**late**?	Can you tell me	**whether**	they	**were late**?

Notes

- Indirect questions often appear after introductory phrases, such as *I wonder*, *I don't know*, *Can / Could you tell me*, *Do you know*, *I'd like to know*, or *Would you mind explaining*.
- We always use statement word order in indirect questions. The subject always comes before the verb.

UNIT 8, LESSON 3 *WILL, MAY,* AND *MIGHT* TO EXPRESS LIKELIHOOD

Use *will* to talk about something that is certain to be true in the future. Use *may* or *might* when you are unsure of something.

Subject	*Will / May / Might*	*Not*	Base form of verb
It	**will**	**not**	**solve** the problem.
You	**may**	**not**	**be** connected to the Internet.
The problem	**might**	**not**	**happen** again.

Notes

- Use *will (most / very) likely* or *will probably* to talk about something that is expected to be true.
  *That **will most likely** solve the problem.*
  *That **won't likely** solve the problem. That **likely won't** solve the problem.*
  *That **will probably** solve the problem. That **probably won't** solve the problem.*
- Use *will definitely* to talk about something that is going to happen for sure.
  *We **will definitely** be there tomorrow. We **definitely won't** be there tomorrow.*

UNIT 9, LESSON 2 PAST CONTINUOUS WITH *WHEN*

Use the past continuous to show an action that was happening at a certain time in the past. The past continuous shows the duration of an action, not its completion.

Affirmative statement			Negative statement			
Subject	***Was / Were***	**Verb + *-ing***	**Subject**	***Was / Were***	***Not***	**Verb + *-ing***
I	**was**	**cooking** dinner.	I	**was**	**not**	**taking** the train.

Yes / No question			Short answers	
Was / Were	**Subject**	**Verb + *-ing***	**Affirmative**	**Negative**
Was	it	**raining**?	Yes, it **was**.	No, it **wasn't**.

Information question				Answer		
***Wh-* word**	***Was / Were***	**Subject**	**Verb + *-ing***	**Subject**	***Was / Were***	**Verb + *-ing***
What	**were**	you	**watching** yesterday?	**I**	**was**	**watching** a movie.

Use *when* + the simple past for actions that interrupt the action in the past continuous.

Affirmative statement				
Subject	***Was / Were***	**Verb + *-ing***	***When***	**Simple past**
She	**was**	**waiting** to pay	**when**	she **saw** him.

Notes

- Use the simple past, not the past continuous, for actions that were completed without interruptions. *Jim* ***dropped*** *his phone and* ***broke*** *it.*
- In sentences with *when*, the past continuous shows the action that happened first. *Everyone was* ***eating when*** *Scott* ***got*** *home. = First, they began eating. Then, Scott got home.*

PREPOSITIONS

about	below	from…to	outside
above	beneath	in	over
across	beside	in front of	past
after	besides	inside	round/around
against	between	in spite of	since
ahead of	beyond	into	than
along	but	like	through
among	by	near	throughout
apart from	concerning	next to	to
around	despite	of	towards
as	down	off	under
at	during	on	until
away from	except (for)	onto	up
because of	facing	on top of	with
before	for	opposite	within
behind	from	out of	without

METRIC CONVERSIONS

Volume		Length and distance		Weight	
1 fluid ounce	29.57 milliliters	1 centimeter	.39 inch	1 ounce	28.35 grams
1 milliliter	.034 fluid ounce	1 inch	2.54 centimeters	1 gram	.04 ounce
1 pint	.47 liter	1 foot	.30 meter	1 pound	.45 kilogram
1 liter	2.11 pints	1 meter	3.28 feet	1 kilogram	2.2 pounds
1 quart	.95 liter	1 yard	.91 meter		
1 liter	1.06 quarts	1 meter	1.09 yards		
1 gallon	3.79 liters	1 mile	1.61 kilometers		
1 liter	.26 gallon	1 kilometer	.62 mile		

Photo Credits

Cover

Javier Osores/EyeEm/Getty Images (front); Tovovan/Shutterstock (back).

Frontmatter

Page ix (p. 18 Diana) Pearson; ix (p. 18 storm) Circumnavigation/ Shutterstock; ix (p. 18 lightning) oriontrail/123RF; ix (p. 18 clear up) septian intizom/Shutterstock; ix (p. 18 get cloudy) dink101/123RF; ix (p. 18 thunderstorm) Nomad_Soul/Shutterstock; ix (p. 18 thunder) Luis Molinero/Shutterstock; ix (p. 18 get dark) JannisKoertge/Shutterstock; ix (p. 18 start rain) rzemyslaw Koch/123RF; ix (p. 18 snowstorm) Greg Dale/ Getty Images; ix (p. 18 rainbow) pedrosala/Shutterstock; ix (p. 18 windy) Lenz/Alamy Stock Photo; ix (p. 18 start snow) Fernando Pegueroles Pons/ Shutterstock; ix (p. 5 market stall) Carlo Morucchio/robertharding/Getty Images; ix (p. 19 Diana) Pearson; ix (p. 19 [1]) Malte Pott/Shutterstock; ix (p. 19 [2]) 4Max/Shutterstock; ix (p. 19 [3]) Vasuta Thitayarak/123RF; ix (MyEnglishLab) Pearson; ix (workbook) g-stockstudio/Shutterstock.

Welcome Unit

Page 2 (top): VGstockstudio/Shutterstock; 2 (top row, left): Stockbroker/ MBI/Alamy Stock Photo; 2 (top row, center): Bavorndej Prakit/123RF; 2 (top row, right): Wavebreakmedia/Shutterstock; 2 (bottom row, left): Dolgachov/123RF; 2 (bottom row, center): Syda Productions/Shutterstock; 2 (bottom row, right): Ammentorp/123RF; 3 (top): Javier Osores/EyeEm/ Getty Images; 4 (all images): Pearson Education.

Unit 1

Page 5: Carlo Morucchio/robertharding/Getty images; 5 (bottom, right): Pearson Education; 6 (top, right): Pearson Education, 6 (soccer): Dolgachov/123RF; 6 (baseball): Mtaira /123RF; 6 (tennis): Isitsharp/E+/ Getty Images; 6 (theater): Kozlik/Shutterstock; 6 (museum): Shutterstock; 6 (gallery): Africa Studio/Shutterstock; 6 (hike): Baranq/Shutterstock; 6 (travel): Beer5020/Shutterstock; 6 (cook): Daxiao Productions/ Shutterstock; 6 (charity): Amble Design/ Shutterstock; 6 (politics): Pressmaster/Shutterstock; 6 (community): Shutterstock; 7: Pearson Education; 8 (top): Pearson Education; 8 (top, left): Westend61/Getty images; 8 (top, right): Morakod1977/Shutterstock; 8 (bottom, left): Patrizio Martorana/Shutterstock; 8 (bottom, right): Viorel Sima/Shutterstock; 9: Pearson Education; 10 (top, right): Pearson Education; 10 (antique): Robyn Mackenzie/Shutterstock; 10 (glass): Bugtiger/Shutterstock; 10 (metal): Mmaxer/Shutterstock; 10 (shiny): VPC Coins Collection/ Alamy Stock Photo; 10 (dull): VPC Coins Collection/Alamy Stock Photo; 10 (old fashioned): Malivan_Iuliia/Shutterstock; 10 (modern): Cla78/ Shutterstock; (ML2) Cla78/Shutterstock; 10 (cotton): Valentyn Volkov/ Shutterstock; 11: Olivier Le Queinec/Shutterstock; 12 (top, right): Pearson Education; 12 (bottom, right): Jacob Lund/Shutterstock; 14 (top, right): Pearson Education; 14 (center, right): Kzenon/Shutterstock; 14 (center, background): My Good Images/Shutterstock; 16 (top, right): Sirtravelalot/ Shutterstock.

Unit 2

Page 17: Hiroyuki Matsumoto/The Image Bank/Getty Images; 17 (bottom, right): Pearson Education; 18 (top, right): Pearson Education; 18 (storm): Circumnavigation/Shutterstock; 18 (lightning): Oriontrail/123RF; 18 (clear up): Septian intizom armedi/Shutterstock; 18 (get cloudy): Dink101/123RF; 18 (thunderstorm): Nomad_Soul/Shutterstock; 18 (thunder): Luis Molinero/Shutterstock; 18 (get dark): JannisKoertge/Shutterstock; 18 (start rain): Przemyslaw Koch/123RF; 18 (snowstorm): Greg Dale/National Geographic/Getty Images; 18 (rainbow): Pedrosala/Shutterstock; 18 (windy): Lenz/Alamy Stock Photo; 18 (start snow): Fernando Pegueroles Pons/Shutterstock; 19: Pearson Education; 19 (1): Malte Pott/Shutterstock; 19 (2): 4Max/Shutterstock; 19 (3): Vasuta Thitayarak /123RF; 20 (top, right): Pearson Education; 20 (tornado): Minerva Studio/Shutterstock; 20 (hurricane): Warren Faidley/Corbis/Getty Images; 20 (blizzard): Igumnova Irina/Shutterstock; 20 (drought): Bibiphoto/Shutterstock; 20 (wildfire): Christian Roberts-Olsen/Shutterstock; 20 (landslide): Fabiodevilla/ Shutterstock; 20 (earthquake): Maudis60/123RF; 20 (rain): Mac99/E+/ Getty Images; 20 (snow): Tom Tom/Shuttertstock; 20 (winds): Jim Lopes/ Shutterstock; 20 (freeze): Oleg Doroshin/123RF; 20 (icy road): Zakhar Mar/Shutterstock; 20 (flood): Dariush M/Shutterstock; 22 (top, right): Pearson Education; 22 (evacuate): Arena Creative/Shutterstock; 22 (lost power): Cosma/Shutterstock; 22 (flooded street): Welcomia/123RF; 22 (fallen trees): Sheri Swailes/123RF; 22 (road closed): Northallertonman/ Shutterstock; 22 (icy road): Ken Tannenbaum/Shutterstock; 22 (closed): Zynatis/Shutterstock; 22 (damaged homes): Leonard Zhukovsky/ Shutterstock; 23: Pearson Education; 24 (top, right): Pearson Education; 24 (center, right): Kuco/Shutterstock; 26 (top, right): Pearson Education; 28 (top, left): Yevgenia Gorbulsky/Alamy Stock Photo.

Unit 3

Page 29: Hinterhaus Productions/DigitalVision/Getty Images; 29 (bottom, right): Pearson Education; 30 (top, right): Pearson Education; 30 (left): Picture5479/Shutterstock; 30 (center, left): Cookie Studio/Shutterstock; 30 (center, right) Kues/Shutterstock; 30 (right) AshTproductions/Shutterstock; 31: Pearson Education; 32 (top): Pearson Education; 33: Pearson Education; 34 (top): Pearson Education; 34: Dean Drobot/Shutterstock; 36 (top): Pearson Education; 36 (bottom, background): Dmitry Guzhanin/ Shutterstock; 38 (top, right): Pearson Education; 40 (top): Ivan_kislitsin/ Shutterstock; 40 (center): Dean Drobot/123RF.

Unit 4

Page 41: Tongo51/Shutterstock; 41 (bottom, right) Pearson Education; 42 (top, right): Pearson Education; 43: Pearson Education; 44 (top, right): Pearson Education; 44 (sci-fi): Aranami/Shutterstock; 44 (comedy): Coast Entertainment/Courtesy Everett Collection; 44 (suspense): Brocorwin/ Shutterstock; 44 (action): DreamWorks/Courtesy Everett Collection; 44 (rock): Lightfieldstudios/123RF; 44 (pop): Olegdudko/123RF; 44 (hip hop): Kzenon/Shutterstock; 44 (jazz): FabrikaSimf/Shutterstock; 44 (painting): Boyan Dimitrov/Shutterstock; 44 (sculpture): Svetlana Pasechnaya/Shutterstock; 44 (dance): Yakobchuk Viacheslav/Shutterstock; 44 (photography):Banana Republic images/Shutterstock; 45: Pearson Education; 46 (top, right): Pearson Education; 47: DavidTB/Shutterstock; 48 (top, right): Pearson Education; 48 (bottom, background): Charlie Sperring/Shutterstock; 50 (top, right): Pearson Education; 50 (center, left): Lassedesignen/Shutterstock; 52 (top, right): Dwphotos/Shutterstock; 52 (center, right): Flamingo Images/Shutterstock.

Unit 5

Page 53: Webphotographeer/iStock/Getty Images; 53 (bottom, right): Pearson Education; 54 (top, right): Pearson Education; 54 (bland): Ian Dyball/Shutterstock; 54 (greasy): Papaya Salad/Shutterstock; 54 (fresh): Matthew Dixon/Shutterstock; 54 (stale): Millenius/Shutterstock; 54 (cozy): Fizkes/Shutterstock; 54 (formal): Igor Link/Shutterstock; 54 (casual): Olena Yakobchuk/Shutterstock; 54 (crowded): Clara/Shutterstock; 54 (rushed): Cultura Motion/Shutterstock; 54 (efficient): Corepics VOF/Shutterstock; 54 (slow): BlueSkyImage/Shutterstock; 54 (poor): Pressmaster/Shutterstock; 55: Pearson Education; 56 (top, right): Pearson Education; 57: Pearson Education; 58 (top, right): Pearson Education; 58 (chips & salsa): David P Smith/Shutterstock; 58 (guacamole): Larisa Blinova/Shutterstock; 58 (cheese & crackers): MSPhotographic/Shutterstock; 58 (pretzels): Alexei Logvinovich/Shutterstock; 58 (hummus): Alexander Prokopenko/ Shutterstock; 58 (chili): kabvisio/Shutterstock; 58 (donuts): Viktar Lenets/ Shutterstock; 58 (cheesecake): Marina Pylypenko/Shutterstock; 59 (top, right): ESB Professional/Shutterstock; 60 (top, right): Pearson Education; 60 (center, left): Photosphere/Shutterstock; 62 (top, right): Pearson Education; 62 (center, top): Tmon/Shutterstock; 62 (center, bottom): Jacob Ea/Shutterstock; 64 (top, right): Mybeginner/Shutterstock; 64 (center, right): Shutterstock.

Unit 6

Page 65: Anouchka/iStock/Getty images; 65 (bottom, right): Pearson Education; 66 (top, right): Pearson Education; 66 (weight training): Dolgachov/Shutterstock; 66 (spinning): Satyrenko/Shutterstock; 66 (cycling): La India Piaroa/Shutterstock; 66 (climbing): Nejron Photo/ Shutterstock; 66 (jogging): Dotshock/123RF; 66 (marathon): Hero Images/Getty Images; 66 (kickboxing): MilanMarkovic78/Shutterstock; 66 (stretching): Javi_indy/Shutterstock; 67: Pearson Education; 68 (top, right): Pearson Education; 68 (right, top): Sirtravelalot/Shutterstock; 68 (right, bottom): Mimagephotography/Shutterstock; 69: Pearson Education; 70 (top, right): Pearson Education; (MR) Rido/Shutterstock; 72 (top, right): Pearson Education; 72 (bottom, right): Maridav/Shutterstock; 74 (top, right): Pearson Education; 74 (top, left): Lzf/Shutterstock; 76: Andrey_ Popov/Shutterstock.

Unit 7

Page 77: Rawpixel.com/Shutterstock; 77 (bottom, right): Pearson Education; 78 (top, right): Pearson Education; 78 (delete): Francois Poirier/Shutterstock; 78 (download): Supernick299/Shutterstock; 78 (upload): Supernick299/Shutterstock; 78 (copy): Arafat Uddin; 78 (paste): AVIcon/Shutterstock; 78 (attach): Sergii88/Shutterstock; 78 (install): LVM/ Shutterstock; 79: Pearson Education; 80 (top, right): Pearson Education; 81: Pearson Education; 82 (top, right): Pearson Education; 84 (top, right): Pearson Education; 84 (Tarek): Zurijeta/Shutterstock; 84 (Siguri): Natu/Shutterstock; 84 (Kim): Jennifer Hogan/123RF; 84 (Vinod): Ranta Images/Shutterstock; 86 (top, right): Pearson Education; 86 (center, left): Chizimger/Shutterstock 88 (top, right): Robinsphoto/123RF; 88 (center, right): Mangostar/123RF.

Unit 8

Page 89: Robert Daly/Caiaimage/OJO+/Getty Images; 89 (bottom, right): Pearson Education; 90 (top, right): Pearson Education; 90 (allergy): Budimir Jevtic/Shutterstock; 90 (food poisoning): Ljupco Smokovski/Shutterstock; 90 (flu): Elnur/Shutterstock; 90 (migraine): Kamil Macniak/123RF; 90 (fever): Uniquely india/Getty Images; 90 (sneeze): Shutterstock; 90 (stuffy nose): Dmitry Ageev/123RF; 90 (indigestion): Image Source/DigitalVision/ Getty Images; 90 (stomachache): NamtipStudio/Shutterstock;90 (rash): Pumatokoh/Shutterstock; 91: Pearson Education; 92 (top, right): Pearson Education; 93: Syda Productions/Shutterstock; 94 (top, right): Pearson Education; 95 (top, right): Pearson Education; 95 (bottom, right): PR Image Factory/Shutterstock; 96 (top, right): Pearson Education; 96 (chai tea): Ivan Dzyuba/123RF; 96 (salsa): Oleksandr Prokopenko/123RF; 98 (top, right): Pearson Education; 100 (top, right): Francesco Dibartolo/123RF; 100 (center, right): Lightfieldstudios/123RF.

Unit 9

Page 101: AleksandarGeorgiev/ E+/Getty Images; 101 (bottom, right): Pearson Education; 102 (top, right): Pearson Education; 103: Pearson Education; 104 (top, right): Pearson Education; 104 (center, right): Shutterstock; 105: Pearson Education; 106 (top, right): Pearson Education; 106 (right, top): GaudiLab/Shutterstock; 106 (right, center): Antoniodiaz/ Shutterstock; 106 (right, bottom): Luna Vandoorne/Shutterstock; 107 (center, right): Kaspars Grinvalds/Shutterstock; 107 (piano app in phone): Chornii Yevhenii /123RF; 108 (top, right): Pearson Education; 108 (bottom, background): Majcot/Shutterstock; 110 (top, right): Pearson Education; 108 (center, background): Zamurovic Photography/Shutterstock; 112 (top, right): Yellow Dog Productions/ Iconica/Getty Images; 112 (center, right): Piotr Adamowicz/Shutterstock; 112 (center, right [image on laptop]).

Unit 10

Page 113: Borut Trdina/E+/Getty Images; 113 (bottom, right): Pearson Education; 114 (top, right): Pearson Education; 115: Pearson Education; 116 (top, right): Pearson Education; 117 (center, right): Pearson Education; 118 (top, right): Pearson Education; 119: imac/Alamy Stock Photo; 120 (top, right): Pearson Education; 120 ("Reducing Waste" letters): Jibon/ Shutterstock; 122 (top, right): Pearson Education; 124 (top): Monoforma/ Shutterstock; 124 (center): Michael Simons/123RF.

Grammar Practice

Page 125: Zsolt_uveges/Shutterstock; 126: David Acosta Allely/ Shutterstock; 127: Olga V Kulakova/Shutterstock; 128: SKLA/E+/ Getty Images; 129: Meghan Pusey Diaz/123RF; 130: Narongsak Nagadhana/123RF; 131: Stephen Coburn/Shutterstock; 135 (left): Cathy Yeulet/123RF; 135 (right): Daniel Ernst/123RF; 136: Adam Vilimek/123RF; 137 (top): Karandaev/123RF; 137 (bottom): Stockbroker/MBI/Alamy Stock Photo; 138: El Nariz/Shutterstock; 140: Tyler Olson/Shutterstock; 152Z: Andriy Popov/123RF.

Illustration Credits

418 Neal (KJA Artists), John Goodwin (Eye Candy Illustration), Anjan Sarkar (Good Illustration)